"After 45 years of being born and rais
3HO community, I finally came to tern
who left long ago, forgotten by many. May our stories help others evaluate their experiences and recognize the massive abuse and unnecessary
harm inflicted. I know how hard it is to look back at your life and face
hurtful truths. It's time to be kind to ourselves, listen to our inner voices,
and tear down the pedestal we placed Yogi Bhajan on. He betrayed his
position, the community, and his legacy. I have compassion for those
struggling or looking the other way. Let's acknowledge that no one
wants to join a cult or harm their children."

> Sat Pavan Kaur Khalsa, born and raised in 3HO,
> groomed, and abused by Bhajan, a second-generation
> survivor voice in *Under the Yoga Mat.*

"What we discover hidden *Under the Yoga Mat* is astonishing in its
depth and magnitude. Ms. Coenen has pursued and shared here the
fruits of her own research. Like a private investigator, she identifies and
brings forth the many levels of deception and corruption carried out
under the guise of assembling an enterprising community of people
with a 'mission' of service to a New Age. The gulf between the idealistic
vision expounded by Yogi Bhajan, and the degree of corruption he
employed, is mind-boggling. Ms. Coenen has managed to share these
many facets and avenues of abuse and exploitation and also to help the
reader understand the ways in which such charismatic leaders seduce
and exploit their followers. Hers is a cautionary tale that reminds us of
the importance of looking beneath the surface."

> Pamela Saharah Dyson, the first secretary general for
> Bhajan's organization, author of *Premka:*
> *White Bird in a Golden Cage: My Life with Yogi Bhajan.*

"Our collective spiritual health demands that we recognize the potential dark side of the teachers and institutions we turn to. They can
inspire, illuminate, and transform our lives for the better—and, at the
same time, they can abuse, wound, and traumatize. In this well-

researched book, Els Coenen makes an important contribution by exposing the egregious actions of the once-prominent Yogi Bhajan and his 3HO organization. The lessons in the book can make us all more spiritually mature."

Philip Goldberg, author of *American Veda: From Emerson and the Beatles to Yoga and Meditation, How Indian Spirituality Changed the West.*

"*Under the Yoga Mat* is an engrossing, beautifully written account of the systematic and heart-breaking abuses that occurred in the 3HO community under Yogi Bhajan. By interweaving historical sources and the very human testimonies of survivors, *Under the Yoga Mat* proves a master class in the psychology and harm of cults. Anyone who supports or works with cult survivors should have a copy. I intend for it to be required reading for our lawyers."

Carol Merchasin, Lawyer, Of Counsel Sexual Abuse in Spiritual Communities, McAllister Olivarius, mcolaw.com.

"*Under the Yoga Mat* is an essential and eye-opening book that delves into the potential dangers lurking within spiritual teachings and communities. Els Coenen's unwavering commitment to uncovering the truth offers a valuable service to survivors and is a cautionary tale for all. With a discerning eye, Coenen emphasizes the importance of understanding spiritual teachings' complete context and origin, especially when associated with controversial figures. This thought-provoking work is a powerful reminder of the importance of critical thinking and awareness when engaging in spiritual pursuits, empowering readers to make informed choices and navigate the complex terrain of spiritual movements."

Dr. Steven Hassan, Author of *Combating Cult Mind Control* and *Freedom of Mind*, Cult Expert, freedomofmind.com.

UNDER THE YOGA MAT

UNDER THE DESERT

UNDER
THE YOGA MAT

The Dark History
of Yogi Bhajan's Kundalini Yoga

ELS COENEN

with Excerpts from GuruNischan's
Uncomfortable Conversations Podcast

IZZARD INK
PUBLISHING®

IZZARD INK PUBLISHING
PO Box 522251
Salt Lake City, Utah 84152
www.izzardink.com

LIBRARY OF CONGRESS CONTROL NUMBER:

Designed by Daniel Lagin
Cover Design by Andrea Ho
Cover Image by Hendrika De Hantsetters

First Edition
Contact the author at els@undertheyogamat.com
www.undertheyogamat.com
Paperback ISBN: 978-94-6475-213-7
eBook ISBN: 978-94-6475-214-4

In honor of Kirantana († July 26, 2022).

This book is dedicated to Kirn Jot and all Yogi Bhajan's rape victims.

Proceeds from this book go to nonprofit initiatives that support recovery from sexual violence, child neglect, and institutional abuse.

CONTENTS

FOREWORD

by GuruNischan

I am one of the thousands of children born and raised in the 3HO (Healthy, Happy, Holy Organization) Kundalini Yoga community. Yogi Bhajan, my parents' spiritual leader, was revered as all-knowing, a grandfather to many, a living saint to some, a master of Kundalini Yoga, and a spiritual leader of the Sikhs in the Western Hemisphere. I refer to him as YB.

Under his influence, my parents, like many of his followers, became Western Sikhs, resulting in our foreign-sounding names. We, the children of 3HO, were groomed to be perfect yogi-warriors, divine souls. We were born to ensure the survival of humanity as we usher in the Aquarian Age with the 3HO lifestyle and Kundalini Yoga technology. Being a child in this community meant that we were expected to live up to the image of the bright and evolved souls YB promised we would become. Our parents' lives and the future of the planet depended on it.

In 1978, one year after my birth, my mother left the community after rampant infidelity by my father, who exploited his young, pretty yoga students—behavior condoned by YB himself. Prior to her abrupt departure, she counseled with YB and was sent to other ashrams (community houses) to "serve" and learn how to become a "better wife." This included time in service to BibiJi, YB's wife, now widowed and heir to his empire.

After my mom left, taking my brother and me with her, she faced community slander, shaming, and fierce custody disputes. My brother and I ultimately ended up living with my father back in the community. When we visited our mom, she always spoke to us about knowing who we were outside of "the community." She encouraged us to express ourselves, experiment, wear our hair down, and try meat if we wanted. It was confusing, to say the least, and we were often pulled between two worlds, seeking freedom and stability simultaneously.

My mom was made out to be the crazy, erratic, emotional one, while my dad played a lot of manipulative games backed by YB and his leadership. Her house was broken into three times in two years, and her car was damaged more often than seemed "normal" throughout my childhood. Often, community members would ignore her when she arrived to pick us up for our monthly visits, as if looking at her would cause them disgrace.

Nonetheless, I have to say I loved my community and the people who made up my extended family worldwide. I thought it was awesome, and I've always held my upbringing in high regard. By fifteen, I thought I had reconciled the hypocrisy and the abuse patterns that I knew were prevalent with what I thought were the good health habits and spiritual consciousness that seemed legitimate and true as well. After all, didn't governments and all religions have hypocrisy?

My identity was solidified in being "a cultural other." I had a deeply rooted pride in being born different, a Western Sikh (a seeker of Truth) with elevated consciousness meant to change the world. I was a world traveler, outspoken and proud to be unique. While no longer "in" 3HO, this "specialness" still propelled my sense of self throughout my twenties and thirties.

After the book *Premka: White Bird in a Golden Cage: My Life with Yogi Bhajan* was released in early 2020, abuse stories started flooding in online and in private Zoom meetings. While fellow second-generation adults were sharing the impact of being sent to schools in India—nonattachment, bullying, neglect, hunger, trust issues, and other emotional and sexual abuse barriers—I was washed with overwhelming familiarity, even though I had never attended the schools in India myself.

I began to understand that my "resilience" and my "strength" were actually trauma patterns covering up my feeling of anything at all—joy, happiness, lust, love, anger, hunger, and the full range of expression normal to being human. My mind had convinced me that the sensation of deprivation was enlightenment, holiness, and love. It was actually neglect, emptiness, and loneliness. It was "disassociation." It was the mimicry of adults modeling how to give up their power while continuously overriding their needs—all built into the lifestyle itself.

In an eerie, dreamlike way, I remembered KartaPurkh from 1980: she was a princess to my childlike wonder because she was the only one wearing high heels. Come to find out, this young woman was brought in as a child and groomed by her older sister to be horribly and abusively raped by YB, forced to wear high heels as a manipulative control tactic. When she went public in 1985—I was seven years old then—she was discarded and slandered. All this has been in the public record for decades. Yet I had been trained not to look at it. Even to this day, current 3HO members will share YB's anecdote, teaching that "he made her wear heels for her spine and to correct her past life karma."

This helped me realize that the compacted memories in my body were the very ethos of abuse that happened around us every single day. This is the inner terror propelling me into obligatory service and rigorous discipline. This is the horror I've held in my body as tightness and anxious achievement.

I was blown away by each and every story shared, as they reminded me of something I had long since tucked away for mere survival. It was like flipping a Rubik's cube in my psyche. I was stunned to be bearing witness in 2020 to victim shaming, denying, propaganda videos, and written rhetoric from members of 3HO. It was, quite literally, YB's 1985 slander narrative on full display for all of us to view.

I appreciated the private Facebook group Beyond the Cage, which created an atmosphere of support and spoke out loud about uncomfortable truths among survivors spanning several decades. And then, when Krishna Kaur, a senior teacher in Los Angeles, failed to come forward with a statement about the abuse that was surfacing, I called her. I reminded her that silence is not neutral. Silence is abusive.

She was my "Auntie," my only lifeline into 3HO as an adult. She had been around since my birth, privy to what my mom had dealt with prior to leaving. As an early leader in YB's community, she had been the primary communication channel for my father as the head of the Phoenix Ashram. I took Teacher Training Level One with her when I was going through really dark times in my mid-thirties. She had never judged me for cutting my hair and making choices not aligned with the community regulations. So, when she finally released a statement, I was angry because I felt it was subpar and minimizing to the countless children, women, and men who had actually been harmed.

I was perplexed. How can I love someone and be angry with them too? At that moment, I realized my anger was mine, and it was right. I no longer had to pretend that my anger didn't exist. I no longer had to repress or internalize it. I can be angry. I can say it out loud, and I don't have to direct it toward her, anyone else, or myself. I can use it as fuel to create and speak what is true for me.

That realization birthed *The Uncomfortable Conversations Podcast: The Untold Stories of the 3HO Kundalini Yoga Community.* I simply wanted these stories to move from secret, private spaces, into a public platform, a place where the dark part of our history could be accessed and listened to whenever someone is ready. The shackles of my obligatory reverence for "The Teachings" fell, and I realized, *There's nothing for me to be reverent towards.*

From my point of view, we've spoken about the amazing aspects of the 3HO lifestyle long enough. We've felt elevated and communed worldwide. We chanted and drank Yogi Tea together. We're now in a stage where we *must* speak to the predatory abuse in the 3HO community worldwide as well. It's time to talk about the not-so-amazing parts—not by "light-washing" or sugarcoating them, but by facing the realities of harm that have occurred. We do it by shining light into the dark history head-on, by speaking to it clearly and holding the pain, discomfort, resentment, disgust, and rage. We learn to hold the conflicting inner realities of ourselves and begin to examine how we may have participated in propagating false narratives and presenting them as truth. We cannot heal what we do not recognize.

This book leans into the enormous task of illuminating these cultlike characteristics lurking beneath the surface of the Kundalini Yoga community worldwide. It brings a myriad of collective voices, revealing tales woven together to architect the historical and present-day patterns hiding in plain sight. This book is not simply "telling a personal story or two." It tells many stories over many decades on a complex web. Stories that have weaved their own tapestry of discovery, revealing the essential patterns of abuse and criminal tales from the untold, dark history of this Healthy, Happy, Holy 3HO community.

Els Coenen brings us a well-refined compilation from numerous publication sources on this organization spanning five decades. Her artful crafting together of facts and distillation of patterns from various interviews delivers a glaring and accurate view into the lived reality and personal everyday lives of those who've been and are still being impacted by it.

This book reveals what has always been there but has never before been highlighted so clearly. It's the convolution of love and abuse commingled, normalized, and disguised as community, compassion, caliber, and consciousness. Students of Kundalini Yoga as taught by Yogi Bhajan are told that this is the Yoga of Awareness. But those who practiced it for decades were blind to what happened with their children, sisters, brothers, spouses, colleagues, and neighbors.

This book reveals the courageous voices of second-generation children born into this lifestyle or brought in as children, and numerous survivors of sexual, physical, emotional, psychological, financial, and spiritual harm inflicted by YB and other community "leaders" over several decades. It's a compilation of the flood of stories released in audio, video, and print since 2020, as well as many decades before that, since the beginning of 3HO in 1969. It's a diligent effort to make sense of a very dark, secret past that has been hiding in plain sight.

There is nothing easy about speaking out loud about abuse, as we've been trained in YB's lifestyle to discount and be silent. It can be retraumatizing to tell your story or to listen to someone's story of harm. It can feel minimizing to read your life summed up in a well-researched article, a book, or a documentary feature displaying secrets that have been kept confined to the silent walls of your own inner experience.

With this in mind, we honor your courage to listen as each voice reveals a missing puzzle piece for dissolving our collective entanglement. We acknowledge the *RishiKnots* blog, being one of the only voices of the children of this community who've been relentless in speaking out loud about cult and child abuse in 3HO since the 1990s. Their efforts are acknowledged as foundational groundwork for this publication to be possible. A special thanks to the crusaders behind the Wacko World of Yogi Bhajan website. Your fierce pursuit to expose the truth has been a source of respite and recovery for so many people, spanning several decades.

There are numerous other content creators, writers, podcasters, researchers, website builders, and organizers—many of whom are survivors—who dedicated thousands of hours collecting personal testimonies, researching from various sources, and spending countless amounts of time listening to survivors' stories. Their sole purpose is to bring the dark truth about 3HO, and Kundalini Yoga as taught by Yogi Bhajan, into the light. We thank them for their diligence and commitment.

Yet, what Els Coenen has done by bringing it all together in one manuscript is a priceless feat that surely will create a ripple effect worldwide. It's a clear, transparent stand for the complete telling of the TRUTH. Her efforts to amplify the voices of survivors from this community in a coherent, digestible, and easily distributed form will prove to be life altering and shattering for many. Many, like me at one point, were dedicated, devoted, and fully convinced that it's entirely possible to "follow the teachings but not the teacher."

What you're about to read, in part, is what changed that misnomer for me. We welcome you to have an experience of your own.

April 2023

GuruNischan

Writer, trauma-healing activist, and consultant in personal and professional reinvention; host of *The Uncomfortable Conversations Podcast: The Untold Stories of the 3HO/Kundalini Yoga Community,* and the *Uncomfortable Conversations on Predators in Business Community and Culture* podcast publication.

GuruNischan.com

@gurunischan

Those who cannot remember the past
are condemned to repeat it.

GEORGE SANTAYANA IN 1905

INTRODUCTION

Come and sit on your heels. Let me show you what we are going to do. Just watch me first. You will raise your arms straight up like this. Fold your hands. Then, extend your index fingers, so they touch each other and point to the sky. Allow your upper arms to softly touch your ears. If they don't, turn your elbows toward each other, and they will. Keep your shoulders relaxed. Do not bend forward, and make sure your back is straight, not hollow like this. Tilt your pelvis a bit if needed. Smile. There is no need for strain in this position. Your eyes will be closed and focused on the spot between your eyebrows.

We will use the mantra "Sat Nam." Remember that "Sat" means truth, and "Nam" means identity. So, as you chant "Sat Nam," you call upon your true identity, your soul. On "Sat," you pull the navel point in and up. Keep in mind that the navel point is slightly lower than the belly point and more inward. On "Nam," relax the navel point. We will repeat that movement on a steady rhythm of about eight repetitions every ten seconds. The breath will regulate itself. You don't need to worry about that. Questions? No? Please come into the position. Are you all set? Inhale . . . and exhale . . . Make your upper body light. Inhale . . . exhale . . . and here we go. Sat Nam. Sat Nam. Sat Nam . . .

Hundreds of thousands of yogis worldwide will recognize the instructions of Sat Kriya. The Sanskrit word *Sat* means truth, and *Kriya* means an action to achieve a specific result. Sat Kriya is a photogenetic practice from Yogi Bhajan's legacy that can be performed on its own or can be part of a yoga set with multiple exercises. It is said to strengthen the sexual system and stimulate its natural energy flow.

Kundalini Yoga as taught by Yogi Bhajan has hundreds of different yoga sets and meditations with promising names: Kriya to make you Enchantingly Beautiful, Kriya to Develop Human Power, Kriya to Relax and Release Fear, Kriya to Throw off Stress, Kriya to Release Pain and Refresh Yourself, and so on. Some kriyas are relaxing or prepare you for deep meditation. Others are intense, physically challenging, and exhausting. Yoga teachers and practitioners can pick and choose from a wealth of materials available in books and on the Internet. They will always find something to fit the needs of the moment. It never gets boring.

Yogi Bhajan often combined classical yoga postures with eccentric exercises such as snoring, walking like an elephant, chewing like a cow, or pretending you are a giant crocodile, strong and mighty, slithering along a riverbank.

Typical for this yoga style are the mantras woven through the sets, released in rock-and-roll, upbeat, psychedelic, or angelic-sounding compositions. They help maintain a steady rhythm during energetic and challenging body movements. For example, they give you strength while holding your arms like a halo above your head with your hands folded for eleven to thirty-one minutes. Or they support meditation and relaxation sessions. It is common for students to slip into a light trance through the repetitive rhythms of breathing patterns or while chanting mesmerizing mantras. Most practitioners enjoy being in such an altered state of consciousness and look forward to achieving it in every yoga class if possible. The mantras come mainly from the Sikh tradition since Yogi Bhajan was a born Sikh. They add considerably to the charm of his yoga.

While hundreds of thousands practice and enjoy Kundalini Yoga as taught by Yogi Bhajan, many more people worldwide drink Yogi Tea. Only a minority of them know that the creator of their favorite yoga sets and the spiritual father of the Healthy, Happy, Holy Organization (3HO) in which Yogi Tea originated was a cult leader, sexual predator, child abuser, gay basher, and successful but fraudulent businessman.

In 1968, when Yogi Bhajan arrived in the US, he portrayed himself as a yoga master. A few years later, he claimed to be the Chief Religious and Administrative Authority for Sikh Dharma in the West. Sikh leaders and academics from Punjab questioned the legitimacy of this position. Nonetheless, it was in this capacity he met with Pope Paul VI in 1972 and Pope John Paul II in 1984. These popes probably did not know they were dealing with a criminal and a rapist.

There are pictures of Bhajan with President Nixon, the Dalai Lama, and several other secular and religious leaders. He was a generous political donor to both the Democrats and the Republicans. He maintained good relations with the governor of California and established strong ties with the governorship of New Mexico. Former governor Bill Richardson considered him a trusted advisor and loyal ally.[1]

While other cult leaders were exposed in the 1970s, 1980s, and 1990s,[2] Bhajan remained at large. He played it smart. However, as early as 1977, an article in *Time* magazine used the word "cult" while revealing issues within 3HO.[3] Nonetheless, there was never an official investigation. In 1986, lawsuits were filed against Bhajan for sexual abuse and other misdeeds. Yet, they were all settled outside the courtroom. Over the years, his accomplices were imprisoned for drugs and arms-related felonies and financial and business fraud. He himself was never convicted.

In the early 1990s, the assistant district attorney of California (ADA) told a former community member that the FBI was one handshake away from Bhajan.[4] Unfortunately, they could not close the gap. The ADA compared his gang activities with the Chicago Mafia. "At that moment, Yogi Bhajan fled from California to New Mexico," says the ex-member, "not to return for many years."[5]

Two weeks after Bhajan died in October 2004, the *Los Angeles Times* wrote:

> Before he was Yogi Bhajan—kundalini master, Sikh missionary, lifestyle sage and political advisor with 300 yoga centers and 4,000 instructors, more than a dozen corporations, and $1 billion in government contracts for security—he was Harbhajan Singh Puri, an ex-civil servant who landed in Los Angeles at the dawn of the city's guru boom and inspired the hippie masses with his movie star charisma and exotic health regimen. . . .
>
> Bhajan's legacy wasn't immune to controversy. While many see him as a tireless missionary whose only goal was to serve humanity, others considered him a brilliant cult leader and masterful con man who lived the life of a rock star by exploiting his followers.[6]

At the death of Yogi Bhajan, the flags of government buildings in New Mexico flew at half-mast. Six months later, on April 6, 2005, the US Congress agreed to honor Yogi Bhajan in a two-page resolution listing his achievements and concluding with the words:

> . . . be it resolved by the House of Representatives (the Senate concurring) that the Congress
>
> (1) recognizes that the teachings of Yogi Bhajan about Sikhism and yoga, and the businesses formed under his inspiration, improved the personal, political, spiritual, and professional relations between citizens of the United States and citizens of India;
>
> (2) recognizes the legendary compassion, wisdom, kindness, and courage of Yogi Bhajan, and his wealth of accomplishments on behalf of the Sikh community;
>
> (3) extends its condolences to Inderjit Kaur, the wife of Yogi Bhajan, his three children and five grandchildren, and to Sikh and 3HO communities around the Nation and the world upon the death on October 6, 2004, of Yogi Bhajan, an individual who was a wise

teacher and mentor, an outstanding pioneer, a champion of peace, and a compassionate human being.[7]

In September 2005, the Yogi Bhajan Memorial Highway was inaugurated in New Mexico.[8]

In September 1968, the almost forty-year-old Harbhajan Singh Puri gave up his job as a customs officer at New Delhi airport and traveled to Toronto, Canada. Three months later, he moved to Los Angeles, California. By his own account, he was a master of Kundalini Yoga and became Yogi Bhajan. With his handsome looks and charisma, he soon gathered a core group of followers around him who helped launch a new spiritual movement. Under his influence, masses of young people stopped using drugs and alcohol and became fully-fledged vegetarians. They started growing their hair and wearing turbans as their spiritual leader introduced them to Sikhism. He determined that they should wear white to expand their auras. Each day at half past three in the morning, they took cold showers before engaging in a two-and-a-half-hour ritual, including Sikh prayer, yoga, meditation, and chanting. At the simple request of their beloved teacher, they married complete strangers and moved to faraway cities in other states and countries to establish spiritual centers. These community houses, called ashrams, mushroomed and attracted new followers.

In those days, many young Westerners read *Autobiography of a Yogi* by Paramahansa Yogananda. That book taught them that guidance from a guru was needed if you wanted to live a meaningful life. Yogi Bhajan's followers believed he was such a guru. They considered him as all-knowing and larger-than-life, a man of great wisdom who would lead them to liberation, eternal freedom, and happiness. Utterly uncritical, they surrendered control of their lives to him.

Shortly after Bhajan had won the trust and devotion of many gullible seekers, he began to abuse his power and status until he died in 2004. Over the years, his hunger for power grew along with the brutality and cruelty of his actions. Hundreds of ex-community members are still actively working on trauma recovery.

A former secretary of Yogi Bhajan estimates that he sexually assaulted more than a hundred women. At least a thousand children who grew up in 3HO suffered greatly from his child-unfriendly distance therapy and other sectarian policies.

In 1969, the Healthy, Happy, Holy Organization, was officially established. Over the years, more nonprofit organizations were added, as well as for-profit companies. Yogi Tea and Akal Security, a security company that earned billions from US government contracts, became successful thanks to the cheap labor of devotees in the early years. When small businesses born from the creative minds of 3HO members began to make money, Yogi Bhajan took them over. More than once, he pushed the founders and investors aside.

Bhajan was a genius and master in controlling everyone and everything, always. He did it so no one else could understand what was happening in his empire. Entity names, organization structures, and leadership changed randomly.

The current leaders still use the same tactic. The financial flows from for-profit entities to nonprofits were and still are a well-kept secret. In 2021, the names of the for-profit companies suddenly disappeared from the organizational chart on the website of the umbrella organization, the Siri Singh Sahib Corporation, the SSSC. *Siri Singh Sahib* is an honorary title that Yogi Bhajan took on in the early 1970s.

Because 3HO was the first officially registered entity of the organization, its name is often used to refer to the totality of organizations and businesses. That's not correct, but it serves a practical purpose.

Yogi Bhajan preached his own version of Sikhism. In 1973, the Sikh Dharma Brotherhood was recognized as a religious organization in the US. 3HO Sikhs often refer to their community as "the dharma." In Sikh tradition, "the dharma" means the path of righteousness and proper religious practice. The official purpose of this nonprofit organization, later called Sikh Dharma International, was to spread Bhajan's Sikh teachings in the West and support the rapidly growing number of 3HO

Sikhs. 3HO's status as a religious organization helped to keep prying eyes away from the nefarious and illegal activities of the master and his accomplices. Moreover, it created opportunities for all community activities to benefit from the favorable tax regime that a religious association enjoys in the US.

In 1975, the State of California approved the creation of a corporation sole. This legal entity, also used by the crown of England, was the ultimate solution to grant Bhajan overall power and authority.[9]

Since the early 1990s, many 3HO-related entities have headquarters in Española, a small town in Santa Fe County in New Mexico. The Santa Fe ashram, which had begun as a hippie campground, moved in late 1971 to a house on a modest plot of land in Española. Over the years, the community bought more properties as the number of members increased. In 1975, 3HO bought "the Ranch."[10] Bhajan stayed there when he visited Española and lived there after he fled California in 1992. Many atrocities occurred on that ranch.

In 1977, Yogi Bhajan influenced a faithful follower to spend about a million dollars of her inheritance to buy 150 acres (61 hectares) of land some miles outside Española. Big events for the worldwide community were and are still hosted there. He named it Ram Das Puri. "Ram Das" refers to Guru Ram Das, the fourth guru of the Sikhs, who lived in the sixteenth century and whom Yogi Bhajan considered his personal guru; "Puri" is Bhajan's birth name. Events held in that high desert wilderness brought, and still generate, a lot of money. Gigi, the woman who bought the land and "donated" it to 3HO, ironically became homeless in recent years.

GRUESOME STORIES COME TO LIGHT

2020—The Masks Fall

For decades, the 3HO–Kundalini Yoga–Sikh Dharma community managed to outwardly maintain the Healthy, Happy, Holy façade. At the beginning of 2020, fifty years after the abuse had started, the masks finally fell. The massive revelation of wrongdoings began with the publication of the book *Premka: White Bird in a Golden Cage: My Life with Yogi Bhajan*, written by Pamela Saharah Dyson. In 1968, twenty-five-year-old Pamela fell under Bhajan's spell and decided to devote her life to him and his mission. He called her Premka which meant "the beloved of God," he said. In 2022, she learned it is the Punjabi word for "mistress."

For sixteen long years, Bhajan presented her as the second in command while she was a gullible puppet in his hands, like every other leader he appointed. At the end of 1984, Pamela left 3HO to finally live her own life. Her book *Premka* tells a story of devotion, hard work, dedication, love, loneliness, abuse, lies, exploitation, harassment, pain, and loss.

Because Pamela/Premka played a prominent role in 3HO, her voice could not be ignored in 2020. Combined with the #MeToo zeitgeist, this encouraged many others to finally speak out. As more accounts of terror and abuse emerged, and still do as I write this, the true extent of the damage done became, and still becomes, clearer every day. Some survivors had testified before but were never listened to. Now was the time.

For many years, RishiKnots, the Wacko World of Yogi Bhajan, and the Gurmukh Yoga Forum brought the issues into the open,[11] but they received no attention and were shunned and ridiculed. After the publication of *Premka*, the private Facebook group Beyond the Cage was launched and joined by thousands. To this day, it is a space where survivors share stories, give and receive support. Second-generation adults have set up private groups, and like-minded Kundalini Yoga teachers have formed communities to share and reflect on what happened and how to deal with it.

The Siri Singh Sahib Corporation (SSSC), the Healthy, Happy, Holy Organization (3HO), the Kundalini Research Institute (KRI), the International Kundalini Yoga Teachers Association (IKYTA), Sikh Dharma International (SDI), and the 3HO-related profit-making companies like Yogi Tea and Akal Security had not seen it coming. The yoga of awareness turned out to be the yoga of deafness and blindness.

In the spring of 2020, the flood of allegations forced the SSSC, the umbrella organization, to scrutinize the fast-growing number of claims of sexual abuse by their founder and spiritual leader. An Olive Branch (AOB), a Buddhist-inspired organization that guides spiritual groups in examining ethical issues, was called in to do the job.[12] They contacted three hundred people, half deniers of the abuse, and half believers. At the end of July 2020, they released following findings: ". . . based on reports of harm from 36 people, the investigation concludes that it is more likely than not that Yogi Bhajan engaged in several types of sexual misconduct and abused his power as a spiritual leader." The AOB team acknowledged that "it is likely that not all individuals who had been harmed by Yogi Bhajan came forward to participate in this investigation."

The major limitation of the AOB report was that it only considered allegations of sexual abuse of women. Claims involving child abuse, exploitation, homophobia, life threats, financial abuse, and other misdeeds were not investigated.

Early 2023, an expert report was made public that focused on the abuse of 3HO children. Cult expert Dr. Alexandra Stein drafted her "Report on Themes and Impacts of 3HO Childhood"[13] at the request of a group of second-generation adults. It is a tough and raw but necessary reading.

Here are some of the former 3HO kids' experiences cited in Stein's report that indicate the extreme levels of neglect: they ate rose petals and drank water to give themselves a feeling of being full, food served in schools contained bugs, worms, cigarette butts, and other foreign objects. Children suffered from continuous sleep deprivation. In Indian schools, the latrines were often filthy and scary. They constantly had to deal with lice, boils, diarrhea, parasites, or wounds that took months to heal. One person testified they deliberately broke their arm to get much-needed attention and care. Bullying was pervasive. Many kids had suicidal thoughts and no one to talk to. Higher education was discouraged, and culture and arts were not part of the school curriculum. Harsh caning in schools resulted in injuries. Punishments consisted of holding physical positions for a long time while kneeling on gravel. Children were isolated, verbally abused, and humiliated in front of others. There was sexual abuse by teachers, American staff members, and older students. The kids were made to believe that Yogi Bhajan could read their auras and minds, which was experienced as extremely invasive. They were told that their parents were neurotic, and Yogi Bhajan was the only adult to trust.

Stein's report analyzes the impact the abuse had on the survivors' lives in adulthood.

3HO was and is a cult, she says, and she includes the evidence that supports this claim in her report.

Since the 2020 revelations and the AOB report, the yogic nonprofits 3HO and KRI have quietly but unmistakably repainted their façades. Yogi Bhajan's name, picture, and quotes have been removed from the forefront. No more all-in-white and whites only, many fewer turbans on websites and social media. The new outer image of 3HO and KRI is colorful and focuses on diversity and inclusion. Bhajan has been relegated to the back burner.

Sikh Dharma International and the umbrella Siri Singh Sahib Corporation play a different game as they still openly honor Yogi Bhajan as their spiritual leader. Their income seems less dependent on "what the outside world thinks about them."

Following the AOB report, the SSSC launched the Compassionate Reconciliation Program.[14] I was a member of one of its advisory teams for almost two years. At the end of 2022, I stepped out as it felt like I was part of a window-dressing operation. The focus during our meetings was not on healing the wounds of the past but on finding ways to put a bandage on those stinking injuries without coming near them, looking at them, smelling them, hearing the screams, or feeling the pain. One day I asked, "Why is this not a 'Truth and Reconciliation Commission,' like most other initiatives pursuing Restorative Justice?" They told me that the word *truth* was left out because, in this community, in this situation, different people have different truths. Everybody should respect that.

Desmond Tutu would have furrowed his brows at such an answer. In 1996, he chaired the South African Truth and Reconciliation Commission, established in response to the atrocious misdeeds of the apartheid regime. In his *Book of Forgiving: The Fourfold Path for Healing Ourselves and Our World*, he described four steps to healing. The first step is admitting the wrong and acknowledging the harm. Next, the stories need to be told, and the pain and damage should be witnessed. After that, forgiveness can eventually be granted. Finally, reconciliation can be sought, and a new way of living together may be explored.

In May 2022, most probably triggered by juridical actions of second-generation adults, the SSSC launched the Independent Healing and Reparation Program (IHRP).[15] People harmed by Yogi Bhajan or any other community leader or at any of the schools in India were invited to file a claim for reparations. Over six hundred claims were reportedly filed. Other complaints, like those linked to financial abuse, exploitation and homophobia, did not qualify for the reparations program.

On April 28, 2023, Dr. Nirinjan Kaur Khalsa-Baker, born and raised in 3HO, spoke at the Harvard Divinity School spring conference on the topic, "Healthy Happy Holy? Harm and Healing in Sikh Dharma's Kundalini Yoga Community."[16] She talked about the awakening of her community to the reality of sexual misconduct, manipulation, and abuse by their spiritual teacher.[17] "The second-generation adults are discussing what accountability could look like when some of their parents continue to hold fast to their loyalty to Yogi Bhajan rather than believe their own children, continuing to demonstrate patterns of silence and denial. They're asking what it takes for their voices to be heard, to receive acknowledgment, accountability, and how to prevent future abuse with some organizing lawsuits and others participating in the reparations program," she said. There were community leaders in the audience as she spoke in an often trembling voice. They kept silent.

On June 11, 2023, a group of a hundred Second Generation Advocates wrote an open letter and launched a petition to make their voices heard in response to the abuses that they experienced in the community. Many are currently participating in the Independent Healing and Reparations Program, which may have been well-intentioned but is being poorly executed and is causing re-traumatization.[18]

Less than a week later, just before the 2023 3HO summer solstice event in New Mexico started, another shock wave went through the community. The president of the highly divided board of directors of the Siri Singh Sahib Corporation, Sahaj Singh Khalsa, a second-generation adult himself and an advocate for change and truth telling, resigned from the board and as a Sikh Dharma minister. In his resignation letter circulating on the Internet, he recounted how he and his family were attacked, threatened, and abused because of his stance.[19]

Purpose of This Book

To Keep You Vigilant

This book is not about the battle between the ardent worshippers of Yogi Bhajan, deniers of the abuse, and people within 3HO who see the need for acknowledgment, reparation, and change. Neither is this book about the issues with the current reparation and reconciliation programs. The reason is simple: as long as the enormity of the abuse and malpractice remains underestimated, any remedial initiative will also be inadequate and insufficient.

Nor is this book written to keep you away from yoga. Scientific studies provide evidence that yoga practice can have a positive impact on brain health.[20] And healthy brain is what you need when you choose a spiritual practice, a teacher, and an organization for guidance. "Do not leave your brain behind," says lawyer and investigator of sexual abuse in spiritual communities Carol Merchasin,[21] and always remain vigilant.

By highlighting the pain, suffering, and shady practices in 3HO, *Under the Yoga Mat* aims to show you why you should be wary of teachers and organizations who claim they know what is good for you better than you do. Trust your own sensing. Training programs that have sleep deprivation built into their schedule, and starve you, are influencing you in an unhealthy way. Euphoric states numb your critical thinking.

Call for Rectification!

This book is written because it is time to adjust the world's perception of this not-so-saintly man and not-so-holy organization. Part of the public injustice inflicted could be righted by amending the 2005 resolution of the US Congress and changing the name of the New Mexico highway to one that honors the survivors rather than the perpetrator.

Inform Those Who Want to Know

The information shared by current leaders about the wrongdoings is shamefully limited. At best, they say, "There was abuse, we acknowledged it, and we will help those who suffered harm." That is far from enough. When it dawned on me that they would not do more anytime soon, I decided to write this book to fill the gap in the truth-telling part of the healing process.

Newcomers, practitioners, and teachers have the right to know to be able to answer the question, "Can I separate the teacher from the teachings?" in a well-informed way. Everyone should be able to choose to look at the whole story, the light and the dark side of it, or not. Teachers or trainers who keep people from this knowledge show how the cult nature is still active in them.

Since mid-2020, I have spent hundreds of hours listening to and reading survivors' stories. In 2021, I summarized and structured what I learned on abuse-in-kundalini-yoga.com. The site and this book compile fragments of publicly available testimonies from children and adults who lived in different periods and locations. Together they provide a broad picture of the atmosphere and culture of 3HO. The selection is made to give an overview of the extent and diversity of the crimes committed and the damages incurred. We cannot represent the lives of thousands of people over fifty years in one book, let this be an invitation for many more to follow.

Under the Yoga Mat shows how Bhajan used his yoga, lifestyle, and religion as a cover-up for his criminal activities and to create conditions to manipulate, use, and abuse his devotees and their children to his advantage. Bhajan's methods and tools carry the potential to control people. It is that simple.

Trigger Warning

Reading this book may be confronting and can be (re)traumatizing for those who were or are still involved in high-demand groups or cultic organizations. **If that is your case, make sure there are people you can reach out to if you get triggered. Contact a trauma-informed and preferably a cult-informed therapist who can assist you.**

Piercing the Myth

Yogi Bhajan told his followers they were privileged and special human beings. They were lighthouses for humanity, more conscious and enlightened than "normal people." Many 3HO members and Kundalini yogis still strongly identify with that image. They believe they possess the exquisite and unique technology, lifestyle, and values to bring salvation and solve all ills. Blinded by that important quest, many are unable or unwilling to see what went on for decades under that holy veil. Bhajan said, "When everyone else goes down, we remain upright. We are the saviors, the spiritual warriors, the chosen ones, the pure ones."

Today, there are still teacher trainers who continue to preach the specialness of this path and how it is different and superior to other paths.

Reading this book may pierce this myth. It may reveal that instead of being more aware than others, we—I count myself as an ex-member of this cult—were more asleep than others. **Letting go of a cult identity is ultimately liberating but can be extremely confronting, frightening, painful, retraumatizing, and complex. It should be done under the guidance of specialized counselors and therapists.**

By retelling the survivors' stories and calling Yogi Bhajan a cult leader, *Under the Yoga Mat* deliberately scratches the wounds to drain the pus, which is very uncomfortable, unpleasant, and painful but necessary.

Cult Nature of 3HO

Cult expert Dr. Steven Hassan developed a model that helps to evaluate cases of exploitation, mind control, thought reform, and undue influence. It is based on four components: control of behavior, information, thoughts, and emotions, and is therefore called the BITE model. I performed a BITE analysis of 3HO at his request using my experience of being showered with survivor stories for three years. It was amazing how easily I could map the 3HO situation to his model[22] as if he developed it for 3HO. The results make it difficult to deny that 3HO was a cult when Yogi Bhajan was still alive.

Alexandra Stein argues in her 3HO-childhood report that 3HO was and still is a cult: "Note that after his [Yogi Bhajan's] death the group has apparently loosened up and may now be moving away from at least some of the elements listed. However, though there have been some incremental improvements, many of the same elements of neglect, abuse, coercion, and isolation from the mainstream as noted above [*she refers to her report*] have persisted at least until 2019."[23]

By describing various aspects of life in 3HO, *Under the Yoga Mat* is of interest to people who want to understand or research high-demand groups and cultic organizations. It will also help readers to recognize situations of undue influence and mind control more quickly.

About Cults

Cults have existed throughout history and come in many different forms. Expert Dr. Steven Hassan gives the following definition in his book *Combating Cult Mind Control*:

> A destructive cult is a group that violates its members' rights and damages them through the abusive techniques of unethical mind control. It distinguishes itself from a normal, healthy social or religious group by subjecting its members to systematic control of behavior, information, thoughts, and emotions (BITE) to keep them dependent and obedient.[24]

How can sane and intelligent people join such groups? It is hard to understand for people who never consciously dealt with cults. Fortunately, academic research has dispelled some myths and misunderstandings in recent years. One such myth is that only weak people can be caught up in them. Here is what Dr. Alexandra Stein has to say on this topic:

> I want to emphasize that the people who find themselves in cults, extremist groups, or even totalitarian nations are ordinary people who did not choose that situation. Rather, the situation—or the group—chose them. . . .

None of us are immune, given the right come-on and the right situation, yet those who do become victims are demonized. This demonization prevents us from recognizing our own potential vulnerability.[25]

In her book *Terror, Love, and Brainwashing*, she explains cult dynamics and how cult leaders create a relationship of disorganized attachment to gain complete control over people's lives.

Dr. Jajna Lalich, another cult expert, explains in her book *Bounded Choice* what she calls the bounded choice perspective:

I have struggled intellectually with issues of belief and coercion, which I see as the heart of the matter. I have concluded that there is a particular state of being, which I call "charismatic commit- ment," that can take root quickly, so that people become easily enmeshed and, in some cases, trapped, at least psychologically. This is the point at which there is a fusion between the ideal of personal freedom (as promised in the state goal of the group or its ideology) and the demand for self-renunciation (as prescribed by the rules and norms). At that point, the believer becomes a "true believer" at the service of the charismatic leader or ideology. In such a context, in relation to personal power and individual decision-making, that person's options are severely limited—hence my overall conclusion is that the best way to understand why cult members do what they do is to consider them in a state of ever-present bounded choice, a narrow realm of constraint and control, dedication and duty.[26]

In their respective books, Jajna Lalich, Steven Hassan, and Alex- andra Stein cite testimonies of survivors of high-demand groups or cultic organizations in various situations. The similarities between their stories and those coming from Bhajan's 3HO community are remarkable.

Setting the Stage

One-on-One Interviews

After reading *Premka* in early 2020, Kundalini Yoga teacher Mina Bahadori felt there was a need in the community to connect and openly discuss what was surfacing. She started interviewing survivors and experts on her Instagram account. In November 2020, she wrapped up after more than thirty revealing and intense live interviews. GuruNischan, born and raised in 3HO, continued this critical work. She created a new podcast/YouTube platform with the all-telling name: *The Uncomfortable Conversations Podcast: The Untold Stories from the 3HO/Kundalini Yoga Community* and invited (ex-)3HO members who felt ready to share their stories in the open. At the time of publication of this book, more than a hundred interviews are available on Instagram, YouTube, and various podcast channels.[27]

The responses to these testimonies show how important they are for other survivors who are often inspired by listening to peers to bring their own stories into the light or seek support.

GuruNischan's first interview was with a good-humored couple in their seventies, Guru Bir Singh and Gur Siri Kaur, who entered 3HO in 1974. Yes, reader, I know. Guru Bir Singh and Gur Siri Kaur. Those names! How are you going to remember such strange names? To keep it simple, I will call this couple Bir and Gur.

Intermezzo on Spiritual Names

Like other cult leaders, Bhajan gave his followers new names to drive them further away from their own identity. 3HO's spiritual names follow the Sikh tradition. Men have Singh as a second name, which means lion. Women are called Kaur, meaning princess.

Baptized 3HO Sikhs use an extra name: Khalsa. It means "pure" and stands for the Sikh ideal of the "warrior-saint." While most Punjabi Sikhs are not initiated into the Khalsa, 3HO Sikhs join the Khalsa more easily. Again, unlike Punjabi Sikhs, baptized 3HO Sikhs use Khalsa as their surname, and Singh and Kaur become middle names. (Are you still with me? If not, no worries. This is not crucial, but still, I need to explain a minimum.)

In 1974, Yogi Bhajan established the Khalsa Council. Initiated members, called ministers, could/can perform Sikh initiations, marriages, and death ceremonies. Initially, only his confidants, mostly community or business leaders, had seats on the Khalsa Council.[28] According to khalsacouncil.com, in 2022, there were seventy-one active ministers, most from the US. Male members are addressed as Singh Sahib and females as Sardarni Sahibas.

Many 3HO members of the first generation renounced their birth names. Their spiritual name became their official name, a solid and clear sign of their commitment to their new lifestyle. This played into the hands of Bhajan, who encouraged his followers to distance themselves from their natural family, especially if relatives were not interested in joining "the dharma."

When Yogi Bhajan was still alive, 3HO parents would call him to receive a name for their newborn. There is a story of a boy to whom Bhajan gave the same name as his brother.

The parents said, "Oh, sir, but you already gave this name to our firstborn."

He replied, "Very well then, that is their karma. They will bear the same name."

Children born in 3HO got those strange-sounding names from birth. GuruNischan, for example, says she often needs to spell her name.

Exiled after Eighteen Years

"Why do you want to share your story?" GuruNischan asks in her very first *Uncomfortable Conversation* with Gur and Bir on November 20, 2020. The husband, Bir, replies:

You know, in our community, everybody loved everybody. We worshiped together. Every morning we did our sadhana [morning practice] together. We went to yoga class together. We washed each other's feet going into the gurdwara [the house of prayer of the Sikhs]. . . .

And then, suddenly, we were told, "Oh! These people are gone. They betrayed our leader and the dharma. They are no longer welcome. Don't let them in whenever they show up at the door." Nobody knew what had happened to them. We never guessed that one day it would be our turn [*Bir and Gur laugh*].

People asked us, "What happened to you? Where did you go? You disappeared from the face of the earth?"

We told them, "No. We didn't."

So, that's why we're here, to share our story.

Bir prepared a summary of what happened to them and read it aloud.

We started awfully long ago, in 1974, in 3HO and the world of Yogi Bhajan, Kundalini Yoga, and ashram life. We've named this our 3HO graduation story. In short: On April 30, 1992, I was arrested, handcuffed, and transported to jail. My arrest was on the evening news on television and front-page news in the morning paper. As a result, I lost my business, my wife lost her job, our children were bullied in school, and we lost our house.

For eighteen years, we had been the beloved son and daughter of the Siri Singh Sahib [Yogi Bhajan's title often used by his devotees]. Overnight, we were exiled from our community.[29]

We will tell Bir and Gur's story in more detail later, but you can already sense that what this family went through had nothing to do with sexual abuse.

After the publication of *Premka* in early 2020, most of the talk was about Bhajan's sexual abuse. Bir and Gur's story is different but equally harsh. It shows how Yogi Bhajan did not shy away from taking everything from an innocent family with two children, turning their lives upside down, to save his skin. Many stories covered in this book show that Bhajan's lack of ethics was monstrously multifaceted.

Faithful until the End

GuruNischan grants her guests ample time to share their experiences. Most Zoom interviews last between ninety minutes and two hours. And yet there is one that tops it all: the interview with Siri Nirongkar, whom we will call Siri. It lasts three hours and thirty-eight minutes. Though long, there is never a dull moment.

Siri was nine when he and his mother entered 3HO in 1976. They lived in the ashram because they could not afford their own flat. Siri was sent to the single men's room where the guards lived who worked for Akal Security and often served as Yogi Bhajan's bodyguards. Over the years, Siri was assigned to three or four different men. They were supposed to care for him as his mom was busy working as a nurse for one of 3HO's medical doctors. Siri recounts:

> She thought she did the right thing. She had no time. I only saw her once in a while.
>
> Growing up with all these guards meant that nobody took advantage of me or beat me and that I was not sexually abused, but I was neglected. I was clothed and fed, and my physical well-being was not in jeopardy. Though nobody gave a shit if I did my homework. Nobody guessed how my day at school was. Nobody gave me a hug. Nobody cared if it was my birthday because I didn't know it myself. To this day, I don't celebrate my birthday. "What's the point?" you know.
>
> These guardians weren't mean. They weren't purposely not asking how my day was. I was not their kid. I bet they didn't even want me. I bet the Siri Singh Sahib, or the head of the ashram, told them, "You're taking a kid." . . .
>
> I once lived with the head of the ashram in Española, New Mexico. That was interesting. I watched the power dynamic as people

came in and out of the house and how they ran things. When people left the community, I heard the conversations about them. As a kid, you're soaking it all up. You're watching and discovering, "Ha, this is how it works." . . .

I wasn't the only kid living with the guards. When I was in Española, there were probably seven or eight of us. We became good friends. We loved to disappear. We played in the irrigation ditch and climbed around in the old barn. We threw chunks of dirt at each other. Because ten-year-old boys aren't the brightest, we got caught from time to time. As a punishment, we had to do push-ups or frogs [one of Yogi Bhajan's favorite exercises: you sit as a frog, fingertips on the ground, stretching your legs up and sitting down again, up and down, up and down]. Then, I would say, "You want me to do frogs? I can do frogs." So, I just busted out frogs. My ability to keep doing that . . . [laughs and shakes his head]. What I figured out as a kid was that I could take punishment longer than they were interested in punishing me. . . .

We knew how to play the game. It was not that difficult. I learned how to quietly do what I wanted. How to make my own plans, and how to avoid problems. I knew the power dynamic and became more and more able to deal with it. We learned to lie like the best. There was no other way. Everyone was lying, and hypocrisy was the norm. But don't get me wrong. I don't mean to make it sound like it was all good. I remember being lonely. How I longed for an adult who would hold me. Someone who would genuinely care about me. I went to a different school every year. I had dreamed of going to military school, but, at the age of fourteen [in 1981], I was sent to a boarding school in India together with other 3HO kids.

Soon after the children arrived in Mussoorie, at the foothills of the Himalayas in the Uttarakhand region, where the school was, the two American adults who had accompanied them from the US to India returned home.

I watched them walk away, and I remember thinking, *There goes my only connection to the US. I don't know how to make a phone call to the US. I don't know how to write a letter to the US. I don't know anything. That's my only connection to the US that just walked away.* That was a strange feeling. Wow, that was like, *OK, I am really on my own now. I am really on my own.* . . .

After all, India was the most stable part of my childhood. I appreciated that part of India. At least I knew where I was going to school next year, and I wouldn't have to make new friends.

Siri stayed in India for the next five years. A few days after he had returned to the US, he was having lunch with seven fellow students at a community gathering. Yogi Bhajan joined them at the table.

"You will all go to college," he said. "None of you will have to pay for it. I will pay for you all."

Later, when the boys inquired about how they would get the money, they were told, "He didn't mean that. It was just a joke."

Siri started working for Akal Security and often served as a personal bodyguard to the master.

I was willing to give my life for him because he was serving something big. And I was serving him to do that. I threatened people for him. I heard him say to people, "You're going to be a prostitute." He told a friend, "When you get to Saint Peter's gate, I will be there. I will make sure you don't get in." My friend wrestled with this for years. Rationally, he knew it was a bunch of shit, but in the back of his mind, he was afraid it might be so. I watched the Siri Singh Sahib do those things. And I should not have stood by. But I was twenty-two years old, you know.

At one point, Siri's boss at Akal Security was a young woman. He thought she was incompetent, arrogant, and a bully. However, she was protected by the Siri Singh Sahib. Regularly, Siri and his teammates were called to the ranch. On those occasions, Yogi Bhajan yelled at them for their behavior toward her. Then, one day, they were called in again.

I had a principle I took to heart: "I bow to no man. I bow only to the *Guru*." [By *Guru*, Siri means the holy book of the Sikhs, the *Guru Granth Sahib*.] So, I never touched Yogi Bhajan's feet as most people did. That day, he told me to get over to him. My body language was probably one hundred percent showing, "I don't give a shit. Can we just get yelled at, so we can leave?" He asked me to massage his feet. I thought, *OK, I don't give massages, I am awful at doing it, but I will do it.*

"What are you doing?" he shouted.

"Massaging your feet."

"Come here."

He got up from his chair. We walked to the back of the ranch toward his bedroom. He opened the door. I walked in first. He hit me so fucking hard in the back of the neck and then punched me in the head. I saw stars. I hit the floor, and he kicked me hard while I was on the ground. He kicked me into a fetal position. I'm not small. I had my body armor on and was wearing a gun.

He looked down at me and said, "You are fucking useless."

I was shocked. I jumped up and said, "Give me one minute to explain."

He looked at his watch.

I said, "If you want to turn this company around, fire the boss. And get in some people who know what they are doing. So, if you want things to work, we need to do this, this, and this . . ."

He looked me up and down. Then he said, "I will burn that fucking business to the ground around her before I ever fire her. Your whole job is to make sure she looks good." He walked out. He was not interested in making that business better. If you have enough of those experiences, you realize you are working to improve things, but the system is not designed to make the place better. The weird thing is that it didn't even hurt me. It was worth it to have him hit me that hard, so I had a moment to say what I needed, so to get it off my chest. If that was what it took to have him open up and listen to me for a minute ... I felt so much better just being allowed to speak out honestly.

In 1992, when Siri was twenty-five, he decided to finally pursue his old dream. He started making arrangements to go to military school.

But Yogi Bhajan pulled me in and said, "The kids are moving to Amritsar [in India, where 3HO was building a new school]. I need somebody to go over there and take care of these kids. You know India. You know the program. You know these kids. You can do this."

Of course, he promised me many things he never delivered. But he knew me. Once I got there, it would be about caring for these kids. It wasn't about me. I would make it work because I cared about these kids. So, I got there, and it was horrendous. We had a hundred kids living in a house. Fifty boys stayed downstairs, and roughly fifty girls upstairs. I had three bathrooms for fifty boys. They had just come from another pretty crappy school in a pretty crappy situation. The academics in the school they were going to was a joke. The living conditions were subpar, for sure. . . .

I didn't have enough food for the kids. Even the little ones had to wash their own clothes, as I had no money for the laundry service. And meanwhile, the Siri Singh Sahib called me regularly to run political errands and get things done for him [in India].

I said, "Sir, I need these things, and these things, to run the school and to do the things you are asking me."

"Yes, I will get them for you."

He never kept his word. Then he called me, "Did you do what I asked you to do?"

"No, because you were supposed to give me this and that."

He always had excuses every time. It slowly started to dawn on me: If my word is supposed to be ironclad, isn't your word even more important? If you're going to take the perks of being in charge, you also get the responsibility, and you are held up to a higher standard. That's just how it works. If you have any honor, that's how it is supposed to work. So, I started to get disillusioned. I said, "Look, I need half a dollar a day per kid to feed them. Why don't I have enough food for the children?" I started to challenge him directly, always polite but firm. . . .

Things were really disjointed and disorganized at the leadership level. It was a mess back in America and in India. We uncovered fraud in the building of the school. Nobody cared. There was embez-zlement of funds. People told me, "We know what the kids are pay-ing." But the money was not there. We did not know where it was. So I said, "I hope you can figure it out. I gotta go back and take care of those kids." I did not have the bandwidth to deal with all that.

After two years, Siri returned to the US. He was determined to do his own thing and became a paramedic. He worked for a few years on his own account. When Yogi Bhajan's health started deteriorating, the nurses regularly called Siri to the ranch to give the master his injections.

He was such a baby about needles. He was terrified of needles. I said, "You're a big strong man. Give me your hand." And boom! I didn't give a shit. Can't you handle a needle? Harden the fuck up, son [laughs].

"You know, all these cheese sticks, pizza, and all that shit are what got you here."

Do you know what he used to do at the movies? How he got his popcorn?

GURUNISCHAN. Yeah, with M&M's at the bottom and popcorn on top.

SIRI. Not just M&M's. A layer of popcorn, a whole order of nachos, an entire box of M&M's, and popcorn on top so the staff wouldn't see. He ate awful! That's what did him in.

Things really changed between us during that time. I was in the back of the car when he was driven miles and miles to the hospital in Albuquerque. He had heart attacks and missed toes from diabe-tes. He had one kidney, was in constant pain, and was drugged to the gills. His life was miserable. Compassionately I was saying, "I forgive you. Hurry up and die. You have no quality of life. What are you hanging on for?" It felt good I could take care of him in the end. For all the shit he did to people I know and to me. For all that I had watched him do, I said, "I'm going to be big and have a big heart. I am going to take care of you. I am going to watch you die." It got to a point where our conversations were so frank.

The staff asked Siri more and more to visit Yogi Bhajan. "We ask you because you don't want anything from him," they said. "You're not going to be a drain on his energy. You're a distraction, a couple of minutes of entertainment for him. He really enjoys seeing you." So, Siri stopped by occasionally. One day they called him in to give another injection. While everyone else in the room had taken the habit of using whispering voices, Siri just used his normal voice to greet him.

"How are you doing, sir?" I leaned over to listen to what he had to say.

"Well enough to kick your ass."

"Oh, wow," I just stood up and laughed. "No doubt, sir. No doubt at all. OK, what are we here for today?"

That was my goodbye. I felt really good about where we were at.

Two days later, Yogi Bhajan died. Siri had arranged with his boss at the ambulance to drive Yogi Bhajan's dead body to the funeral home in Santa Fe. It was at night. They had to go to a dark alley behind the funeral home, where there was a walk-in cooler. With his bare hands, Siri placed the master's body on a shelf in the steel refrigerator.

"It looked like it could have been an industrial kitchen, but instead, it stored bodies."

He closed the door and stood in the alley looking at the walk-in cooler door and said, "That's quite an end, buddy. Where's all your power, jewels, cars, and people? They're all fucking gone." And that was the end of it. Siri did not go to the funeral. He forgave Yogi Bhajan.

Siri ends his three-and-a-half-hour-long interview with the following words:

> There's obviously a huge fracture in our community right now. For simplicity, there are deniers, and there are believers. I don't know why we can't all get along. Why can't someone who denies all this say, "I can't deal with it. He's still my spiritual teacher who brought me to the feet of the *Guru*. Yoga and meditation work for me, and I will leave it at that. I'm not going to call you a liar."
>
> And for the people who believe all of it. I want to hear compassion from them and say, "He did these things. He's no longer my teacher. I can't deal with him. But you get to have your experience. Just don't call me a liar."
>
> Because the same person can be sensed differently by different people. I don't have a problem with that. Because we are humans. And we are complicated.[30]

YOGI BHAJAN AND HIS YOGA

A Refugee in His Own Land

Harbhajan Singh Puri was born on August 26, 1929. His father was a medical doctor and a Sikh, and his mother was a Hindu. They lived in a small village in a district of the Punjab that was still part of India in those days. He went to a Catholic school run by nuns. His grandfather taught him about the Sikh religion and culture and took him to the gurdwara, the house of prayer of the Sikhs.

In 1947, India became independent from British rule. A separate state was created for the Muslims. The Islamic Republic of Pakistan was born. Harbhajan's village was part of the region that was no longer Indian territory. He, his family, and other village people had to flee. Harbhajan was eighteen. The partitioning was violent, with looting, burning, rape, and genocide. Almost one million people died, including 600,000 Punjabis. Fourteen million people were forced to move from Western Pakistan to India, losing their homes, land, and jobs. After an arduous journey, they arrived as refugees in New Delhi, a Hindu-dominated city. Sikhs were not welcome and had to start new lives in a hostile environment.

In 1948, the University of Punjab opened Evening Camp College in New Delhi for Sikh refugee students. Classrooms were rented from a day school as a base for providing these students with classes. There was no library, meeting hall, canteen, or hostel. Many could not pay their college fees. Through fierce lobbying with the government, the students obtained tents to live in and loans to pay for their college fees. Every evening, they came together on the school grounds to listen to speeches and sing Punjabi songs. Some wept while singing those songs. The wounds of the partition were still fresh.

This difficult situation was described by Dr. Shamsher Singh, a contemporary of Harbhajan who was born in the same part of Punjab and who worked at the World Bank in Washington, DC. He shared his memories in the prestigious 1979 memorial book, *The Man Called the Siri Singh Sahib*, published to celebrate Yogi Bhajan's ten years in the US. Shamsher remembered Harbhajan as an active and ubiquitous member of the Sikh Students Federation in New Delhi. He described him as a tall, handsome, talkative, youthful figure with a barely sprouting beard who was never a loner. "Bhaji the Tall," he was called. "He seemed in a state of ever-preparedness to go on any errand, undertake any task, or assist anyone in need of help," Shamsher wrote.[31]

In 1952, Harbhajan got married. A year after his marriage, he started working for the revenue department of the Indian Government and traveled a lot throughout the country.

One day, something extraordinary happened. Bhajan called it a virtual turning point in his life as he told the story in his memorial book. That morning, he was ready to go off to work. His orderly had brought the car out. Harbhajan had put on his best uniform because he would submit an important case in which he had requested a punishment harder than anybody else could have given. Before he got into the car, his mother came out of the house and asked him what he would do that day at work. She wanted to know all the details. He told her about the case and mentioned the names of the people involved. His mother looked him in the eyes, raised her hand, and slapped him so hard his turban fell off. She told him she was angry because her son did not know how to have compassion that could stand above the law. What had happened was that the offenders knew that Bhajan would not accept bribery. So, they had reached out for his weakest spot: his mother. When he arrived at work, Bhajan put a note on the case file. His mother's involvement had created a prejudicial circumstance. Therefore, he could not decide on the case. In the evening, he asked her again why she had done this to him. She said, "I did what a mother should do. I don't want you to be known as so honest that people should be afraid that you have no compassion left in you."

In the recounting of this story, Bhajan admitted he recognized the same bluntness in his life. "I also understand that there is nobody else on this Earth who can have the privilege to catch me and just slap me in public and still feel it is her right. This privilege belongs to just one person in life."[32]

After a few years in the revenue department, Harbhajan was promoted to customs inspector at New Delhi airport. In all, he served the Indian Government for eighteen years. The memorial book highlights his reputation among senior and junior officers for always being honest and acting with integrity. He was a respected man who could not be fooled because he was able to read auras and knew when people were telling the truth.

One day, a Canadian man conversed with Harbhajan at the airport in New Delhi. He shared how hard it was to find someone to come and teach yoga at the University of Toronto. Customs Officer Harbhajan told the gentleman about his yogic training, and he got the job.

The Conquest of the West

Harbhajan the Yogi

Harbhajan resigned as a customs officer at New Delhi airport, and in September 1968, he flew to Canada. He left his wife and children in New Delhi until it he could bring them over later. In London, his luggage got lost. He arrived in freezing Toronto with the clothes he was wearing and with almost no money in his pocket. When he tried to reach his host, he learned the man had died in a car accident. Harbhajan found a job as a clerk at a book publisher. After work, he taught yoga.

Three months after his arrival, an old New Delhi friend invited him to Los Angeles for a weekend that ended up being years. He sensed that Los Angeles was "the center of the youth's movement toward self-knowledge, self-discovery, and expression of real and meaningful values." He had been led to this place because he had the right knowledge, experience, and technology that could "fulfill the longings of those searching souls." He began teaching Kundalini Yoga at the East-West Cultural Center.[33] Soon, his yoga classes drew large crowds. Several people testified that under his influence, they had rid themselves of drug and alcohol addictions. His vigorous yoga sets and intense meditations brought them to states of bliss as psychedelics and alcohol had done before.

In 1969, Yogi Bhajan established 3HO "to promote a conscious lifestyle of elevation, awareness, and total health."[34] His disciples started calling him the yogi or Yogiji.[35] They followed the dogmas, rituals, and customs he introduced to shape his self-styled version of Sikhism. Bhajan's Sikhs were called 3HO or Western Sikhs. His approach caused discussion and division in the community of Punjabi Sikhs. Some were happy he gave their religion more visibility in the West. Others were resentful because he knew so little about the Sikh faith, mixed it with yoga, and profiled himself as a Sikh leader.

After a few yoga classes, the yogi urged his students to start teaching yoga and spread the 3HO–Sikh Dharma lifestyle in the new ashrams they created in the US, Canada, or Europe. As the community grew and became more geographically widespread, Yogi Bhajan kept the reins tight via frequent phone calls and regular visits. Gatherings were organized to build, maintain, and strengthen the "we-are-all-one-big-family" feeling. The main events were the celebration of the summer solstice and winter solstice, both in the US, and the annual European Yoga Festival in France. These were unique opportunities for 3HO members to meet friends and peers from all over the world. And, not unimportantly, for many, this was "the" chance to meet the yogi in person, to ask his advice on marriage, divorce, children, education, work, health, or whatever. These big events allowed Bhajan to sense and measure his people's loyalty, so he could adjust where needed. They were a time for him to inform his followers about new and changing doctrines.

As of 1977, the summer solstice gathering occurred at Ram Das Puri land in Española, New Mexico. Each year, after summer solstice, the women stayed at the women's camp for six more weeks. Men were sent home to care for the businesses, and kids were transferred to isolated children's camps in the high desert. In his daily lectures at these women's camps, Yogi Bhajan taught women how to become good wives and good women.

Harbhajan the Mahan Tantric

In 1971, musician Peter Macdonald Blachly participated in the summer solstice celebration. In those early days, this event occurred in Paonia, Colorado, at 9,000 feet above sea level, in the middle of the Rocky Mountains. The Tantric Yoga that Yogi Bhajan taught was the most exciting experience in Peter's new 3HO life.

> Every afternoon we gathered, sitting in long rows, men and women facing each other to do exercises as couples under his [Yogi Bhajan's] direction. Never before had I experienced anything either so difficult or so rewarding. Each exercise seemed harder than the last. We would hold our arms straight out with our palms turned up, or our legs raised to 60 degrees, or our arms with palms together stretched above our heads—and hold these difficult positions for 31 minutes, or even 62 minutes at a stretch. Combined with the positions would be long, deep breathing, breath of fire, or chanting of a mantra. And the entire time we would stare into our partner's eyes. People were collapsing or just giving up right and left, only to be coaxed back into the exercise by "monitors" who navigated between the rows to keep everyone in line.

By the end of each day, we were all completely wiped out, but in such an altered state that everything about the experience took on epic, if not magical proportions. On several evenings we broke into spontaneous celebration, with guitars and drums seeming to appear out of nowhere to drive a frenzied release of pent-up emotions in dance and song. These were the moments I loved the best. I would join fellow musicians in improvising rhythms, chords, and melodies to accompany the various mantras we had learned. With 300 enthusiastic voices joining in we could go for an hour or more on the simplest melody. Our shining faces, reflected in the firelight, revealed the ecstasy we all felt. Eyes met eyes with love and absence of judgment. We were, each one of us, "clear channels." Together as a group, we felt we could transform the world.[36]

In the early 3HO days, everyone led tantric sessions, but in 1971, the rules changed. From then on, Yogi Bhajan assumed the title of Mahan Tantric, which means "great teacher of Tantra." It implied that he was the only living individual on earth allowed to teach Tantric Yoga. Not long after that, he started calling it White Tantra.

Sixteen years later, in 1987, White Tantra sessions were recorded on video so that these teachings could continue after Bhajan's death. Another sixteen years later, in October 2004, one week after the master died, Sikh Dharma leadership released a directive: "As the Mahan Tantric, the Siri Singh Sahib planned for the continuation of White Tantric Yoga seminars to be taught as a vital tool for the upliftment of humanity. His subtle body will continue to preside, and the video courses he made over the last 17 years will continue to be used all over the globe."[37]

Certain disciples must have felt cheated when they heard this. From testimonies, we know that Yogi Bhajan had promised several people that they would become the next Mahan Tantric.

Two historians, Dr. Trilochan Singh[38] and Philip Deslippe,[39] expressed severe doubts about everything Yogi Bhajan said and claimed about White Tantric Yoga. They suggested he made it all up, including the title Mahan Tantric. There are no sources other than his own to confirm anything he said about the practice.

Harbhajan the Siri Singh Sahib

On the homepage of the Sikh Dharma International website, you can click to "About the Siri Singh Sahib." The banner shows a picture of a serious-looking Bhajan in white attire in a green hillside setting. He sits on a bench looking sideways, his left arm leaning on a stone wall. The page gives a Bhajan version of his arrival in the US and how he got his titles.

> In 1971, in acknowledgement of his extraordinary impact of spreading the universal message of Sikh Dharma, the president of the S.G.P.C.[40] (the governing body of Sikh Temples in India), Sant Chanan Singh, called him the *Siri Singh Sahib*, Chief Religious and Administrative Authority for the Western Hemisphere.[41]

In 1977, Dr. Trilochan Singh, a Sikh historian whom we'll present to you in the next section, commented on Bhajan's titles:

> I met a very prominent sitting member of S.G.P.C. who is touring the U.S.A. and Canada for an undeclared mission. . . . [I] asked him how on earth could the S.G.P.C. do such an absurd thing. He [the prominent member] had attended all the meetings in 1970–1974 and no such title was ever sanctioned by S.G.P.C. Executive. . . .
>
> A Robe of honor was given to Yogi Bhajan in 1974 on the recommendation of President Taura, but a Robe of honor does not carry any title with it, nor does it give authority of any kind. If Yogi Bhajan had been made any such Chief of the Western Sikhs in 1971 then a Robe of honor in 1974 was meaningless. . . .
>
> There is no such Ecclesiastical title as Siri Singh Sahib, and others ridiculously created by Yogi Bhajan . . . .[42]

Also in 1977, a man representing the highest Sikh authority signed a document declaring that "no such title as Siri Singh Sahib exists" and that it "has never been bestowed by me to any person." The signer told an Amritsar-based newspaper later that Yogi Bhajan could not call himself Siri Singh Sahib under any circumstances and that he was misleading and making a fool of his American Sikhs and devotees in the name of Sikhism. However, Yogi Bhajan kept the myth alive. In 1985 he said, "They took me before the Akal Takhat, [main Sikh body of authority in Amritsar, Punjab], they gave me the sword, they told me, 'You are Siri Singh Sahib.'"[43]

Stop Talking Nonsense

Before historian Dr. Trilochan Singh visited the West in the mid-1970s, he had spent twenty-five years in India, mostly in silence, meditating, researching, and writing. He wrote twenty books and two hundred research papers on Sikh history, philosophy, and comparative study of religions and research-oriented biographies of three Sikh gurus. Besides that, Trilochan also made readable and authentic translations of the holy book of the Sikhs. In the academic world, he was revered for his knowledge of Sikhism and for the many languages he spoke.[44] He died in 1993, "pen in hand and the final manuscript in his lap while discussing it with an editor."[45]

In 1976, Trilochan was invited to London to lecture on Sikh philosophy at six universities. At Oxford, he met Dr. Shamsher Singh of the World Bank and another gentleman who was a professor at Bucknell University in Pennsylvania. Trilochan accepted their invitation to come to the US. In March 1977, he started a five-month lecture tour in the US.

In Washington, he was a guest at the house of Shamsher. It was there that he met for the first time a disciple of Yogi Bhajan. The young man commented on how he saw a Punjabi Sikh meditate and say his prayers. The person who was being criticized by the Bhajan follower was a divine singer from an important Sikh temple in India. Trilochan was outraged. "I have never slapped anyone, but for once, I felt like slapping this incurably arrogant man, but then I thought this is how his Master has trained him."

Next, the 3HO man told Trilochan that many Americans who had left 3HO must have come to see the historian since he arrived in the US to complain about 3HO and its way of working.

I reacted strongly and told him, "Will you stop telling lies and talking all this nonsense? What the hell do you people know about
[names of prayers and singers]? Why do you people live in fear if
you are all saints and Khalsas? Why have you come to me at all? Get
away from here. Do not dare to insult my friends and our revered
Saints. I do not know what you people are up to." [Name of the 3HO
member] probably phoned about this encounter with me and to my
great surprise Yogi Bhajan flew from Los Angeles to Washington
the next day and contacted Dr. Shamsher Singh in his office. He
came home with Shamsher Singh, expecting I would be there.[46]

Trilochan returned to the house of his host late at night when Bhajan had already left. The next day, they met at the 3HO ashram and
spoke for three hours. Trilochan questioned Bhajan about his teachings
and reported the details of this meeting in his book *Sikhism and Tantric
Yoga: A Critical Evaluation of Yogi Bhajan's Tantric Yoga in the Light of
Mystical Experiences and Doctrines*. He wrote it during his US trip in
1977 because he felt it was necessary to document what he had experienced with Yogi Bhajan and his 3HO community.

Tantra (White as he calls it) is his [Bhajan's] basic faith while Sikhism
is only an offshoot of his Tantric system. The reason he gave was that
he believed Sikhism has no meditation techniques. I told him that
Sikhism has more specific, fruitful, and spiritually exalting techniques
of meditation, but his misfortune is that he has never studied *Siri Guru
Granth Sahib*, and never cared to live according to Sikh Discipline.[47]

Later, Dr. Trilochan Singh traveled to Los Angeles, where he met
with half a dozen 3HO leaders who had left Yogi Bhajan. They shared
their positive and negative experiences.

During the last four months [when Trilochan was traveling through
the US], every friend and foe of Yogi Bhajan has come to me and
discussed this controversial man with a streak of genius for

extremely good actions and extremely bad deeds. Yogi Bhajan is a
Sikh by birth, a Mafia Tantric by choice but without training, and
a 'Siri Singh Sahib' and self-styled Leader of Sikhs of Western
Hemisphere by fluke and mysterious strategy. He has undoubtedly
helped many people and taken them out of the hellish pit of drugs
and homelessness, a great contribution by itself; to some he has
given the right path, but the wrong techniques and doctrines
gleaned from his pedestrian knowledge of many Indian traditions.

His disciples beautifully dressed in Classical Sikh style, a thing
charming and courageous by itself, and not easy for those who do
it in this country, are indoctrinated by utterly absurd doctrines of
Tantra and hearsay mantras of Sikhism. Within six years he could
have given them a detailed interpretation of Sikh scriptures and the
best works on Sikh history; but as he is himself gravely ignorant of
them all, and unable to interpret even two pages of *Adi Guru Granth*
[another name for the holy book of the Sikhs], he has been feeding
them with mumbo-jumbo sermons, which sometimes do not make
any sense. I have quoted [in *Sikhism and Tantric Yoga*] innumerable
instances of his abhorrent knowledge of Sikhism which would
make a high school student from the Punjab burst into laughter.

The sincerity of his followers is so deep and profound that even
for their sake one would hesitate to criticize 3HO; but their igno-
rance and misguided faith may lead to a situation when they too
may fall away disillusioned and disgusted with his false doctrines
and blame Sikhism and Sikh savants for not warning them and
saving them. . . . I admire him for many of his qualities which make
him distinguished and lovable like a famous Circus Clown. . . .

I have always paid the price of isolating historical truths from
political campaigns of self-interest of the few. I will do it again. Even
fifty years from now this book will have a meaning and significance
of its own.[48]

Trilochan's prediction proved to be correct. Almost fifty years later,
his book is cited more than ever.

Devotion and Hostility

Dr. Trilochan Singh noted with dismay how Bhajan had so much impact on his followers despite having so little knowledge of the holy book. One of the examples he used to substantiate his claims was the mantra *Sa Ta Na Ma*, frequently part of Bhajan's Kundalini Yoga sets or meditations. Bhajan taught that each syllable had its own meaning: *Sa* – infinity, *Ta* – life, *Na* – death, and *Ma* – rebirth. Trilochan commented, "In the dictionary of no Indian language can one find the meaning of these syllables, Sa-Ta-Na-Ma, as Infinity-life-death-rebirth. Yogi Bhajan has specially invented it for his American followers and, wonder of wonders, they believe him and are prepared to believe any other balderdash in the name of unknown mysteries of Kundalini Yoga."[49]

Trilochan dedicated his book to the 3HO Sikhs:

> Whose devotion to Sikhism is unique and exemplary, Whose passion to learn from historical experiences and the lives of really great Sikh saints is marvelous, . . .
>
> In the Hope and Sincere Expectation that they will reject false doctrines and accept Truth as revealed in Sikh Scripture, that they will reject completely Tantric and other Yogas and be Sikh divines. . . .[50]

In 1977, the Sikh historian was not the only one who felt the need to expose Bhajan's darker sides. The opening lines of a *Time* magazine's article read:

> The leader of 3HO inspires devotion—and hostility.
>
> Nine years ago, he was an anonymous yoga teacher who owned little but a suitcase full of beads. Today he earns over $100,000 a year in lecture fees as Yogi Bhajan, the "Supreme Religious and Administrative Authority of the Sikh Religion in the Western Hemisphere." Thousands of American disciples in his Healthy-Happy-Holy Organization ("3HO") revere the robust, bearded Bhajan as the

holiest man of this era. With equal fervor, opponents denounce him as a charlatan and a heretic.[51]

According to *Time*, 110 ashrams of various sizes existed in the US, Canada, and overseas. Community members worked "twelve hours a day on low salaries and skimpy diets at 3HO small businesses, such as landscaping companies, shoe stores, and quality vegetarian restaurants."

A 3HO spokesman had called Bhajan the equivalent of the pope. Dr. Trilochan Singh had told *Time* that Bhajan's yogic and tantric "sexual practices" were forbidden and immoral. Judith Tyberg, the respected founder of the Los Angeles East-West Center, had questioned Bhajan's knowledge of Kundalini Yoga and shared that she had fired him after three months for reasons she did not want to disclose. *Time* reported that Bhajan had been accused of being a womanizer served "by a coterie of as many as 14 women, some of whom attend his baths, give him group massages, and take turns spending the night in his room while his wife sleeps elsewhere."

Time reported that Bhajan told a man who left 3HO he would suffer 84 million reincarnations and would be reborn as a worm for betraying his teacher. Bhajan refused *Time* an interview, and his chancellor had stressed that "reports of illicit affairs and of women in the yogi's bedroom were 'absolutely untrue.'"

In London, a group of Western Sikhs and their Punjabi Sikh friends protested in front of the Time & Life Building against this article.[52]

In 1979, two years later, the 3HO community celebrated Yogi Bhajan's ten years in the US. At this occasion, he said about himself:

There are three in me.

One is Harbhajan Singh. One is Yogi Bhajan. One is Siri Singh Sahib.

Siri Singh Sahib is a very direct hassler who'll nail you on the spot. He'll find everything wrong with you, analyze you like anything, shatter you like you are nobody.

Yogi Bhajan is that compassionate, analytical, intelligent man who tells you this is this because of that; but it is up to you, son, or daughter, do whatever you want.

Then there is one Harbhajan Singh who will say, "Well, let us all freak out. Don't worry, there is no problem in the world, everything is all right, God and me, me and God are one."[53]

Cult Deprogrammers Circling Around

In his book *Confessions of an American* Sikh, Gursant tells many revealing stories of his time in 3HO. He remembers, for example, how 3HO members reacted to the book of Dr. Trilochan Singh and the cult deprogramming attempts by concerned family members.

The Time article quoted a well-respected Sikh scholar and historian Dr. Trilochan Singh who said, "Bhajan's synthesis of Sikhism and Tantrism is a sacrilegious hodgepodge." . . . If the Time article had been scathing, Trilochan Singh's book was devastating in its assessment of the validity of Yogiji's teachings.

The book was never distributed in the US and very few of Yogiji's students ever heard of it let alone read it. Certainly, it was unknown to me. The few of Yogiji's students who read it dismissed it in this manner: "This guy, Trilochan Singh, knows nothing of the spirit, consciousness, or grace of the Siri Singh Sahib's teachings. He is looking from a very narrow perspective. He is an intellectual Sikh who only values the rituals and ceremonies of Sikhism but not the spirit."

Certain people who styled themselves as "cult deprogrammers" started circling around some of our members. They actually came to 3HO homes a couple of times and dragged some ashramites away, kicking and screaming. We always expected the victims to come back as soon as they got a chance, but they never did.[54]

Since Gursant left the community in 2009, he has been denouncing the ignorant way Bhajan's follower's deal with Sikhism on his site gurmukhyoga.com. His tactics against (ex-)members of 3HO, among other things, have made Gurstant a disliked and controversial figure in 3HO and with many survivors. In 2022, he gained media attention for his fight to rename the Yogi Bhajan Memorial Highway in New Mexico.[55]

Origin of Bhajan's Yoga

The True Kundalini Yoga

Kundalini is a Sanskrit word that literally means "coiled serpent." According to Hindu philosophy, it is a form of divine feminine energy, the creative aspect of Shakti, the primal cosmic energy that is the origin of mind and matter.

Sir John Woodroffe, a British orientalist, was born in Calcutta in 1865. India was still ruled by Britain. He was a lawyer at the Calcutta High Court before becoming a Tagore Law School professor. At the end of his career, he was chief justice of India. Besides his judicial duties, he studied Sanskrit and Hindu philosophy and published books under the pseudonym Arthur Avalon. In 1919, he released *The Serpent Power: The Secrets of Tantric & Shaktic Yoga*. Among Indian scholars, his work in orientalism is considered groundbreaking. He profoundly understood Kundalini. Woodroffe's book is recognized as the most essential document for the study and application of Kundalini Yoga. Yet, this comprehensive work was never cited by Bhajan.

Another renown work never mentioned in Bhajan's teachings is the book *Kundalini Yoga* by Sri Swami Sivananda. The author was born in 1887 into a prominent Indian family. As a successful medical doctor, he observed that conventional medicine only cured superficial symptoms. In 1924, he began a rich spiritual life while continuing to care for the sick. In 1936, he started his own ashram on the banks of the Ganges. He broke with an old tradition by making spiritual reading available to everyone. Bringing yoga closer to the people earned him the name "Yogi Propagandananda." His description of Kundalini Yoga is close to that of Woodroffe's. However, his book is less academic, more accessible, and more practical. The first page shows a picture of the bald author with a Buddha smile. An eleven-leaf Lotus flower with the OM symbol at its center is pictured next to it. Four words are written around it: "Serve, Love, Meditate, Realize."

Those who studied Bhajan's yoga will link this to his "Obey, Serve, Love, Excel" mantra. Was he inspired by Sri Swami Sivananda? A fact is that Bhajan's version is more attuned to his personal goals and interests: "Obey, Serve, Love, Excel" versus "Serve, Love, Meditate, Realize."

Judith Tyberg and Dr. Trilochan Singh did not think highly of Yogi Bhajan's knowledge of Kundalini Yoga, which they felt was inconsistent with the tantric texts they studied.

The question arises: If Yogi Bhajan was not teaching Kundalini, what was he teaching?

Bhajan's Yoga: Copy and Paste

Historian Philip Deslippe researched Yogi Bhajan's past, including his yogic and spiritual education. The information in this section comes mainly from his often-cited article "From Maharaj to Mahan Tantric: The Construction of Yogi Bhajan's Kundalini Yoga."[56] In this study, released in December 2012, Deslippe contradicts what Bhajan always said: that he was a master of Kundalini Yoga at age sixteen. The historian reveals that Bhajan started studying yoga in his early thirties with Dhirendra Brahmachari, a Hindu yogi five years older than Bhajan. In his paper, he shows many resemblances between Dhirendra's and Bhajan's yoga, for example, using breath of fire while holding postures. Deslippe claims that extracts from Dhirendra's books were copied and pasted into 3HO teaching material without crediting the source.

All information about the lineage and practice of Bhajan's Kundalini Yoga, as presented in manuals, books, and 3HO periodicals, came from Yogi Bhajan's own lectures and student notes, says Deslippe. "Yogi Bhajan is best thought of as neither a lineage holder nor an inventor, but as a *bricoleur* who brought together elements of different practices and presented them to his students as a distinct entity with a romantic mythology surrounding it. Perhaps it says as much about Yogi Bhajan as it does about the expectations and hopes of those who believed him."[57]

Sandals on the Bed

Dhirendra was Harbhajan's yoga teacher but not his spiritual master. That was Sant Virsa Singh. A *Sant* is a Sikh saint who has attained spiritual enlightenment and whose power and knowledge come directly from God.

Deslippe found out that before coming to the West, Harbhajan and his wife had served in Virsa Singh's ashram for many years. At the end of his working day, while still wearing his customs officer's uniform, Harbhajan dutifully cleaned the toilets in his master's ashram.

Upon arrival in Los Angeles in late 1968, Yogi Bhajan used to put the old sandals of his master on his bed at night and slept on the floor. A life-size picture of Virsa Singh dressed all in white stood at the center of his altar.[58] In the spring of 1970, Yogi Bhajan changed the protocol and appeared in white himself. Suddenly, his students had to bow to him, and he started using the titles we mentioned earlier. His followers now meditated on his picture, no longer on that of Virsa Singh.[59]

The Clash between Master and Disciple

The most significant changes in the narrative and behavior of Yogi Bhajan appeared after a trip to India at the turn of 1970–1971. Yogi Bhajan took eighty-four of his followers to his homeland for a three-month spiritual pilgrimage. The group stayed at the ashram of Virsa Singh. After a few days, there was a big clash between the master and his disciple. Different people report different reasons for the clash.[60]

Was the dispute about money? Yogi Bhajan had sent money in advance to prepare the sleeping accommodations for his American students. He was not satisfied with the setup.

Or was it because Virsa Singh had declared in front of Yogi Bhajan's followers that yoga had nothing to do with Sikhism? Virsa Singh did not believe in yoga as a spiritual path.

Or was the dispute about image and prestige? To whom did this group of mostly white Americans belong? To whom would they bow?

Or was it because of Yogi Bhajan's wife? She had stayed alone in New Delhi for three years with the children. She was very close and loyal to Virsa Singh, and Yogi Bhajan was far from happy with that. Moreover, she had not greeted him properly on arrival.

Or was it a combination of all these elements, or yet something else?

The fact is that Bhajan's group had to leave Virsa Singh's ashram quite abruptly and in a fairly dramatic way.

After this tumultuous India trip, Virsa Singh, who had been worshiped within 3HO as a demi-God before, became persona non grata. Philip Deslippe wrote, "The sandals of Maharaj Virsa Singh no longer had their place on Yogi Bhajan's bed; in both a literal and a symbolic sense, that space was now his. . . . The original story of Yogi Bhajan cleaning toilets for Maharaj Virsa Singh . . . was turned into washing the floors at the Golden Temple after work."[61]

The historian points out that the Golden Temple, the major spiritual center of the Sikhs in Amritsar, is about 290 miles (470 km) from New Delhi, where Bhajan worked. It is very odd that he would travel such a distance back and forth, every evening.

The Invisible Sant

Soon after the India trip, a new teacher appeared on the scene, Sant Hazara Singh. Yogi Bhajan suddenly started talking about this holy man, a master of Sikh martial arts, Kundalini Yoga, and White Tantric Yoga. A saint who knew the *Siri Guru Granth*, the holy book of the Sikhs, by heart. According to Bhajan, Hazara Singh was a brave man who organized an armed defense of the city of Anandpur, during the partition in 1947. Deslippe wonders why, outside of 3HO sources, no documentation exists on a man with such a track record.[62]

More than once, Bhajan recounted how his teacher, Sant Hazara Singh, recognized him, at the age of sixteen, as a master in Kundalini Yoga. That must have been in 1945, two years before his family and community were forced to flee to New Delhi. Here is how he told this story to his followers in Los Angeles in 1990: Sant Hazara Singh had called on him when he was sixteen. When he was twelve, Harbhajan had received a similar invitation to appear before his beloved master, but nothing extraordinary had occurred then. Four years later, this is what happened:

The law is: Obey, Serve, Love, and Excel. This is the spiritual essence. So, I had the habit to obey my teacher. I went in. I bowed down. I got up.

He said, "Bhajan, it is a very special day. I have called you."

I said, "Yes, Master."

"You ARE the master."

"Yes, sir." Out of habit I said, "Yes, sir."

He said, "That's it. Well, there are certain conditions with it."

I said, "Please let me know."

He said certain things.

"Thank you, sir."

"You can retire now."

I came out. There were twenty-five to thirty people, whatever they were.

"What happened, what happened?"

"Don't you see?"

"No."

"Don't you know?"

"No."

I said, "I am the master. Bow!"

And they all bowed.

I said, "Wow! It works!" I said, "Now rise! This is what happened! That's what the master said, 'I am the master.'"

"Yes, sir."

Because they had the same conscious habit to obey, too. There was no logic, no reason, no debate, no asking, no questioning, . . . nothing. I hope you will carry the tradition, with grace and your utmost dignity, wherever you find fit.[63]

The site of Sikh Dharma International shows a picture of the "one man who changed and directed Yogi Bhajan's life like no other."[64] Shanti Kaur Khalsa writes that she met Sant Hazara's grandson in 2017. He told her that Sant Hazara grew up in a village south of Amritsar, where he studied with Sant Baba Sohan Singh, who came from a lineage of Sikh heroes. When Hazara came of age, his teacher sent him away to start a school in the area where young Harbhajan lived. The article includes a Yogi Bhajan quote from July 4, 1995: "I went through a very tough teacher… He brought out of me, not the man, not the godly man, not the great man, but a real human. There's nothing in the world I can pay to him in tributes, in compliments, and in thanks. He did the most wonderful job. I used to say I was a nut, but he tightened all my nuts so good that I became the best. And that's why [I say that] calamity is my breakfast, tragedy is my lunch, and treachery is my supper… What else do you want after this? Is there anything else which can bother you? If you can eat all these three things and digest them, you are the best person."

On the KRI site, the same author tells a different story. It is not dated. As it is more modest, it could be of a more recent date. For this story, Shanti Kaur spoke to someone who had known Sant Hazara Singh as a child. He told her that the five-year-old Hazara had survived an earthquake that killed all his relatives. The great Baba Sohan Singh took in the child, and Hazara became his devoted student and son. This text ends with: "It is still a mystery where and when Sant Hazara Singh learned Kundalini Yoga. And there is no indication that Sant Hazara Singh studied yoga from Baba Sohan Singh. This is part of the story that, by Guru's grace, is yet to unfold."[65]

Facts and Papers

To summarize this chapter on Yogi Bhajan and his yoga, we can say that some facts are well established: Harbhajan Singh was born in 1929 to a Sikh father in the part of India that is now Pakistan. At eighteen, in 1947, during the partition that killed 600,000 Sikhs, he experienced the violent migration of fourteen million people. He arrived in New Delhi, where Sikh refugees were not welcome. He dedicated himself to improving the situation of the Punjabi students in Delhi. He worked for eighteen years for the Indian government. In 1968, he moved to Canada, and later the US, where he presented himself as and was believed to be a yoga master. Gullible and uncritical American youths, who had read *Autobiography of a Yogi* and were looking for new ways to freedom and happiness, crowded at his feet to serve and enrich him. He could make up titles, invent history, and ignore historians because his followers were convinced that he, and he alone, held the truth.

A review of scholarly research on 3HO in religious studies, anthropology, or sociology faculties can be found in a 2016 academic dissertation on *3HO in the Light of Experience* in the section "Previous studies of 3HO."[66] It notes that 3HO was mentioned in the *Encyclopedia of American Religions* in 1978 and the *Encyclopedic Handbook of Cults in America* in 1992. The review shows how different authors have different views on how Bhajan's Sikh Dharma relates to the Punjabi Sikh religion. Besides briefly mentioning the lawsuits against Yogi Bhajan in 1986, this thesis does not mention the abuse and criminal activities within 3HO.

In 2021, Rob Zabel, a graduate student at the University of Chicago, released an "in-depth study" of Bhajan's Yoga.[67] It relates YB's teachings to other yoga traditions and other expressions of Sikh yoga. It does not address the abuse. KRI, the Kundalini Research Institute, supported the creation of this paper. Much energy goes into proving that there is no incompatibility between Sikhism and yoga, contrary to what historian and Sikh scholar Dr. Trilochan Singh proclaimed. Similarly, many arguments are presented to confirm that Sant Hazara Singh was YB's first teacher. Zabel claims that, since Philip Deslippe's article appeared ten years ago, "a wealth of sources has materialized" showing Hazara existed and is known by people today. To prove that, the author cites 3HO-related sources and his conversation with a Punjabi Sikh.

THE GURU HEYDAYS

You Need a Guru

Autobiography of a Yogi was published in 1946, translated into fifty languages, read by millions, and is included in the list of 50 Spiritual Classics.[68] It appeased the spiritual hunger of many young Western people. The author, Paramahansa Yogananda, looks you in the eye from the cover of his book. If you allow it, he pierces your soul with his Christ-like allure and Mona Lisa smile, making you want to stay glued to his gaze.

Yogananda was born in 1893 in India into a Bengali Hindu family. In 1920, he was invited to Boston to speak at a religious conference. He traveled across the US lecturing and teaching Kriya Yoga, as his teachers had told him he was the one chosen to spread this ancient meditation technique in the West. In 1925, he settled in Los Angeles and installed a worldwide spiritual organization: the Self-Realization Fellowship.[69] He trained disciples, went on teaching tours, and initiated thousands into Kriya Yoga. He died in Los Angeles in 1952 when he was fifty-nine.

In his book, Yogananda leads his readers through his life's journey and encounters with Eastern and Western spiritual teachers. He explains how he became a monk and established his teachings of Kriya Yoga meditation. Steve Jobs read the book as a teenager and reread it after that once a year. George Harrison's interest in Vedic culture started after he read the book.[70] Elvis Presley was inspired by his "hair-dresser-turned-guru" to read it for the first time in 1965 and continued to study it through the 1970s.[71]

Paramahansa Yogananda and his book *Autobiography of a Yogi* were undeniably crucial in the introduction of Eastern spiritual wisdom to the West.[72] He taught American youngsters that a guru was indispensable to a meaningful life. It is likely that Yogananda's popularity spoke to Bhajan and inspired him to call his yoga sets "kriyas." I found no evidence for this, but it does not seem far-fetched. By choosing the word *kriya* for the yoga sets he taught, Bhajan added yet another layer to the confusion he had already created by calling his yoga Kundalini Yoga. Bhajan's yoga sets have nothing in common with Kundalini Yoga or Kriya Yoga. For cult leaders, however, it is interesting to let questions, mysteries, myths, uncertainties, and ambiguity fester in the minds of their followers.

The Zeitgeist of the 1960s and 1970s

"Here is what you need to know about life here in America," says Bir in his interview with GuruNischan. He then paints a picture of the social and political situation in the US in the early 1970s to explain why ashram life was so attractive to young people.

> No computers were smaller than a refrigerator and were certainly not privately owned. We had no cell phones, but public payphones scattered throughout the community and landlines at residence and work. There was no Internet, Google, Facebook, or Twitter. Instead, our social media consisted of a 17-inch to 21-inch television with five channels, a newspaper, and a radio. On November 22, 1963, the assassination of John F. Kennedy, the thirty-fifth president, was broadcast on television and radio. On April 4, 1968, Martin Luther King was assassinated, and we watched this on the

evening news. On June 5, 1968, the president's brother, Robert F. Kennedy, was assassinated. We watched this on television in our homes. The Vietnam War was going on. People of my generation were being drafted. There were 58,000 American casualties, most of them my age. The peak year was 1968: up to a thousand body bags per week were returned to the US. On May 4, 1970, the Kent State massacre occurred at the university, where the Ohio National Guard shot nine students, killing four. From coast to coast, nationwide, there was a vast disconnect between the generation of parents and young adults. The disconnect was just unbelievable.

So, a yoga ashram felt like an oasis: young adults close in age, no drugs, no alcohol or unmarried sex, and mandatory long hair. Well, my hair was already long. Wholesome, healthy, organic, vegetarian lifestyle. Everyone was involved in learning and teaching yoga. Moving into an ashram felt like moving into an oasis. I remember going through that door, meeting people, and being part of that community. Everything was built from there. We did yoga together and made yogurt together and granola. Moving into a yoga ashram was like escaping, walking away from the turmoil that prevailed coast to coast in the sixties. One of the ways our generation communicated was through music. There is a lot of music from back then.

[*Gur takes over from her husband.*]

At university, we took yoga and meditation classes. We did Zen meditation and Raja yoga and experienced different things. We began to connect with our inner selves in a way that brought more equilibrium and balance to our lives than all the discourse around us.

So, it was wonderful. Moving into an ashram felt like an intention to find inner peace. Later, we would be able to go out and share these tools. Finding a relevant, peaceful, and self-empowering place spoke to me.[73]

On a global level, the Cold War, the clash between the US and the Soviet Union, between capitalism and communism, defined much of what happened between the end of World War II and the collapse of

communism. Nuclear weapons were installed in secret locations, leading to psychological warfare; sporting events were used to fight political
battles; and the superpowers' rivalry extended into space.

In the US, anti-Vietnam War demonstrations in 1965 led to a broad
social movement that shaped polarizing debates. In the protests, women,
children, and antiestablishment youth often participated in nonviolent
demonstrations. Peace movements saw their membership numbers
explode, bringing hundreds of thousands to the streets worldwide. Sci-
entists and peace activists protested the testing of nuclear weapons. It
wasn't until the 1980s that discussions about nuclear disarmament
began. These were hectic and explosive times. Change was in the air, but
no one knew which way it would go.

Music to Connect

"One of the ways our generation communicated was through music,"
Bir said.

Rock music was a key ingredient of the hippie movement. Song lyr-
ics allowed youngsters to express their dissatisfaction with the con-
sumer culture, the Vietnam War, and nuclear weapons. It helped them
to address themes such as drugs, sexuality, and free love. Music was vital
for young people to connect with one another and distance themselves
from the older generation and society's turmoil.

Many first-generation 3HO members were musicians, such as Peter
Blachly, whom we met when he described his first Tantric Yoga class
with Yogi Bhajan. This is how he starts his book *The Inner Circle: Book
One: My Seventeen Years in the Cult of American Sikhs*:

> At the age of 20 I was desperate for wisdom. A burning desire for
> truth and meaning, ignited in my teens by reading Plato and Her-
> man Hesse, had not been extinguished by two years of playing lead
> guitar for Claude Jones, a popular Washington DC rock band. The
> ego-gratification for heading the three-piece band I started in 1968

had faded with the addition over time of four other band members, so that by the end of 1969 I felt I was little more than a backup musician for our lead singer. At the time I had not articulated it this way, even in my own thoughts. But I grew painfully aware that the band would not fulfill my original idealistic vision of "saving the world" through music. I was also increasingly aware that my persona as a rock musician was an insufficient balm for the gnawing insecurity I felt about my own lack of real identity. In the peculiar slang spoken by our band members, I felt I didn't have "much of an act." . . .

I was depressed by the gradual demise of the flower power ideals of the "Summer of Love," as the hip culture descended into the widespread use of hard drugs. The symbols of long hair and freaky clothes began to evoke more desperation, squalor, and crime than freedom and joy. By 1970 the dream of a better world through sex, drugs, and rock & roll was going sour. I was ready for a big change.[74]

On a February evening in 1970, his friends took Peter to a yoga class in Washington, DC. He was reluctant because this was not the Kriya Yoga he had read about in *Autobiography of a Yogi*. Nonetheless, after his first experience with Bhajan's Kundalini Yoga, he thought, "'This is it! This is what I've been looking for. This will give me the power to change my own life and effect positive change on the planet.' I was determined to learn this discipline and teach it. It was as simple as that. My mind was made up."[75]

It took only a short time before he started teaching yoga. Soon Peter was fully absorbed into 3HO. He led groups in chanting. He started a musical partnership with two other musicians in the community who lived in different ashrams in other states. Every two or three months, when Yogi Bhajan visited one of the ashrams in the Eastern region, they tried to come together and lead "musical meditations" as a means for achieving altered states. Then, at the summer solstice event of 1972, they devised a plan to create their first cassette tape, called "Jewels from the East."

"We were all thrilled, and the 3HO family responded favorably. The first run of one hundred cassettes nearly sold out at the winter solstice in Florida. Perhaps most importantly, the mix of spiritual songs and traditional mantras set to new tunes provided a unifying musical theme for more than one hundred 3HO ashrams throughout the US, Canada and abroad."[76]

In the fall of 1973, they brought together all the best musicians in the 3HO family, including classically trained musicians playing viola, clarinet, and flute, to record a real vinyl LP album at the National Recording Studios in New York City. They named themselves "The Khalsa String Band."

> The *Spiritual Nation* album was a serious project and had none of the raucousness that marked our earlier cassette albums. In part this was due to the sobering influence of our West Coast and Arizona friends who were for the most part a great deal "holier" than we were. . . .
>
> At the beginning of May [1974], all ten members of the band assembled at an ashram in the suburbs of Detroit for two weeks of rehearsals before the first concert of our tour. We were full of hope and bursting with talent and creativity. Our rehearsals in the ashram attic went well. The vocal blends were rich, the harmonic arrangements snappy and powerful. Occasionally, an instrumental break in the middle of a song would transform into a spontaneous, improvised jam. In these joyous moments we would beam at each other with surprised glances and satisfied smiles, recognizing how good we really were. Our shells of piety and restraint, carefully crafted from years of austerity and chanting mantras, melted away as the rock & roll burst from our souls.

The first concert took place in the basement auditorium of a local church in Detroit for nearly 150 people, mostly yoga students. Every song was greeted by enthusiastic applause. The next day, the Khalsa String Band packed their equipment into a truck and their luggage in three cars and caravanned to St. Louis for their second concert. They toured from Michigan to Arizona for two months, ending with the summer solstice celebration in New Mexico.[77]

Until today, music plays an essential role in the experience of Bhajan's Kundalini Yoga. Hundreds of bands and artists perform creative versions of the mantras introduced by Bhajan or self-composed spiritual songs. For example, Snatam Kaur is a famous singer-songwriter born and raised in Yogi Bhajan's Healthy, Happy, Holy Organization. 3HO musicians are well represented in the international scene of spiritual music.

Harijiwan Singh, who is also called "the toner bandit" because of the fraudulent 3HO businesses he ran that landed him in jail for eighteen months, won a Grammy award for the second time in 2023 with his band White Sun in the "New Age, Ambient, or Chant" category.[78]

We Were Sincere

Tej Steiner was born in the Midwest. In the late 1960s, he led a peaceful march against the Vietnam War at university and was expelled. Two weeks after losing his student deferment, he was drafted. He resisted by moving to Toronto, Canada, where he took his first Kundalini Yoga class. His yoga teacher went on the famous 1970–1971 trip to India with Yogi Bhajan, and on his return to Canada, he started dealing drugs and left 3HO. Yogi Bhajan asked Tej to start an ashram in Toronto and take the lead for the Canadian region. That's what he did for eighteen years.

Three of Tej's siblings also stepped into "the dharma," much to the dismay of their parents. They grew their hair and beards, wore only white clothes, and embraced the 3HO–Sikh Dharma way of life. In his interview with GuruNischan, Tej shares an anecdote: One day, his mother was at the office. None of her colleagues knew that all her children were in 3HO. One colleague looked out the window and saw a group of 3HO Sikhs passing by. She shouted, "Hey, come and see the white penguins." Everyone ran to the window, and so did his mother. She watched as a group with long white fluttering robes and high turbans strode down the street. The laughter of her colleagues hurt her ears and heart, but she said nothing.

Tej shared with GuruNischan why and how Eastern philosophy appealed to his generation.

> These Eastern teachers started talking about nonduality, oneness, "I am I am," about consciousness. You didn't have to believe in consciousness. It was something to experience. Yogi Bhajan brought us this powerful yoga. It blew us out of our bodies and into our bodies. However, he also took us outside our emotional bodies. Along with that, he provided a framework that made sense to us. We were looking for connection, and he provided a yoga style and a way of living that allowed us to connect. In yoga classes, we all did breath of fire and challenging asanas [yoga postures] that united us. Living together in ashrams, we were constantly in this field of connection. We, the yoga teachers and ashram leaders, didn't know what the hell to do with it. We were in charge, but we had no idea how to be inside that field without being authoritarian. The only model we had was this man who was essentially a sociopath.
>
> He used the connected field to his advantage. Every time we would do *Ardas* [a daily Sikh prayer], we brought his name into our prayers. Energetically that's very powerful. He became the center of everything. We created a hypnotic connection with him, and he just empirically sucked it up. He was good at it. Inside our ashrams, we modeled that. We were trying to figure out what we were doing on many, many different levels. But we were sincere. I think we were really sincere. [79]

Search for a Guru

What the Books Told Her

In 1968, Pamela Saharah Dyson, the author of *Premka: White Bird in a Golden Cage: My Life with Yogi Bhajan*, was twenty-five and recently divorced. She worked as an executive secretary in Los Angeles and was looking for "something new" in her life. Curious and longing for spiritual experiences, Pamela experimented with mind-expanding drugs and discovered yoga and meditation. Like many of her contemporaries, she was convinced she needed a spiritual guide.

> What I thought I understood about finding a guru (from books!) was that one must be in the right place, at the right time, and in the right attitude or consciousness. I expected that once I found one, it would then be like having my own personal guide through life: an enlightened being who knew the right way to live and who would be dedicated to keeping me on track and safe in a world where the old rules no longer applied. That's what I wanted: some safety and certainty in the midst of all the changing times.[80]

Her search began on the bulletin board of the HELP restaurant, one of the first vegetarian restaurants in Los Angeles. She spotted the announcement of a lecture given by a Sufi teacher at the East-West Cultural Center. She decided to go and claimed a seat near the front of the hall. After the Sufi teacher was introduced, the audience was instructed to sit quietly. Pamela was eager to listen to the wise words of this real, living spiritual teacher from the East. But he kept his eyes closed, didn't say a word, and just sat there, fidgeting, "not just a little but a lot."

This was not what she expected from a spiritual teacher. The guru she had in mind, who would bring her enlightenment, behaved very differently in her imagination. Distracted, she scanned the audience and noticed a tall, impressive figure standing at the rear of the hall.

> A bright pink turban crowned the head of a dark-complexioned man with a jet-black, short, and curly beard. Like me, his eyes were not closed, as he was also surveying the audience. His features were strikingly handsome, his well-proportioned face accentuated by sparkling black eyes—eyes that met mine briefly across the crowded hall.
>
> Though he was dressed in casual western-style clothes, from the neck up, he looked as though he might have stepped right out of

The Arabian Nights. Even at this distance, Yogi Bhajan had a mag-
netic energy. The charisma, the draw, seemed tangible. During my
recent search of that bulletin board, I had been told by the owner
of the HELP Restaurant that an East-Indian man called Yogi Bhajan was teaching yoga classes right here, at the East-West Cultural
Center. I guessed that this must be him.[81]

A few days later, she made an appointment for a private yoga class with
"the yogi." When she arrived at the East-West Cultural Center, she was
surprised to hear he wanted to interview her before starting the yoga class.

"I'm just wondering, Pamela, what kind of work you do?"
. . . feeling intimidated by his powerful presence, I haltingly
replied, "I'm a secretary at Warner Brothers Records."
"Aha, you are a secretary, I see. So, tell me, have you ever studied
yoga before?"[82]

Pamela told him she had been taking hatha yoga classes for over a
year. However, she wanted to learn more than physical postures, for
example, how to meditate. She first had the idea to go to India to find
her guru but was too afraid to travel alone. Now she planned to go to
Europe instead to find her guru there. She recalls, "The yogi smiled and
nodded thoughtfully, 'Ah, yes, I think that is a much better plan. But I
have another idea—first, you should let me train you as a yoga teacher.'"[83]

. . . his magnetism and his self-assuredness were persuasive, and my
youthful naiveté prevented me from challenging any discrepancy.
I was fascinated, curious, and even hopeful that maybe he was the
spiritual teacher I was looking for. I tentatively extended my hand
and replied, "Okay, I would like to be a yoga teacher." . . .
He looked into my eyes, and taking hold of my hand, he challenged my resolve with one word: "Promise?"
Filled with more questions than answers, I nonetheless responded,
"Okay I promise." [84]

First Yoga Class

Yogi Bhajan led her to the yoga room. He directed her through a series of yoga postures. After a while, he guided her into a posture he called *guru pranam*. She had to sit cross-legged, with her upper body bent forward and her forehead touching the ground. Her arms needed to stretch above her head with palms together. He instructed her to breathe long and slow in this position and wait to get up until he said so. It was a very confining position, and soon discomfort started building in her knees and hips. And then, she heard him leave the room. At first, she panicked but soon reasoned this had to be a test. The books stated that those enlightened master tested their student's sincerity, obedience, and devotion. She wanted to demonstrate she was ready. After what seemed like ten long minutes, Yogi Bhajan returned and asked her to lie on her back and relax. He came sitting next to her.

> . . . relaxing would have been a whole lot easier . . . if he hadn't put his left hand on my right breast!
>
> The really strange thing about his hand on my breast, apart from the fact that it was there at all, was that it seemed to be sort of clinical. He wasn't fondling me, rather, his hand was just there. I attempted to remain calm and unruffled, afraid to insult him with an accusation. I didn't want to alienate him before I even got to know who he was. . . .
>
> He seemed to be meditating, deeply contemplating something about me. Once again, I didn't know what to make of him. *It must be another test.* I had read many stories about the tests of faith and tests of devotion that gurus use to determine the sincerity of their students. I was doing my best to follow the examples portrayed in the books I had read.
>
> He soon removed his hands and seemed to instantly shift from a trance-like state back into ordinary consciousness as he announced, "We are complete. Best if you come at least two times per week."[85]

First Meeting of the Community

After they left the yoga room, Yogi Bhajan directed Pamela to follow him to a library. He reached up to a shelf and pulled out a large volume, showing her a prayer entitled *Jap-ji*, written in an Indian script with English translations beneath. He told her, "I am just requesting that you can type up this English translation for me. I want to make a pamphlet to distribute to my students. You are a secretary, so I am thinking this could be easy for you to just type it up?"

Pamela was flattered and assured him that she could do that for him. Next, he invited her to follow him across the street to meet his students, who all lived in the same building. As it was mid-day, Pamela calculated it was safe. The first student she met was a bearded Afro-American in his early thirties who was exceptionally polite and respectful. A woman in her late teens was straightening up the yogi's apartment. She told Pamela that she had followed him from Canada to the US to study with him.

Next, a woman with dark grey, curly hair in a turquoise blue, single-piece jumpsuit came into the room and brought a special salad for the yogi's lunch. Pulling her by the ear in a playful and mischievous manner and calling her "my little thing," Yogi Bhajan introduced her to Pamela, "Shakti Parwha is the name I have given her, and it means Great Flow of Divine Energy."

Pamela writes about this last encounter:

> Shakti had a distinctly middle-aged demeanor. She was what I would call 'straight,' pretty much the opposite of 'cool.' She was from another generation though she was clearly a bundle of energy and bristling with self-importance.
>
> I wasn't sure why I had been invited to meet everyone, but it did put me more at ease about the yogi. I sensed the family feeling between all of them and the deference and care they were giving to the man they all clearly regarded as their spiritual teacher. [86]

A few days after that first meeting, Pamela went on a picnic with Yogi Bhajan and his students. She became more and more integrated into his small community. Soon she was accompanying him to the yoga classes he gave for his growing number of students.

> [Besides yoga,] he taught about the use of food for health and for healing, including advocating vegetarianism, . . . He taught about living a dedicated life with a balance between work and worship. His teachings were drawn from his native East Indian culture, and he combined streams of yoga philosophy, Ayurvedic medicine, and the philosophy and spiritual principles of his own Sikh religious tradition. For all of us, this information was totally new, and he seemed to be an endless fountain of knowledge.[87]

The yogi soon asked Pamela to get up early to recite a mantra that would set her free. She followed his instructions. Almost overnight, she stopped smoking, drinking alcohol, using marijuana, and eating meat. It happened without effort. Her spare time went into attending his classes, transcribing the morning prayer of the Sikhs—as he had asked her to do that first day—and making the pamphlets for his students.

Aquarian Age Leaders

One evening in late 1968, several hundred students had gathered for a celebration announced by the yogi in honor of an astrological conjunction that heralded the dawn of the Age of Aquarius. He spoke in a thundering voice, using prophetic-sounding words. He proclaimed that he had been sent to the West, not to collect students but to train teachers who would become the leaders for the Aquarian Age, guiding humanity towards God-consciousness.

> "I also want to warn you that I may not live that long. I have seen that time will come when I will be misunderstood, and I may be crucified. That is to be expected. It is part of the destiny of all those who offer themselves to serve humanity. I understand there will be many conflicts along the way. Some of you will question me, you

will doubt me, and even some of you will betray me. I'm ready for that; I'm prepared to walk this lonely path. I have even seen a vision—that my back will look like one big scab from all the stab wounds that I'll receive. But I'm ready for this, and I have faith that my guru is always with me."

His words were so powerful they cracked Pamela wide open.

As I listened intently, they triggered an internal vision. . . . I was 'seeing' a future scenario—where many of these inspired students would be disillusioned and leave this teacher. . . . As this inner vision unfolded, I found myself overcome with sadness and grief. What I, myself, would do in the future was not revealed, but I sensed that my faith would also be sorely tested. . . .

The miraculous experience of having this vision, and the enormous love and compassion it evoked for this powerful and inspiring teacher, drew out of me an urgent inner commitment to serve him, to stand by him through thick and thin.

Within a few months of meeting the yogi, Pamela quit her outside job at his request and moved into a house where he lived with his students. She even gave him her $10,000 in savings. He began to call her Premka, and she assumed the role of his primary attendant.[88]

Night Service

From the beginning, Yogi Bhajan instructed the faithful in his household on precisely what, when, and how things should be done. For example, it was imperative that, at all hours of the day and night, a personal attendant remained alert by his side.

"You all must understand; sometimes, I just leave my body at night when I'm sleeping. If someone is not there to make sure a blanket is covering me, I can just freeze to death. My little dog, Nazee, who

is still there in India, is so devoted to me. Once, when I was just out
of my body, my blanket slipped off, and that little Nazee just grabbed
it with her teeth and pulled it back to cover me. Since then, I understood that I must have someone with that much devotion to watch
over me when I sleep."

At night, the yogi's attendants had to kneel beside him and massage
him to sleep. Pamela shares the following about her night shifts:

He would often pull me into his bed for muffled and secretive sex.
Afterward, though I longed to enjoy lying next to him, hoping to
be held by him, he would inevitably nudge me back onto the floor
to continue massaging him until he fell asleep.

As painfully disappointing as that was, I accepted his explanation that it was critical that I not fall asleep in his bed since other
household members would be coming into his room at 4 a.m. to
begin morning meditation practices.

She agreed to all this because Yogi Bhajan was, to her, "the most
important and precious being on the planet." She felt reassured to have
a spiritual teacher who had the answers for all of life's ambiguities. "If
he said something was right, if he confirmed it was OK, then I need not
question any further."

He told her it was her karmic duty to serve him. "That's your only
option—to fulfill your highest destiny." She bowed her head with relief
and gratitude. She felt special, "knowing it was such an honor to have a
unique destiny to care for him, to serve him. I understood it was a great
privilege, a blessing to be so chosen, to have such a special relationship
with such a master."

At the same time, she felt doors closing all around her. "I perceived
that I was entering a disciplined confinement, a path of service to him
and to the mission he described. And it seemed that, as he often reminded
me, I had no choice."[89]

LIFE IN BHAJAN'S COMMUNITY

In the Cage

Designed and Decorated

Slowly but surely, Pamela entered her golden cage. Yogi Bhajan had given her the pompous title of secretary general and presented her to the 3HO–Sikh Dharma community and the outside world as the second in command. In her book, Pamela describes her struggle to carry the weight of living up to that role. Initially, she tried to fill it but gradually discovered that all these titles and positions were just an illusion. While 3HO members perceived "the leaders" as those who consciously worked with him, they were unwitting, as used and abused as anyone else in his surroundings.[90]

Shakti Parwha, the "straight" woman wearing a jumpsuit whom Pamela had met after her first yoga class, had been with Bhajan for several months. In those early days, Shakti drove the yogi around to the places where he was teaching. Bhajan called her "his manager" in somewhat mocking tones since Shakti took care of his personal and corporate matters. She helped him get his green card and citizenship and ensured his wife and kids could come over. Pamela recounts that Shakti tried to educate Bhajan about Western culture. From early on, she discouraged him from hugging his students. At the same time, she fiercely defended him against any early rumors of sexual impropriety. He called her the "Mother of 3HO," and soon, the whole community referred to her that way.

Yogi Bhajan designed and set up his organizations in consultation and conjunction with Shakti and his attorneys. She was his go-between for lawyers and accountants. His finances, accounts, investments, and tax reporting were her exclusive domain. In 1973, Pamela/Premka was asked to sign corporate papers as the vice-president of the Sikh Dharma Brotherhood. She did not even know this organization was created, nor that she held that position.

Fifty years later, Pamela shares her memories of how Yogi Bhajan and Shakti, together, designed Premka. Like many other survivors, she calls Yogi Bhajan "YB."

They decided how to dress me, so I looked modest enough for public consumption. I was an executive secretary at Warner Brothers Records when I met YB. I wore typical professional-style clothing of that era, which included miniskirts, pantyhose, and high heels. I was never a hippie, and it was a dilemma how to dress me for sitting crossed-legged on floors. (Yoga-style clothing had not yet been designed.) In the year leading up to the 1970 trip to India, YB and Shakti came up with floor-length princess-style dresses—long-sleeved and V-necked, made of corduroy fabric. Once in India, YB had a tailor sew me kurta [loose collarless shirts] and churidar [tight trousers] sets in various shades. My long hair was tied up and draped with a chunni [long scarf] that matched each outfit. Initially they were in bright-colored cotton, not flattering to my whiteness! Over the years, YB determined that white was a better color for me and for all of us.

"Premka" was positioned by YB to be the feminine face of 3HO. I was encouraged to design the turban style and given the task of helping women how to tie their turbans. The original movement that he named "Grace of God Movement for the Women of America," the GGMWA, was put forward by him in the very early 1970s. Premka became the image of grace.

All these names and titles were his creations. I did not like any of them. They sounded so silly and unsophisticated to me: Healthy, Happy, Holy Organization, GGMWA, secretary general as my title, etc. But nobody cared what I liked, nor was I asked. Calling our offices "the Secretariat" and giving everyone titles! I found it embarrassing in its exaggeration.

Master of Deception

I agree that I was a good "cover", validating him to a wider audience. I had the right look, the appearance of innocence and purity.

I tried to "be him" when it came to public speaking, and I did strive to be the epitome of grace. I made the mistake of being a tool in his hands. He used my skills and talents to serve his own ends. But YB never shared power with anyone. He was clever enough to make you think you had some influence, like Shakti and all the community leaders, including the Khalsa Council. That was part of his mastery.

I am not particularly proud of it, but I functioned as a good secretary to YB and for the ongoing evolution of the International Headquarters. He counted on me to take dictation from him and rewrite his broken English so that he came out sounding literate. He instructed me to rewrite the existing crude translations of Sikh scriptures and published this work under my name as *Peace Lagoon*. I didn't know he was having the book printed, nor did I choose that title.

Although I was editor-in-chief of the *Beads of Truth* [3HO magazine], he would often meet with me as I was designing the next issue, sometimes dictating an entirely different direction than I had planned. We fought about the issue with all the photos of the dead and bloodied faces of Sikh martyrs who were slaughtered at the Golden Temple [in Amritsar, during a government attack in

1984]. I was horrified at the idea of publishing those photos. He sometimes directed the magazine more toward the Indian Sikhs than his Western followers.

I protested when he wanted my picture in the *Beads of Truth*, the one that is now on the cover of *Premka*. He loved that picture and insisted it would be filling a full page. I don't recall any explanation for why it was there, and I frankly was not pleased with it. Anyone with direct access to him, who attempted to confront or challenge him, was soon pushed away. It happened to me in 1972 or 1973.

Bhajan was a master at keeping everything compartmentalized; one hand did not know what the other was doing. For years, he kept Pamela/Premka in the dark about his sexual activities with other women. He lied to her when she confronted him. The constant struggle to keep trusting and believing him was very confusing. Shakti Parwha and other staff members were deliberately excluded from knowing anything about his "other activities." Each staff member had a different vantage point and a different level of participation. He kept each one vying for his approval. One of Bhajan's skills, which he deployed tactically, was that he knew how far he could push each person. The staff members renounced the right to personal life, family, and payment, so they had no independence. Their only reward was their private access to Bhajan. That was the essence of his manipulation.

A big part of Pamela's turning point was when it finally hit home that she had no authority despite all his claims and pronouncements. She came to see how they all served as his "cover" and how they magnified him with all their whiteness. He never guided her to believe in herself. It took many years before she learned those things. The extent of the abuse became clear to her only after her book in 2020 brought out other survivors' stories.[91]

Double Standards

Bhajan was not only a master of false promises, cover-ups, and secrecy, but he also maintained double standards, for example, regarding yoga and meditation practice. Besides performing selfless community service and having regular jobs, his followers were expected to do a two-and-a-half-hour morning sadhana, say their Sikh prayers at set hours, and attend or lead yoga classes. They also had to do their personalized daily yoga practice, a particular kriya or meditation, to repeat for forty or one thousand consecutive days. "This is the yoga of the householder," he said. They all bent over backward, not to disappoint their spiritual leader.

At the same time, his personal practice looked quite differently, as a former staff member remembers:

> Yogi Bhajan did not do any yoga sets. He did a stretch movement or two before reading his *banis* [Sikh prayers], something he was very consistent with. YB had his own *Nitnem* [book with Sikh prayers] written in Urdu, the primary dialect of his region. He did not know how to read Gurmukhi, the script in which the sacred Sikh texts are written. Over the years, he developed the habit of sleeping very little, three to five hours per night.[92]

Food was another topic for which Bhajan used double standards. For his followers, he devised new diets with clocklike regularity: forty days of rice with beans, or only bananas, or only green, or only white food like rice and milk, or just beets or celery, that kind of oddity. People believed he knew about food, fasting, or had access to divine sources to diagnose and heal.

At the same time, his own diet was "different." Siri told us about the nachos and M&Ms hidden under the movie theater popcorn. Sat Pavan, born to 3HO parents in the mid-1970s, remembers this:

> One day, I was around twelve, YB took my sister and me to the movie theater. He asked us which kind of candy we wanted. I said I didn't know. He said, "She'll have one of everything." I never had

that. My parents were constantly told to follow his healthy diet. "You don't feed your kids sugar." And then, all of a sudden, the spiritual leader, the grandfather, the person making all these rules, is saying you can have the junkiest candy!

So, while my parents kept me from those things, he was fun. Consequently, he was the one I wanted to be around. It seems like such a small thing, but it created a mental state and feeling like, "He's my grandfather, and he is breaking the rules." And yet, at the same time, he was creating them. If he had seen my mom giving me junk food, he would have screamed at her, "How dare you? What are you doing? Are you trying to destroy your daughter's immune system? Are you trying to kill her? Or to ruin her brain?"[93]

Marina, who lived in Bhajan's court for three years from 1999 onwards, recalls that his diet was mostly not yogic. He was seventy when she arrived in his inner circle, and his health was poor. He had diabetes, his kidneys were malfunctioning, circulation through his legs was poor, and his heart regularly gave out due to his terrible eating habits.

Only on days when he got blood test results, which always showed that his cholesterol was too high, a secretary reminded him to eat healthily, but the next day it was forgotten. While his doctors encouraged him to eat simple foods, we usually went to restaurants in the evening. He sometimes had wounds that were difficult to heal because of diabetes. For example, there was a wound on a toe that was very ugly. There was an infection on it that did not heal. When the staff took care of the wound, they did not remove the scab, so the pus stayed behind it, and the infection grew deeper and deeper.

One day Marina commented that they should remove the scab, but Yogi Bhajan waved at her that it was fine as it was. Gangrene set in, and the toe had to be amputated.[94]

They All Want to Fuck Me

Marina's memories above date from 1999. In 1983, when Gursant Singh became the driver of YB's team, the master was fifty-four and still in better shape. Gursant describes below how he perceived YB's secretaries. The ladies' names have been replaced here by "A, B, C, ..."

His secretaries were a handpicked team of women, always single, who traveled with him everywhere. The story was that they were celibates, having "dedicated all their creative energies to the life-long service of Yogiji." Kind of a perfect hybrid of Charlie's Angels and the Stepford Wives. Like us all, they dressed completely in white, but added gossamer veils to their turbans. They were like angels, from afar, until you looked into their eyes.

The secretaries spent their time massaging Yogiji's feet, serving his food, fanning away flies. Whatever went on behind closed doors between them and Yogiji—they never talked. In return for their service to him, the secretaries had total control over who saw Yogi Bhajan and when. They also made decisions about ashram-owned businesses. They hired and fired. If one of them didn't like you, you would get the worst ashram housing, worst job, worst of everything.

They slept in the same room with him, too. One at a time, two at a time, or more, or so I've heard. No one knows what really went on, but we were assured by Yogiji himself that he was too pure for any sexual hanky-panky as he had committed himself to celibacy.

One of his secretaries in particular was the one who got me my job. "A." That voice! Angelic! She was so sweet, so soft-spoken—utterly feminine in every way. I'm sure Yogiji was as captivated by her as I was. Soon after taking her on as a secretary, he had an intuition that she had a certain "car karma."

Bhajan felt that if she drove herself, she was liable to get into a horrible accident and die, so A wasn't allowed to drive anywhere. I would pick her up and take her grocery shopping or wherever. Over time, we became friends of a sort, but only in the way that "ashramites" could ever really be friends: as fellow devotees, always turning their conversations to the exalted source, to Yogi Bhajan.

Although A was my favorite, I ended up driving all the secretaries and developed a limited friendship with each one. This was as close as anyone got to them outside of Yogiji. In fact, I felt like I knew them even better than they knew each other. Although the secretaries, as a whole, presented a united front, believe me, they were not friends with each other.

Premka Kaur was Yogiji's favorite and above us all, even the other secretaries. Unapproachable.

A lady of great intensity, she was Yogi Bhajan's "Secretary General of Sikhs in the Western Hemisphere."

B was a bossy Jewish girl that handled events and entertainment. She set up meetings with the pope, the Dalai Lama. Heady stuff! She was hot to trot—always in the most expensive cars and designer kurtas.

C was a spicy Italian girl. She handled everything about Yogiji's appointment book, living quarters, the kitchen staff, you name it. When you received an answer from Yogiji, she was the one who typed the directives from the great man.

C would spend most nights with Yogiji in a converted garage in the back of the Guru Ram Das Ashram on Preuss Road [Los Angeles]. After my all-night security duty at the ashram, I'd see her walking Yogiji's white dog and white cat.

"Sat Nam, good morning, C."

"Sat Nam Guru Sant Singh."[95]

Shakti Parwha Kaur was the only secretary older than Yogi Bhajan and had been with him from the very beginning, even before he first started teaching yoga at Jules Buccieri's antique store at the top of Robertson Boulevard in Beverly Hills. Shakti didn't like to drive much so I would act as her chauffeur. Every week we would drive to the Wells Fargo bank on Wilshire Blvd in Beverly Hills, to retrieve a different set of jewelry for him to wear.

On my first visit to the bank, my eyes almost popped out of my head. Within the safety deposit boxes, I saw literally dozens of trays of expensive and ostentatious jewelry. Each week Yogiji demanded a fresh array of pendants, necklaces, and rings; different kinds of gemstones to align his auric body with the vibrations of different planetary positions and conjunctions. It was highly scientific and Yogiji had it all figured out.

"Let's go get the crown jewels, Guru Sant Singh."

"OK Shakti, will we be taking the Rolls or the Benz today?"

D was a Harvard graduate who edited the ashram magazine, and E—also Jewish—was a short, pushy girl. I don't know what she did except incite conflict.

Then there was angelic A. All she had to do was hang around and be sexy.

She did it well.

Some secretaries stayed with him for life, but over the decades, many came and went from his service. Some would eventually meet a guy and leave Yogiji to get married, others would pursue careers or simply leave for unexplained reasons. There were always more women willing to accept the honor.

Mostly Yogi Bhajan chose his secretaries for their intelligence or skill in some area. He had secretaries to write books for him, do his taxes, manage his businesses, and do his homework so that he could get his online PhD. One thing about his secretaries: all were smart as whips. Many had *Ivy League* degrees. The whole arrangement was a stroke of genius. He had a team of people with the best educations money could buy, and he got it all for free. They did it to serve God, and, I assume, for the status.

Bhajan used to say he kept the secretaries' auras aligned, like a "super husband," while Bibiji (his wife) and their kids lived in a palatial estate nearby, almost forgotten.

Those secretaries spent a lot of time listening to Yogiji, taking down his every word for posterity. What they liked about me was that I actually listened to them. They always had plenty to say, but it never amounted to anything other than bitching about each other. It was like living in a big swarm of bees: everybody buzzing, everybody stinging, everybody after the honey. And if the lady got a drink of nectar—a little personal attention from Yogiji—all she wanted was more. Even A wasn't above it. She would jump into the fray just like the others, stinging deeply with soft, delightful words.

It was lust. Pure and simple.

By denying or shunning one of them, he would only make her want him more. It was the same thing he did with all of us, only more intimate.

He once told a fellow disciple: "See these women?" He waved his arm around his living room which was full—as usual—with his staff. "They all want to fuck me, but they know they can't because of my vow of celibacy. So, you know what they do instead? They fuck with my head."

They tended to fuck with everybody else's head as well.[96]

Dysfunctional Structures

Peter Blachly, the musician from the Khalsa String Band, wrote about the impressive power structure that Bhajan had set up:

By 1976, the 3HO Community was a well-developed organization with established, though dysfunctional, social, and administrative structures, and a deeply engrained religious culture—most of it focused on Yogiji. At the nominal apex of the religious hierarchy was the Siri Guru Granth Sahib, the holy book of the Sikhs, and the sacred memory of the ten Sikh Gurus who had lived through the 16th and 17th centuries. For most of the people in 3HO, however, Yogiji served as the ultimate temporal and spiritual authority. Next in line was the "Secretariat" of Sikh Dharma, which was made up entirely of Yogiji's secretaries, whom he appointed or removed at will, and to whom he dictated virtually all policy and administrative details.

Next was the Khalsa Council, made up of Yogiji's appointees, all of whom held impressive religious titles bestowed by Yogiji, and most of whom, besides me, were directors of ashrams. The Khalsa Council was supposed to work in an advisory capacity, but it had absolutely no authority to make decisions about policy, no access to the organization's budget or books, and no authority to make financial decisions. Khalsa Council meetings, therefore, were little more than giant encounter groups.

Another layer of the organization's administration was the five geographical regions and their respective regional directors, all longtime students. . . . The exception was the Los Angeles area, which was over-loaded with so many longtime students, most of whom were endowed with enormous egos and considerable ambition, that power struggles and conflict were inevitable. The Los Angeles region, therefore, was under Yogiji's direct supervision.

Finally, came the administrative structure of the individual ashrams. Generally, the ashram directors followed the authoritarian model demonstrated by Yogiji. In fact, it seemed to be every director's greatest aspiration to be a cloned replica of Yogiji. Many even imitated his Indian accent and mannerisms.[97]

Love and Terror in the Ashrams

Warm Welcome

Despite all this pompousness, Peter held fond memories of his 3HO time.

One of the great joys of being part of the 3HO family in those early days was that by 1971 we were never more than a day's drive from an ashram, and the feeling of family among us was generally so close that we were always guaranteed a warm welcome, especially in the smaller "outposts" in places like St. Louis or Kansas City.

Most of these smaller ashrams were in low to middle-income, inner-city neighborhoods. . . . All were set up as communes with the head teacher in charge, usually along the same kind of authoritarian model that we had in Washington, DC. There were some advantages to this model. The ashrams were always fairly clean, the meals communal and well organized, and the logistics for overnight stays easy to arrange. In every ashram the largest common space was the living room, which served as both the classroom for public yoga classes and the communal space for morning sadhana. As the religious aspect of Sikh Dharma gradually gained dominance, this space also served as a temple, and both before and after solstices it served for several days as a kind of hostel for travelers visiting from other ashrams. In most cases it was a lot of fun to travel by car to a solstice celebration, for it gave an opportunity to visit with old and new friends along the way, and the people in smaller towns were usually as glad for the company as the travelers were for a place to spend the night.[98]

Routine in the Ashram

Most 3HO members living in ashrams had no idea what was happening in the inner circle of Bhajan's household. Bir and Gur, for example, who entered 3HO in 1974, tell us about their peaceful life in the Los Angeles ashram.

BIR. My involvement in the community was limited to a yoga class with Yogi Bhajan once a week and going to gurdwara [house of prayers for Sikhs] on Sunday. And I participated in whatever little task was assigned to us, like washing people's feet as they came to the gurdwara. I didn't work on Preuss road [where the Los Angeles ashram was] but outside the ashram for forty hours a week. I was more out of the community.

GUR. I was really involved in the community daily. Usually, I did sadhana in the morning. I brought my children to sadhana at 4:00 a.m. We went to the gurdwara afterward. I came home in time to make breakfast, took the children to school, returned to the ashram, and gave a yoga class at 10:00 a.m. I read my *banis* [Sikh prayers] every day, which took a lot of time. I did *seva* [selfless and unpaid service], for example, putting together 3HO programs on topics like oriental beauty secrets and prenatal and postnatal advice.

So, unlike my husband, I was pretty immersed in the community. And even in the evenings, we would attend Yogi Bhajan's lectures or gatherings in the gurdwara. We were Amritdhari Sikhs [Sikhs who had gone through the initiation ceremony], and we were ministers of the 3HO Sikh Dharma organization.[99]

Ashram Heads Ran Mini Cults

Sat Pavan told us how Yogi Bhajan bought her candies at the movie theater. In 2022, she shared memories about her upbringing and life in various ashrams.[100]

> The heads of ashrams ruled everything. Interestingly, a lot of them were the first to leave the community. It was as if they were more part of the "behind-the-scenes" bullshit than the rest of the people who were clueless, naive, devoted people. When those leaders left, they often said, "Oh, I figured it out long ago. I knew how fucked up everything was."
>
> That always bugged me inside as they were part of the problem, part of doing things to other people. There is no apology. It's more like, "When he finally messed with you and went too far, that's when you left, but as long as you had power over everybody else, you were more than happy to stay." So, I don't have much respect for many of those people. It's like the bully saying, "I am not going to be bullied by somebody else."

It is said that some of the ashram heads were worse than Yogi Bhajan. Sat Pavan's mother suffered from the authoritarian behavior of one of them.

> When I was one year old, my mother and I were dropped off at the Connecticut ashram. My father was sent to Boston to get settled.

He would be sending for us. My mom was twenty-one, pregnant with my sister, and we had no money. We had absolutely nothing. We had been dropped off and were supposed to be taken care of in this ashram. The ashram director had complete authority over everyone who lived there. He had a landscaping company. Everyone in the ashram worked for him, room and board. My mom was assigned as his wife's attendant. She was also pregnant. My mom's job was to cook for her, serve her food, and massage her feet until she said, "You can go now."

During all this time, I was separated from my mother. The ashram head had separated all the children from their parents except his daughters. They were often with him and could see their mother whenever they wanted. But the rest of us were sent off to whoever he designated to be in charge of the kids. This separation from my mother made me very emotional. I cried a lot. My mom would often see me at night and give me a night kiss. When I woke up, I cried because I saw her, and I wanted her. The ashram director would scream, and they would come to get me. My mom says this man was pretty horrible to a lot of people. Many left the community because of him.

Today, my mom feels a lot of guilt that she didn't protect me from him. But she was twenty-one years old and pregnant. She didn't want to do something that could upset him and throw us out on the streets. He probably knew that she had to put up with it. When he screamed at me, I would cry.

He told my mom I was too attached and too emotional.

Six months later, we finally moved away from this dreadful ashram to the ashram in Boston. My parents worked downtown, my mom in a community-owned restaurant, and my dad in a community-owned shoe store. I was sent to a children's program in New Hampshire. On Sundays after the mandatory Sikh service in the gurdwara, Mom and Dad tried to get to New Hampshire to see me. And again, they were told the same thing because I cried a lot: "She's too attached." I only saw them for a short time.

People often told me my emotions were inconvenient for the leadership. They were convinced that something was wrong with me. I grew up with the idea "something is wrong with me." My dad's family was from New England. They're all very loud, very emotional, and very passionate. I have a lot of that in me. My mom is very quiet and keeps a lot inside. Also, my sister was very still. I was constantly told, "You're really emotional like your father. Your sister is very sweet, like your mother." Like it's a negative thing to share emotions and a positive thing to keep them inside.

No Turban Equals Bad Mother

My mother joined 3HO because she loved yoga and was never really into religious practices. My father was the opposite. He had joined because he was interested in Sikhism.

One day my mom decided to take her turban off. The community in Boston freaked out. The directors at the ashram decided that she was not a fit mother. That she was crazy. The ashram directors had money, and they pulled on my father.

"We can get the best lawyers here in Boston. We will help you get full custody of your kids. We'll help you get a divorce. She's not a good example for your two daughters to grow up with. You need to get away from her."

My parents were very different. They never fell in love but were pushed into marriage. It would not have been completely insane for my father to agree to a divorce. But that is not what he did. He said, "No matter what, this woman is the mother of my children. She is a good person." He knew that. And he knew that she was a good mother. So, he did this: we left the Boston ashram with nothing. My parents had been paid five dollars a week in the community businesses. We had nothing. My dad took us to his great aunt's house in Maine. She was like an angel.

Because we could no longer go to the gurdwara, I loved to go to church to sing, as I loved singing. The pastor said I was one of the most enthusiastic churchgoers he had ever had. I was five or six at the time. All of a sudden, we became "normal kids."

All this happened in the summer of 1981. Sat Pavan's father left his wife and children in the care of his auntie and traveled to the ashram in Florida, where they had been happy before. After six months, he found a job there and called his wife and two daughters to Florida. They were together again.

Intrigue and Slandering

Friends Became Foes

We return once more to *Premka*. In 1982, it had been fourteen years since Pamela had taken her first yoga class with the handsome yogi. She had observed people who got attracted to the yoga, met Yogi Bhajan and soon after became yoga teachers, finally, Sikhs. She saw them taking their marriage vows and rejoiced when their children were born. Nonetheless, she was disillusioned in many ways and about many things. Yet, she continued serving the yogi and playing the role of the untouchable secretary general.

I had also witnessed many of the people I had known the longest, heads of ashrams, and members of the Khalsa Council, as . . . they found themselves compelled to make an independent choice, one that didn't fit with the ever stricter and more confining rules defining the community. I was heartbroken whenever someone finally took off the turban and left, often in the dark of night.

Each departure was quickly condemned by the yogi. He would explain it away by describing a side of them we hadn't noticed before, a whole new, fatally flawed image of them. Through the power of his words, one of our previously exalted peers would be transformed into a pariah and effectively cut off from the whole community.[101]

More and more, Pamela considered the possibility of leaving. Yogi Bhajan did his very best to prevent this in devious, cunning, and despicable ways. Her book tells us all about it. When she finally left at the end of 1984, her healing process could begin.

The Courage of the 3HO Khalsa's

Tej, who was appointed by Bhajan to be the leader for the Canadian region, explains to GuruNischan why he left 3HO–Sikh Dharma after eighteen years of loyal service.

One day in the late 1980s, he got a phone call.

Yogi Bhajan said,

"Tej, your sister is freaking out. Go down there, and don't worry about the speed limit. Get her back in the dharma. Put her mind at ease. Get this nonsense taken care of. Do it now! Go!"

So, I was already packing my bag when I said, "Yes, sir." I went down from Toronto to Chicago to see my sister, speeding the whole way.

She said, "Did you know he's been having sex with everybody in the secretary area?"

"No, come on."

"Yeah."

"Well, how do you know?"

"Why don't you call Premka?"

"What do you mean? Call Premka?"

I had Premka's number with me. So, I might as well. We had known each other all these years. She had left the community one and a half or two years earlier, whatever it was. I called her. I said to her, "Premka, is it true?" She said, "Yes." [Tej shows how he hung up the phone.]

That was it. The whole thing... I still feel emotion... [*closes his eyes*]... It felt like Santa Claus was coming down the chimney and raping my kids. That's what it felt like.

And then, the drug bust happened with Gurujot Singh on the East Coast in the Virginia ashram. [Gurujot Singh was the head of that ashram.] The DEA [Drug Enforcement Administration] came in, and they busted the ashram. Gurujot was obviously involved in some pretty severe drug and arms smuggling. When that happened so close to my finding out about Yogi Bhajan, I thought, *Game over. We're going to have a look at what we do now. The teacher is not who we thought he was.* So, I started talking to people, and it was like, "No, he didn't do it. Who says Gurujot is not innocent?" It was like it didn't happen [*Tej shakes his head and his voice sounds as if he still cannot believe it*]. There was not only denial but also "You have fallen from grace yourself suggesting it." All I was saying was, "We gotta be able to talk about this. Yogi Bhajan slept with all these women...." But no. We can't talk about it. We can't say it out loud. You can't say anything.[102]

On March 25, 1988, two years after Tej had heard that his spiritual teacher slept with his secretaries, he wrote an open letter to Yogi Bhajan. It was supposed to be shared with community leaders and members of the Khalsa Council. He had planned to resign from his post as Canadian regional director. However, he did not need to do that, as Bhajan had already replaced him. Tej wanted to express openly and publicly why he wanted to step down. Below are some extracts from that letter. When he talks about the "two women," he refers to Pamela/Premka and KartaPurkh, another woman who had left 3HO after being abused by YB.

An Open Letter to: Siri Singh Sahib Harbhajan Singh Khalsa, Yogi-Ji

Dear Sir, ...

When I talked with you about what both women had told me, you mainly spoke of how mentally sick they were. When I felt sick inside at your response, I went deeper into my own confusion.

. . . as I looked back over the years, . . . I never understood the seemingly feudal system of organization in which most of the temporal affairs of the Dharma seemed controlled by you, with little input . . . from the rest of us. I thought this would change as we matured, but it didn't. . . .

My experience has been that if I or others question your personal conduct or your organizational judgment, you put out very strongly that to do so is "slanderous." You have also made it clear repeatedly that the penalty for slandering you, our spiritual teacher, is basically spiritual death. That is a pretty harsh sentence knowing how seriously everyone in this family takes both their spiritual lives and your word concerning their lives. . . .

If I state that I think it's healthier . . . to have the Khalsa Council share much of the power you now hold alone, I've experienced that my "faith" in you or "lack of it" becomes the issue rather than the questions I am raising . . . .

I finally had to write this open letter to you when I heard that Gurujot had been arrested. Enough is enough. . . . Whether Gurujot is guilty or innocent, I don't know . . . I do know one thing from my own experience, and that is wherever Gurujot went, he seemed to create around him a climate of secrecy and intrigue: so much so that it became a family joke.

I don't know what you encouraged him to do or not do, but again, from my experience, you seemed to share that same secrecy and intrigue when he was around you. You had him partner with Al Ellis, knowing Al's drug background. You lived in their expensive quarters and experienced their free-flowing money. You encouraged them to travel to Thailand together with Premka and Ram Das Kaur, where the two men carried on "business" while the women played *kirtan*. In general, you gave Gurujot a license to be secretive by creating for him the Office of National Affairs Advisor, a post secretive by its very nature.

Outside of Gurujot, I'm aware of the degree of secrecy that exists elsewhere in our organization. The amounts of money we raise and how we spend it are kept secret; you don't disclose our financial statements. Our dealings with Indian, US, and Canadian governments are secretive; these dealings only you know about in full. Our positioning and relationship with the Indian Sikh community are secretive; one minute, we are sending telegrams of encouragement to the President of India after he signed the order to storm the Golden Temple, and the next, we are working with the Babbar Khalsa, an alleged terrorist group. No explanation for the discrepancy is talked about openly.

. . . the only real response to all this is to create an environment of openness wherein everyone in the family is encouraged to ask the questions that naturally arise by these momentous events. This questioning may be painful, but we have to do it. . . .[103]

Four months after his open letter to Bhajan, which had not been shared with others as he had requested, Tej sent a letter to the heads of the ashrams and the members of the Khalsa Council. This was his request to his former colleagues and friends:

Can we openly question our spiritual teacher's actions within our family/organization? My answer to this is that we not only can, but we must if we are to remain Sikhs. Those who lead the most are the most accountable. If we hold any leader "above" this accountability, we move from being in Dharma to being in a cult. To me, this kind of questioning of our leader's actions is not "anarchy," it is common sense, and it is not "intellectual" if it is done with kindness—without blame or bitterness.[104]

Everything could have been different from then on. The abuse could have stopped in 1988 instead of 2004. The silence and secrecy could have been broken thirty years earlier, but the courage was missing. The 3HO family did not dare to look their spiritual leader straight in the eye and ask for clarification. Tej's proposal to openly question Bhajan's integrity was rejected. As a reward for his bravery, he was slandered, shunned, and scolded. From then on, he was a traitor.

In his interview with GuruNischan, he explained how Bhajan dealt with traitors.

The second to last time I saw Yogi Bhajan, and he knew that I knew, he took me and my ex-wife aside in a room. I am going to use his accent here a little bit.

He said, "You know GuruTej, I want you to know that in this organization, everyone loves me so much. They're crazy with how much they love me. And if anybody talks out against me, I don't know what they would do. And so many of them have guns."

[*GuruNischan listens with her mouth open. "Wo-o-ow," she says. A silence follows.*]

I went home, I sat down, saying, "OK, God, internal self, whatever, you tell me what to do because this is serious stuff." And so, internally, this voice said, "Pick up a pen." So, I picked up a pen and then I wrote this:

[*Tej closes his eyes, and his right hand makes a writing gesture in front of him.*]

"Like a cat be still. Until one-pointedness directs the pounce. Patience pays. Hold the brush high until the heart moves the hand. This is art. Judge not at all until the facts speak first. Act only then. This is all written."

[*GuruNischan utters a "Wo-o-ow" again.*]

So, I withdrew myself into a little room in the ashram. I realized I was involved in a much bigger, much more complicated, and layered system than I thought it was. I understood that this was a time to become really still. I had to work it out: What was I doing that I sent my kids to India and gave my allegiance to a man without questioning? Where was my shadow? Where was my crack? I used my experience to explore my own shadow while at the same time I missed the beauty of community. I had devoted all these years.[105]

Life at Bhajan's Court

The stories covered so far date back to the 1970s and 1980s. Here we will listen once more to Marina who arrived in Yogi Bhajan's household in 1999. She describes the atmosphere and culture she experienced at the heart of the inner circle. The master was seventy and his health was deteriorating. He was still traveling, but less than before. This did not prevent him from controlling everyone and everything.

Twenty-three years earlier, in 1976, eighteen-year-old Marina had begun practicing yoga in her home country, Italy. In 1981, she discovered Kundalini Yoga as taught by Yogi Bhajan and started following the 3HO lifestyle without being fanatical. Four years later, she met Yogi Bhajan for the first time in Barcelona. Marina became part of the team that cared for him when he visited Italy. Yogi Bhajan would call her out of the kitchen because he liked to chat with her and wanted massages or healings from her.

"Yogi Bhajan told me that I had been a great healer in previous lives," Marina says. "It felt good that he recognized my healing skills and gave me so much attention. That was something I had missed during my upbringing."

Introducing Marina to you means I also need to talk about Guru Dev Singh, who played a key role in her life. Bhajan gave him the title Master of Sat Nam Rasayan. SNR is a meditative healing technique linked to Bhajan's yoga. In 1990, Guru Dev had moved to Rome to start the International School of Sat Nam Rasayan. Marina was soon hooked on this healing technique and became an active member of the European SNR community. Her relationship with Guru Dev became very close, and shortly after she divorced, he began to have sex with her. She asked him if this was OK because Guru Dev was a devout Sikh, married with children. These were Tantric experiments, he said. The sexual energy would increase their healing powers. She believed everything the master said and was eager to learn. Her affair with Guru Dev ended abruptly when Marina's eighteen-year-old daughter Olivia revealed to her mother that Guru Dev had repeatedly sexually abused her. The abuse occurred during so-called healing sessions and lasted almost a full year. Marina was devastated. Guru Dev did not deny the abuse. But he also did not apologize or acknowledge the harm done. He decided it would be better for everyone if Olivia left home and moved into the ashram in Amsterdam. That's what happened. The last chapter of this book reveals the abuse that occurred under the cover of healing in the SNR realm.

After all this, in 1999, Marina's life was a mess. She was forty-one and had no idea how to move on, shocked and paralyzed as she was by what Guru Dev had done to her and her daughter.

That spring, Yogi Bhajan came to Italy. Because of problems with his legs and hips, he could hardly walk and wanted a massage from Marina. The next day he was on his feet again, praised her healing skills, and requested her to give him a daily massage during his trip through Italy.

One day he asked her, "Would you not like to be married again?"

"Yes, if possible, I would love to," Marina replied.

"Then marry me, come and live with me."

"What will we do then? You, me, and your wife?"

"For the hard work, I will find you someone else," he had replied.

They had a hearty laugh about it.

As Marina shares this story, she remembers how Yogi Bhajan always knew how to make people move in the direction he wanted without explicitly forcing them to do so.

"He was never direct. His manipulation was very subtle. For example, he never told me directly that I should remarry on this occasion. He made me say it myself. He made you do things so he would not need to take responsibility."

After Italy, Yogi Bhajan traveled to Hamburg in Germany. The next day he called Marina to tell her he had found her the right husband; she had to come over immediately. The "right man" was Dharma, an American Sikh of forty-six whom he considered his spiritual son. If she married him, she could come and live in Española. Yogi Bhajan had engineered what he wanted: Marina close to him. Having no other options, she flew to Hamburg. Barely arrived, Yogi Bhajan officiated the marriage. Marina and her new husband stayed in Germany for a few days to get to know each other on an improvised honeymoon. Dharma informed her he was Yogi Bhajan's chauffeur, took care of his finances, and had just divorced his first wife. His eight-year-old daughter lived with her mother outside the community.

Marina returned to Italy to plan for her final move to the US, where she would end up in Yogi Bhajan's household. Her knowledge of English was limited, and the American culture was foreign to her. This context makes Marina's account of her experiences in Bhajan's "inner circle" unique.

When I arrived at the airport in Albuquerque, I was exhausted. Dharma came to pick me up. I discovered that my bags were not with me. I was tired and upset. Nevertheless, he insisted on driving first to Santa Fe, so he could introduce me to his daughter. Meeting his ex-wife was embarrassing and painful for me, her, and her friends who were with her. The only ones who were not uncomfortable were Dharma and his little daughter. She looked beautiful and was very happy to see her father.

As soon as we moved on to Española, Dharma started a long tirade. [Marina had experienced these "tirades" in Hamburg.] My low-cut T-shirt bothered him a lot. I loved this gorgeous T-shirt, handmade by my aunt. Dharma was sure it convinced his ex-wife that Yogi Bhajan had given him a prostitute as a wife, because of that T-shirt and because I was much younger than her. It was clear that he intended to educate me. For the rest of the trip, he gave me a detailed account of all the ladies and gentlemen sitting with Yogi Bhajan in the big room at the ranch and instructed me on who I should be and how I should behave.

Arriving in Española, I was eager to visit my new home but instead, I was taken to greet Yogi Bhajan who was resting. I was brought into a bare side room. As soon as I entered, he turned around, asked me to come closer, and with a huge outpouring, he embraced me in such a way that I had no choice but to roll on the bed with him.

"Finally, you are here," he said.

I was surprised, pleased, and felt embarrassed by this strange welcome. I did not know what pose to give myself. Yogi Bhajan was going to show me America and kept repeating I should not worry about anything. My karma was over. The fact I had arrived without possessions was a good omen. He had also entered America with nothing, and I could see where he stood now. The same would happen to me.

When we arrived at my new home, I discovered it had been colonized by two Indian families and a bunch of their relatives. Dharma treated these people as if we were all visitors to the same hotel. He seemed to be only polite to them because they were Yogi Bhajan's guests. We would live in the room he used to occupy with his wife and daughter. It had a bathroom and a closet.

And so, the image I got of America, was not America but a community of white Sikhs, and suddenly found myself in India. Political tensions were tangible beneath the surface of so-called friendly relationships.

Soon, inner circle members showered me with instructions on how to behave in Yogi Bhajan's presence and in respect of his "court," strictly organized according to a complex system of ranks and merits. Guru Dev had strongly advised me to be friendly to everyone but to deal only with first-class people.

Not knowing the language was a huge handicap. Sometimes I had the impression they used vulgar words, but that could not be true. Such words would never be used by the Master, the people of his Inner Circle, or Dharma, my husband. My self-esteem was low. When choosing the right point of view, mine was always different from the others. I was constantly criticized. In my childhood I had been criticized, and now I wanted to be accepted. So, I was willing to learn. And I had to learn to be like the others and become like those close to Yogi Bhajan.

Everyone told me how lovable, outstanding, and intelligent I was and what a great healer I was. Nobody knew me or anything about me, but everybody praised me. I had no idea what to think about this. Everything and everyone in this new environment amazed me. I understood nothing.

My husband and I were not sadhana freaks. I don't remember anyone complaining about that. Dharma was a yogi of a particular kind. Every morning he did "his kriya." It consisted of four or five exercises that, he said, lasted three minutes each. According to my observation, his three minutes lasted three breaths. As a groupie, I went, like most people of the Inner Circle, to all lectures and yoga classes of Yogi Bhajan and participated in all the exercises. That was almost every evening at seven o'clock.

When Yogi Bhajan was "home," usually in the afternoon, we spent time at the ranch. We sat with him to keep him company. People who came to see the Master had to put up with us as spectators. Yogi Bhajan liked to watch TV—Doris Day or Bollywood films. Often, he and I were alone to watch those films because the others disliked them. Ever since I was a child, I have loved watching junk. We enjoyed these moments. Later I discovered that the most viewed program in the community, and my husband's favorite, was the *Howard Stern Show*. It is said that Yogi Bhajan watched porn. That may be, but he would certainly not do it in my presence. Maybe he did it at night or when I was not around.

Without my suitcases, I missed my clothes. I wandered uneasily in these rooms full of icy women in silk dresses, with perfect turbans and fluttering veils, and proud, stern men with long beards. Their looks were unemotional, their allure martial, and their manners ceremonial and pompous. Regardless of gender, they were laden with jewels.

As I did not understand much of what they were saying, I used my healer's skills to keep my eyes and ears open and to contemplate what I sensed. I was listening from another level. What I felt was not reassuring. I smelled risk and danger. I saw many tight-lipped smiles and sensed mistrust, plots, and venom. A den full of vipers.

After a while, the Indians in my house became my friends. I preferred their company over the contact with the others. Dharma didn't like that and immediately publicly reported it to the boss. Yogi Bhajan had a good laugh with it. He decided that from then on, my house would be a place of reference for visiting Indian guests. And indeed, that was the case that summer and afterward. Meanwhile, our days were filled with sitting with Yogi Bhajan in his living room, attending chaotic meetings with or without the Indian neighbors, or watching TV at the volume of premature deafness.

It frequently happened that everyone suddenly rushed out to get into Yogi Bhajan's car and drive to a restaurant, even though the cook had just prepared lunch for everyone. Everything always happened in a great hurry to fulfill the master's will, which could fall like the sword of Damocles unexpectedly and at any moment. These were the appointed places in the car: Dharma was driving, Yogi Bhajan was sitting next to him, Hari Nam Kaur, the secretary for the day, was seated behind Yogi Bhajan, I sat in the middle, and Peraim Kaur, the secretary for the night, sat behind Dharma. All others followed in a parade of other cars. There was much pushing and shoving to get into the second or third car. Or, at least as close to Yogi Bhajan as possible. After four or five days, it was pointed out in polite or impolite terms, depending on the lady who addressed me, that it would be good if I understood what my place was. The fifth place in the car was not meant for me, even though I was the new wife of the driver. And so, I switched to the second car in the procession.

I was still considered privileged because Yogi Bhajan often asked me how I was doing. He inquired about my new home, my relationship with the Indian neighbors, and with the new daughter who visited us every day. He asked me how I felt in this fantastic new family, by which he meant the community and, above all, the Inner Circle. Yogi Bhajan did not stop educating me, as I was considered kind of wild.

Dharma's first wife, he said, was a lousy Sikh as she had cut her hair and was eating meat. Her influence on the little girl was evil.

Soon, Dharma's daughter would start to see her real mother in me and return to her father and to her real family, the Sikh family, the family of her soul. I still get goosebumps when I think of the next episode. To witness the construction of the lesbian image of Dharma's ex-wife was awful and highly confusing to me, as I still believed Yogi Bhajan was a good person.

The first time my husband's ex-wife was mentioned was in the car. Yogi Bhajan threw it out: "This woman is a lesbian."

Hari Nam or Peraim downplayed it: "Come on, sir, what are you saying now?"

Yogi Bhajan insisted, "So, what do you think is the reason why she left him?"

And Dharma said, "You may be right, sir."

When I heard this, I thought I must have misunderstood again. These were assumptions, and Yogi Bhajan would never go so low as to speak ill of anyone, would he?

The lesbian story continued in the living room at the ranch. There it became the official truth. Yogi Bhajan put the question to the group again. What could be the reason that woman—he never called her by her name—had left a husband like Dharma? Why would she leave such a home, a prosperous life as Dharma had offered her, and such a high social position? Now she had nothing. But it was fortunate for me because I now had everything. At that moment, Yogi Bhajan kept quiet. Someone said she was indeed a strange woman; another one said she was childish, yet someone else remarked that she always saw her, almost exclusively, with other women, with this or that girl. But, you know, she had been under the impression that Dharma's ex-wife was a lesbian or had become one. On the other hand, you could also tell she was a slut. Maybe she wasn't a lesbian; she was just a slut. "No!" Dharma intervened. She was not a slut, as she was not very interested in sex, at least not with him.

And so, my husband's ex became a lesbian. She was called ugly, old, and fat. No one ever thought of Dharma as a lousy fuck, an arid, unaffectionate, and selfish man. I saw this treatment of Dharma's ex-wife repeated on many other occasions. Whenever someone had fallen from grace or left the community, events that had never happened and nonexistent circumstances were invented and shaped out of thin air. It was an established and customary practice in the living room of Yogi Bhajan. Whenever such scenarios were created, I usually thought I misunderstood because it was so strange, so far-fetched. There was always someone, sometimes Yogi Bhajan himself, who would repeat the concept to me in more and different words to ensure I understood. On such occasions, Yogi Bhajan would pin me down with his eyes to seal my agreement and silence. When it was my turn three years later, I was called a filthy, awful, dirty, farting, nymphomaniacal slut.

Yogi Bhajan asked me every now and then, "What do you think?" I said, "I am watching."

I watched the relationships, how the secretaries hated each other, how there was no friendship. I watched the lies, the theater . . . . It was a dangerous place. I captured all that and wondered if one day I could deal with it better. I often wanted to run away from it all, but I had just gotten married. I had just sold my house in Italy. I had sorted everything out with my ex-husband regarding my youngest daughter, who was coming over, ... I was a proud woman. I was not ready to tell anyone I had made a big mistake. If only I had been humbler ... [106]

We Were Different

Another way to get a sense of what it was like to live in the 3HO–Sikh Dharma community is to look through the eyes of a child. Here are the memories of Sat Pavan who, as a child, sang with equal fervor in gurdwaras or churches, as we saw earlier.

Yogi Bhajan differentiated us from the rest of the American people and Punjabi Sikhs by our dress code. White represented all colors, so we had to wear white. With our long dresses, in which everything was covered up, we had an Amish look.

Wearing a turban was the most normal thing in 3HO. Men, women, children, everyone wore turbans. Initially, 3HO members did not know that Sikh women in India only wear turbans when baptized. Cutting your hair in 3HO was one of the most awful things you could do. YB's position related to the 3HO uniform was: "This is the only way to do it, else it is not correct." Now that I understand his narcissistic personality, I see it was all about creating an identity that people recognized as linked to him.

He always said, "Be perfect." If he asked, "How are you?" and you said, "I don't know," or "I am OK," that was not enough. Your answer had to be, "Everything is great and wonderful." Time and time again, he told me, "Smile, smile. If you walk into a room and you are not smiling, the entire room feels darkness." As if I was responsible for everybody else's happiness. Everybody had to be smiling, happy and positive, especially us kids. We had to make everyone believe that everything was perfect in our lives. If you were upset, in a bad mood or had a negative emotion, you should not show it. If you did, you were screamed at, not just by him but by other 3HO adults, "What's wrong with you? You didn't meditate enough!" For many of my generation, it meant we had no clue how to talk about our feelings or things that bothered us. If we did talk about such things, we felt bad for doing so.

Only in 2020 I started looking at this and realized how exhausting it was. It all seems like lifetimes and lifetimes ago. My sadness is that I was part of it for so long. I'm in my forties now. To start my life in my forties is not exactly what I ever wanted to do, but I guess I can count myself lucky that at least I get to start my life, figuring it all out. Many haven't figured it out and will never do so, and that's so sad.

We were also supposed to live, look, and appear as perfect Sikhs. Much time was spent on meditation and spiritual activities, and we had to take those seriously. Keeping your eyes closed during meditation was rewarded. People said they were proud of you and that you looked like an enlightened being. Yogi Bhajan told our parents we were more enlightened than they were because we were born in 3HO. Our soul had chosen this.

Being constantly told how to be and how not to be, we did not know how to be ourselves. Outside the community, we were supposed to represent the community rather than ourselves.

As a child born into 3HO, you were part of one big family. Besides your parents, every adult in the ashram was your auntie or uncle. Biological aunties and uncles were cast aside if they were not in the community. In "the family," a lot of discipline was expected, and we had many rules to follow. Rules about how to eat, how to dress, how to behave, how to talk, and whom you hung out with. Children who lived in the ashram had to become your friends. Friends from school who were not part of 3HO could not be visited at home. You didn't hang out with them outside the classroom.

The weird thing is that Yogi Bhajan seemed to forget his rules over the years. When our children were born, he said, "Don't make just anyone aunt and uncle of your children. You have to be clear about that." As if our parents had made a mistake. He probably adapted his rules to whatever suited him best at the time.

There were all these little things that Yogi Bhajan would say to us kids. We had a "best practices" list to keep in our pockets. For example, he would say, "Don't flirt. Be alert." From a very young age, we heard that "flirt" was a dirty word. We did not know what it meant but knew we were not allowed to fool around with the opposite sex. We were brought up to be asexual beings. "Look at each other as brothers and sisters," they said.

In the school in India, the local kids wore a regular school uniform. Yogi Bhajan had negotiated that the American kids could wear a Sikh uniform and their *bana* [Sikh symbols]. So, we were separated by sitting apart and how we were dressed. For us, boys and girls wore the same clothes. They didn't have girls' or feminine-looking outfits. All were the same, and they were really thin. For a lot of us, puberty started late. I don't know why. The way we were raised, we wouldn't even recognize things were happening until they were happening. I remember being thirteen and somebody coming up to me, saying, "You need to be wearing a bra. It's disgusting."

We had no sex education apart from "Stay away from boys. Don't flirt. Dating is bad. If you like someone, you need to stop liking that person." If you didn't follow the rules, you were being rebellious. That was seen as negative.[107]

CHILDREN IN 3HO

Isolate to Dominate

Distance Therapy

It is estimated that at least one thousand children were born and/or raised in the 3HO Sikh Dharma over the forty years of Bhajan's reign. Exact figures are not available. Their experiences vary according to their birth year, the ashrams they lived in, the schools they attended, their parents' level of education, their financial and professional status, and the extent to which Bhajan controlled their lives. Once a family was in his sights, his influence was usually pervasive.

While each situation is unique, many 3HO children share similar wounds inflicted by Bhajan's "distance therapy." Programs were set up for children aged eighteen months to seven years. They lived, played, and slept together under the motto "Peers are the best teachers." Bhajan swapped children between families and ashrams as this would protect them from the ill effects of attachment to their parents.

This child-swapping led to many dramas and issues that reached the big chief's ears. Second-generation survivors testify about being malnourished, beaten, and abused as house slaves by their "guardian parents." Because Bhajan did not like to be bothered by such complaints, in the early 1980s, he devised another plan. He would send the children to a boarding school of his choice in India. Family ties would crumble even faster at a greater distance.

Why was this distance therapy so interesting to Bhajan? Dr. Alexandra Stein answers this question in her book *Terror, Love, and Brainwashing*. She mentions a quote from Hanna Arendt, famous for her sharp analysis of totalitarian systems: "It has frequently been said, and it is perfectly true, that the most horrible aspect of totalitarian terror is that it has the power to bind together completely isolated individuals and that by so doing it isolates these individuals even more. Only isolated individuals can be dominated totally."[108]

Sat Pavan remembers how Yogi Bhajan taught them that the first teacher is your mother, then your father, and when you are eight, you must let go of your parents.

> From then on, their job was only to "pa-rent, pay-the-rent," as he would say. After that, as a child, your spiritual teacher was your guide in life. If he said, "Do this," you had to do it. Your parents would say, "Do it because he is your spiritual teacher." Consequently, kids were missing parental security. A small group of parents did not send their kids to India or did things "differently." They were made to feel like they had no respect for their spiritual teacher. Undoubtedly, their child was facing a ruined life. So, when a child turned eight, parents were no longer needed. For some people, this was comfortable, like, "OK, I will not be blamed for anything my child goes through in life because I am no longer the decision maker." Other parents were hurt, as they still wanted to have a say.[109]

Schools to Mold Saints

In September 1974, an article titled "Education of the Future Generation" appeared in the 3HO magazine *Beads of Truth*. Yogi Bhajan had received a loud and clear message that the first 3HO generation should lay the foundation for this new spiritual era. The 3HO family was blessed with the opportunity and privilege to hear and live "the Truth." 3HO marriages had a consciousness to live selflessly, giving birth to "the children of the future," who needed to be prepared for their role as "Saints" in coming spiritual America. Yogiji had helped to clean out the parents' mental distortions enough to allow their infants' pure and innocent souls to enter a life dedicated to service. The 3HO Creative School for Spiritual Children was blossoming in Phoenix, Arizona. At the entrance was a large picture of Yogi Bhajan surrounded by children welcoming kids from San Rafael, Los Angeles, Colorado, etc., who would live with guardian parents.

After glorifying the Phoenix Children's Program, the article moved on to the next topic:

> Then there came the question of how to educate our older children, and the solution was part of a greater lesson in non-attachment for many parents. Yogiji's two younger children have continued their education in a private school in Mussoorie, India, . . . a school which is highly disciplined, where the basic spiritual foundation is reflected in every aspect of daily life and teaching. So Yogiji recommended to some mothers that they send their grade-school and high school age children to India to study in this school along with his own children. The experience of studying in a foreign land, where the values and morals are still basically intact, studying in a school whose tradition follows the spirit of the Sikh Dharma, learning a new language, and relating to a totally different culture, is one which will enhance and enrich the lives of those fortunate ones who have been sent there. . . .
>
> Not every child can be sent to India to study, and we have the challenge before us of developing a total system of education which can fulfill all of the requirements of the society in which we are living, and still give our children the spiritual foundation which they need to grow into the responsibility of guiding a spiritual nation.[110]

A World of Their Own

One year later, in 1975, Sikh Dharma Brotherhood reported on the evolution of the children's school program in Washington DC.

> Children of the same sex and age group share dormitories together. Children of the same age group share daily sadhanas together, take meals together, enjoy "resource periods" using Montessori materials, make frequent visits to museums, zoos, garden farms, and take lots of time to play in parks and wooded areas. They bathe together, read stories together and, in short, enjoy group consciousness existence with each other even before they have learned to walk.
>
> Group consciousness is one of the most powerful aspects of the Children's Program. Living in large groups, as opposed to unitary families, children gain a more balanced perspective on their place in the world. . . .
>
> Of course, "Mommy" and "Daddy" remain very special people with very special roles. They serve as the primary models for their children's behavior and continue to supply a basic security, but they do their best not to eclipse their children in their own shadows, and to avoid overgrown emotional attachments. . . .
>
> A goal of the Washington program is for all adults in the community to have the attitude of "universal parents" toward all the children, and for the children to develop the independence and security to feel comfortable in the care of many different qualified adults.[111]

In 1975, in another communication, Sikh Dharma Brotherhood informed parents on the setup of the school system to prepare 3HO children for their Holy Mission to change the world. The parents could and should stay relaxed and strong in faith, strengthen their sadhana (spiritual practice), and remember that their physical presence was not necessary for the children. It was through projection that they would be able to shape their children's destinies.[112]

Sat Pavan shared how her mother felt about all this.

My parents, especially my mom, felt bullied out of any decision makings in my life because I was going to India at age eight. She felt that her opinion, her desires, and whatever she wanted for me didn't matter. If she spoke up, it would be like she was going against him, and that was a huge NO. Besides that, there was the power of the community. People would say, "No, this is what you need to do. How dare you keep your daughter from her destiny!"

As we were told that we were more enlightened than our parents and that we knew what our soul wanted, if we didn't get something, we would say, "If you don't let me have this, you are denying me."[113]

Yogi Bhajan on Distance Therapy

A Funny Idea

Below follows a direct quote from Yogi Bhajan, not polished by any of his staff. We must warn you that his reasoning is not always logical, his words sound strange, and his sentences can take weird turns. We quote him verbatim to give you a realistic idea of how he spoke to his disciples.

In the summer of 1975, Yogi Bhajan shared a "funny" idea that had occurred to him as he pondered ways to apply his "distance therapy." He had wondered what use this life was if children had to suffer the same things as adults. He had given 3HO children distance therapy so they could stand and understand how to live and what to live for.

None of our children will suffer. You know I was thinking about that day when I was talking to Larry [one of his first ashram leaders]. I said, "Larry, we should do something very funny."

He said, "What?"

I said, "It's really very funny. You know what? You should have Siri Singh Sahib Corporation to adopt all children and when you leave them for residential purpose with their parents."

He said, "What?"

I said, "Man, if they will know they are on leave they will at least behave. And when they don't behave, I'll have to get my little ones back. . . ."

He said, "Yogiji, idea is great, but already people are very much in trouble."

I said, "I know that."[114]

Bhajan never pursued his adoption idea. However, he did about everything else to make his distance therapy a success. At the summer solstice event in 1975, he addressed the 3HO mothers about it.

I want you not to be emotional in deciding the fate of your children. . . . There is a security of distance. If the child is not given the security of distance, he will, after eleven years, try to run away from the parents. If we will not raise our children away from us, then they will run away from us anyway. Remember, don't pass on your negativity to your children. . . . You have to learn to be parents before you can expect your children to be children. We will allow those to be parents who can be parents to all the children, not those who want to be parents only to their children. Khalsa is the parents.[115]

You Are Neurotics

Two years later, in 1977, he said:

We have experimented in 3HO the distance therapy. When the child is little, send him to a training school. Let him come in the holidays, he will long to come [home]. Love him and tell him one thing: "My dear child, you are born out of me, but you are born to learn, and your real parents is the learning institution. My dear child, your mother is the mother universe, and your father is the heavenly divinity and the dignity.

[*While he spoke softly at first, now he starts shouting, spitting out certain words, bolded here.*]

... you have to **go away,** the child has to live **without you** and make him **strong enough** that **without you** it can always **feel you** within him. As the child was **within** you, he must **feel** the **parents** within **him.** And this is called the **balance,** this is called the **equilibrium, without that** there is **no child complete.**

[*He switches to a mean tone:*] **Hah,** you don't know a **thing; 250 million** people of United States of America do not know this thing at all, basically.

[*Shouting in a high-pitched voice:*] **Everything is balanced,** when the **child** is **in you,** when he is **out of you, you should be in him or in her.**

[*His tone softens again.*] There is no distance. Then time and space will never upset you.

[*A longer silence follows, and then he says mockingly:*] You are just, you are just like fools, run after the child, "my child, my child, my child."[116]

Six years later, in 1983, he was pretty clear about his intentions:

Forget about some of you who are neurotics I have nothing to do with you, you can do whatever you want, but finally, I want to have, in two generations, children which are competent, capable, who can stand stress, absolutely make no suffering with allergies, absolutely do not have any major disease, such as cancer, such as this, such as that or main five–six killing disease can be totally eliminated, . . . that's what my purpose is and that's what I am teaching [at] ladies camp. . . .

The doctor is very much involved . . . there is a difference between a 3HO child and the other child. 3HO child will smile openly, others won't. 3HO child will get into a trauma [and] forget it very fast. . . .

Everybody is against me here [about sending children to India]. It's a very hot subject and I know you are very insane Americans, and you will never understand what I am talking to you today. . . .

Children have no future without you, this is what you think. I think children have brighter and better future without you. Totally and I am very convinced of it. . . . you are neurotics, what you are going to inject your neurosis to the children? . . .

What I believe is we will have the most intelligent and self-contained child for tomorrow. For that, I need a woman. I don't need a traumatic, idiot, good-looking prostitute. Neither I am looking for very intellectual, sad, neurotic person. I need a very simple, honest, God-loving woman. Simple woman, very simple, very beautiful, very creative. And I need a very honest, very truthful, and very together, God-loving man. It is essential. Seed and the ground. . . .

We believe in one, or two or three generations, we'll be in a position to produce according to all human scriptures a race of people who can understand, who can raise, and who can have children worth to be the proud of.[117]

A few months later he preached about the same topic in the gurdwara: "To save our children from drug and sex orientation, which is a terrible disease of this country and this modern age there is hardly any corner to. We have sent our children twelve thousand miles away into Mussoorie, just to be away from that effects. See, it is not our irresponsibility, rather it is our love and affection and our graceful attitude towards our children."[118]

Younger rather than Older

In July 1984, Sikh Dharma announced the next year's school program in India.

The letter mentioned that in 1984, 108 American Sikh children attended the school in Mussoorie in the Uttarakhand region. Most of them had been there for two years. Now, applications were expected for the following year's program. The final directive was, "As far as at what age to consider sending your child, we recommend younger rather than older. Again, this year many five- and six-year old's will be going."[119]

People Are Not Kangaroos

In that same month, July 1984, Yogi Bhajan lectured at women's camp in Española on the topic "The Art of Communication." He invited women to stand up and confront him in a one-on-one conversation. They were allowed to bring difficult questions and even attack him. He would show them how to neutralize offensiveness in a conversation.

Different women accepted the challenge. One asked why so many people had left 3HO in the last six months. He used this question to show them how to create duality if challenged. They should always remain courteous, extremely firm, and absolutely confusing to the other party. During an interrogation, if you cannot confuse, you have already lost the case. "Never offend people with whom you communicate. It doesn't matter how neurotic they are. Confuse them." The teaching was: never enter a fight but confuse and defuse people and their personalities.

After closing this case, the next brave woman stepped to the microphone and launched her question, "What is the best way to run an ashram?" After some back and forth, the smooth and polite conversation ended. She went back to her seat.

I switch to the present tense here to give you a better sense of the atmosphere in the following conversation.

"Next," shouts Bhajan.

The video camera focuses on "the master" sitting on stage, cross-legged, in a crisp white robe and ditto turban. His amused eyes follow the new candidate walking to the microphone. A mocking smile appears on his face. He shuffles back and forth.

"Oh wow. Now it's going to be fun."

The giggles in the audience tell us that they too know this can get spicy. The camera turns to the skinny young woman who is the subject of all this commotion. She seems unable to keep her upper body still as if she is standing on a wobbling surface. She's dressed all in white like everyone else, with a long white veil pinned to the front of her towering turban. A princess among princesses. Although she seems nervous, her high voice sounds sharp and clear. Her gaze remains fixed on Bhajan.

WOMAN. I hear you people like to send your children away to the other side of the world.

[*This is the third year 3HO children are sent to boarding schools in India.*]

YB. Oh yeah! Do you mean the other side of the world, beyond or within the Earth?

[*The audience chuckles at his joke.*]

WOMAN. No, specifically, I have heard that you send all your children away to India.

YB: Oh, when did you hear that?

WOMAN. I have just been around in the ashram. People tell me their children are gone.

YB. Gone! [*Yogi Bhajan feigns surprise, which prompts laughter from the audience.*] And did they tell you why they are gone?

WOMAN. Well, I asked them if they miss them.

YB. No, no, no, wait a minute. Wait a minute, wait a minute. First, you heard that children are gone. Don't we agree to that?

[*The audience laughs nervously; the young woman joins in and wiggles even more.*]

WOMAN. Yes.

YB. And did you hear why they are gone?

WOMAN. No, can you tell me why they are gone?

YB. Oh no. Ask them!

WOMAN. Well, I wanted to ask you because . . .

YB. I am not gone. I am not a child.

WOMAN. Well, I can't afford the airplane ticket to ask the children, so I thought I would . . .

YB. No, no, ask the parents from where you heard . . .

WOMAN. Well, they got the idea from you. So, I wanted to ask you [*stresses the word "you"*].

YB. They got the idea from me? [*Again, he fakes amazement, eliciting loud laughter.*]

WOMAN. Yes.

YB. What was the idea?

WOMAN. To send the children away.

[*It is very quiet now.*]

YB. No, we didn't send them away. Children are very much with us. [*Laughter reappears.*] No, no, my dear sweet lady, please, for God's sake, our children are with us very much, every day, every minute of the breath. We love them. We have them. We are very good parents.

WOMAN. Well, I think this is such a great country that I just don't understand why you want to send them where everyone is poor? [*Nervous giggles well up again. Bhajan shakes his head in the negative and his voice grows more serious.*]

YB. Our children are with us. They are very rich. They are in a very beautiful environment, and they are very rich. They are very great Americans. But I don't think people should not have the right to visit. They are just great Americans and have the right to visit, don't they?

WOMAN. They do. But I think they are going to get brainwashed.

YB. Oh, thank God, with what? [*The audience again bursts into frenetic laughter.*] With soap? Brainwashed with what?

WOMAN. You know, brainwashed where they won't have the same American values as great people in this country.

YB. Oh yeah? And people get brainwashed here? In America, is there a place for brainwashing here?

WOMAN. No, we are a free country.

YB. That's what it is. They are free children. Nobody can brainwash them.

WOMAN. But did they really want to go? [*She stresses the word "really." Yogi Bhajan is silent for a moment and looks her straight in the eye. And when he starts speaking, he articulates each word loud and clear.*]

YB. That it seems to be a situation of reality. [*A long silence follows.*] But do you really think they have gone?

WOMAN. They seem to be gone! [*Nervous giggles add to the palpable tension. Bhajan straightens his back as if to end the conversation here.*]

YB. Well, basically, you can live with your misunderstanding. And please understand our children neither are gone nor they are gone to be brainwashed, nor they are gone away from us. The basic idea is that we wanted them to be grown as great people. They wanted to be experienced. They want to run around. They want to see the whole world, and they are just here.

WOMAN. OK, you can have your feelings, and I have mine. [*A nervous laugh accompanies her words.*]

YB. That is true! And perhaps one day, as a mother, you will like to request me to send your child on the world trip too.

WOMAN. Oh no, I would miss them too much. They need me! [*The audience laughs loudly as if they know what she is bringing down on herself. He smiles.*]

YB. Well, you must understand some people are like kangaroos. [*Exuberant laughter.*] And they keep their children in their belly bag. Some people want to give them values, that they can grow, and be strong, and walk their own foundation, and feel themself. I think that's what America is about. But I never knew in America lot of kangaroos have taken birth in human bodies. I am pretty confused.

WOMAN. I am insulted. [*She mutters this while her whole body shakes in laughter, or perhaps weeping. There are no tears though. The audience laugh their heads off and Bhajan laughs along while he seems to be bothered by something.*]

YB. You said something I didn't hear.

WOMAN. Oh, it was insulting to me that you were saying I was like a kangaroo because I . . .

YB. I didn't say . . . My God, please, lady, I said "some" people are like kangaroos. Please, that's not the idea. You are not a kangaroo. I mean, you are not. I can see you are a beautiful lady! Oh, you know what I mean is: Some people are like kangaroos. They feel that they have to have a belly bag and keep the kid in there and run around and . . .

WOMAN. Well, that's the natural way to keep your children with you. God created us to have them. . . .

YB. My basic idea is: why to deliver them after nine months? Why not deliver after six years? It's a matter of thought, you know. It's a matter of feeling. My personal feeling is this.

[*YB starts speaking very fast now. He is rattling on, in fact.*]

A child is born in the grace of God, and has the domain, and has the destiny, and has to walk, and has to be, and all that. As parents, we can do and keep them in the love, and keep them in the bondage of our own love, and affection, and vibration, and keep them wherever they are. They are within the reach of our prayer, and they are within reach of our projection. We are very beautiful people, but we are not kangaroos. We are not. We want our children to see the whole planet. We want the children to rule the planet. We want them wherever they go. They spread the light. They are the most innocent angels of God. We don't want to take away their rights. They are all over the world. I think somebody might have tried to misinform you.

WOMAN. Well, thank you for enlightening me.[120]

Childhood Memories

Self-Made Kid

It was freezing cold on December 30, 2020, wherever Siri was sitting in front of his PC. He was waiting for his interview to begin. As he listened to GuruNischan, who was reading aloud the intentions of her *Uncomfortable Conversations Podcast*, Siri stared to his right. Sunlight illuminated his face. He had wrapped himself warmly. During the interview, he regularly pulled his gray alpine hat further down over his ears. His long, curly, gray-black beard stuck out wide. A small square wood-framed window behind his chair suggested he was in a mountain hut.

Throughout the more than three-and-a-half-hour interview, the room gradually grew darker. When Siri's profile almost blended with the background, he moved to another room. This was the only interruption in the nonstop telling of his life story.

It is a story of a self-made kid who maintained himself in a unique, sometimes playful, sometimes clumsy way in this child-unfriendly 3HO community. In an earlier chapter, Siri recounted how in 1976, he and his mom joined 3HO. And how, twenty-eight years later, in 2004, he shoved Yogi Bhajan's dead body into the funeral home's cooler.

Here we dive a little deeper into Siri's childhood. He grew up in Boston in the late 1960s and early 1970s. He was the first grandchild on his father's side, whom everyone loved. "They called me a super child." Every autumn, his parents gave up their jobs to travel to Vermont, where they went skiing all winter. Then, in spring, they returned to the beach. "Living close to the ocean was heavenly."

Siri was five when his parents divorced. His mother, a nurse, decided to continue her studies at university. Through yoga classes, she encountered 3HO. And so, when he was nine, Siri traveled with his mom by train to Los Angeles to start living in an ashram. He had to leave behind everything and everyone he knew: his father, his grandparents, his family, his friends, and his school. It was a shock. On the train, he ordered a hamburger.

"This is the last burger you will ever eat," his mother said.

"What? Wait a minute. What? Why? Hamburgers are delicious!"

Soon after he arrived at the ashram, he was introduced to Yogi Bhajan, who gave him a new name, Siri Nirongkar. Why would he need a new name? His name was OK! As his mother had predicted, this was the immediate start of a hamburger-free existence. After a short time in Los Angeles, they moved to Española.

"When we arrived there, the entire ashram was on a fast. In the morning, they served plain Japanese yogurt and raw onions. 'This is breakfast,' they said. I said, 'No. This is not breakfast. I don't know what this is, but it is not breakfast.' I also remember the fanaticism in those days: getting up at 4:00 a.m. to take a cold shower."

Because his mom was too busy working as a nurse, Siri was assigned to male caretakers. In the following years, he would change guardians and hometowns several times: from Los Angeles to New Mexico, back to Los Angeles, then to Oregon for a while, and back to New Mexico, more or less in that order. He does not remember exactly.

Public schools in the US were hell for Siri. There was always fighting everywhere—in class, in the playground, and on the way home. As a boy with a turban, he was the target of ridicule, exclusion, and violence. When the school found out he was a vegetarian, they sent him to the infirmary, as they deemed that unhealthy. When American hostages were murdered in Teheran in 1989, Khomeini's name was hurled at his head. One of his teachers called him a white nigger. Another teacher bullied him for wearing a turban, provoking Siri into a fight.

The highlight of the entire year was the summer solstice event in Española. We had so much fun hanging around with friends, the same friends every year. First, we had summer solstice celebration and afterward, children's camp.

We were all bullied at school. Most of us lived separately from our parents. We liked to sneak around looking for food because the banana curry at the festival was inedible. We knew that the leadership had something else in the fridge. For us, children living with the guards, looking for something better to eat was our favorite activity. So, we made new plans to break into the kitchen every day. One day we got caught. They tied us in the pantry with our arms up. Someone broke free, so we ate our fill and tied ourselves up again. The guards did not notice a thing.

Supervision at the children's camps was a joke. Siri and GuruNischan recall announcements over the loudspeaker during the summer solstice event. If you didn't know what to do or needed a job, you could sign up to chaperone the children's camp. The only qualification required was that you were free. However, some of these unqualified guides were able to create memorable experiences, as Siri recounts.

At those camps, we mostly had to keep ourselves busy. Some of the youth guides were outdoor people. When they were around, we had a great time. They liked to share their knowledge with us and took us on treks through the wilderness. One summer, we went out every weekend. Away from camp and the ashram, our guides switched to a diet that matched our activities. On the trek, they left behind all the strict community rules. One of the best memories of my youth was when we went on a six-week hike with a dozen boys and two guides.[121]

I Was in Charge of Myself

Meeri was born in 1975 in the 3HO ashram of Phoenix, Arizona.

When I was between two and three years old, Yogi Bhajan forced my mom to divorce my dad. His big crime was his interest in marijuana. Today that sounds so silly. But in those days, Yogi Bhajan was branding his empire as being super healthy, antidrugs, and anti-AIDS. I even think he was involved in federal contracts to get people off drugs. We were single for a year before my mom got into another arranged marriage. We moved to LA and then to New Mexico. I was probably four when I was sent to this random family in Española. They abused me, not sexually but physically. He spanked me really hard.

Meeri wonders aloud why children were separated from their parents and sent to people who didn't like kids and who beat them.

I suffered from so many things as a result of being born in 3HO, but the main thing was being forced as a kid to raise me. I realized that I had this feeling of being an orphan. Looking back at it, I was in charge of myself. My parents were not there for me. They were busy doing the cult.

Undoubtedly, they suffered as well and still are. Now, didn't they give up a lot of the responsibility of being parents? I remember doing incredibly adult-like things as a four-year-old.

I remember cleaning the bathroom at the Broadway ashram in LA at ages three and four. Can you imagine kids doing that today? . . . The fact that I had no dad plays a role in my story. Yogi Bhajan told me I was gay because I had no proper dad to tell me how to be a man. But he was the one who forced my parents to divorce![122]

Touching His Feet

"Yogi Bhajan was the person we were supposed to revere," shared a former 3HO member. "We were expected to stand up when he entered the room. Our parents brought us in front of him when the class was over. We had to bend down and touch his feet. Mom and Dad were overjoyed when we did that, and for us, it was just doing what we were told. Other than that, we had no personal connection with him."[123]

Miserable Children's Camps

A second-generation adult shared her experiences of the exhausting six-week children's camps in the remote mountainous desert of New Mexico that took place every year after the summer solstice event. Children were sent to an undeveloped part of Ram Das Puri land. Their mothers stayed downhill attending the women's camps, and their fathers went home to work. Whether there was running water in the mountains where the kids stayed in tents, the survivor does not remember, but for sure there was no hot water. She was five years old when they started doing that. The purpose of these camps was to detach.

"From time to time, our mothers would drive by in the bus. We wouldn't get to say hi to them or hug them. They would all be waving happily at us. We would be in tears not understanding why our mother just drove by."[124]

Bear Mush

RishiKnots, an Instagram account containing testimonies and stories from children born and/or raised in the community, shared a post titled "Children's camp in the early 80s" showing a picture of a yellow bus parked on the side of the road. Behind it is a precipice, and to the bus's left, in the distance, loom peaks of rough gray mountains.

Twenty-three children pose for the photographer. They stand neatly, one next to the other, along the side of the bus. The oldest is about five, maybe six. One of the older girls is turned slightly towards the smallest of the gang. She looks at her as the little one sucks her thumb. They could be sisters. To the left is a toddler with round cheeks. Her oversized white turban is twisted thickly around her head. The older girls wear turbans like towers that reach twice as high as their faces, as if in competition. A boy about five years old is picking his nose. A dark-skinned girl stands stock-still as if in a formation. With an open mouth, she looks into the camera. Her turban almost falls over her eyes. The only boy without a turban has his hair tied in a rishi knot that rests modestly on the crown of his head. His apple-blue-sea-green shirt is way too big. They all wear long white or blue shirts, or dresses, with leggings that fall rumpled over their dirty shoes. Loose laces lie in the arid sand. On the left side of the row, kids look dazed, angry, or shy, while on the right side a few timid smiles can be detected.

In the comments on the post, someone asks why these kids look so unhappy. The moderator replies that if her memory serves her well, they had stopped at a viewpoint so the guides could cook a giant pot of porridge. The kids called it "bear mush." It was burnt, but they had to eat it anyway. Another one asks why the turbans were so "fucking big." The answer is, "Because our heads were really tiny."[125]

Bravo!

"Bravo! Toddlers at Ram Das Puri." In Gothic letter type, this title adorns the top of an article in the 1982 Yearbook of the Khalsa Youth Camp. The article reads, "A FIRST . . . and BIG success for Khalsa Children's Camp. Many of us felt that the best thing about camp this year was having one of our one- to three-year-old's run up with a big smile to give you a loving hug. Apart from the daily exposure to *kirtan* [religious chanting], yoga, storytelling, meditations, *banis* [Sikh prayers], gurdwara [Sikh service], and just having plain fun, the toddlers discovered a new sense of independence and self-reliance. How strong they grew!"[126]

Next to the text is a black-and-white photograph of a boy dressed all in white who can barely sit up. His thin hair is tied up in a rishi knot on top of his tiny little head with a white netting drawn over it. He looks at the person taking the picture with questioning eyes. Below the text are more images of young children playing with toddlers.

In a discussion on social media on this topic, a second-generation adult shared that she was eleven when she had to take care of twenty toddlers. She recalls doing her very best. Many, like her, openly wonder what their parents were thinking when they sent them to these camps. They are baffled because all this was normalized for so long within 3HO. The campsite for the toddlers was far away from medical care or other essential services and reachable only via an eight-mile dirt road.[127]

Regulated to a State of Hunger

A recurring topic in stories of 3HO children is the lack of food and its poor quality in the ashrams, the schools, the children's camps, and at the guardian parents' homes. In one of the *Uncomfortable Conversations*, a second-generation adult says that one day, one of her parents had told her their childhood had also been tough.

She had replied, "What? Wait a minute. No, no. You guys went to the movies. You guys ate pizza. We ate rice with bugs in it."

GuruNischan adds:

Are we, the children, the ones who should be compassionate? So many second gens stay silent. It's almost as if their story is "not valid" or "not valuable enough." As if there are hierarchies of trauma. It's all a consequence of our early detachment. We don't look at ourselves as "valuable." We did not bring that upon ourselves. Anyone born into this culture should know that this is complex PTSD. Our healing is about reclaiming our essential self. Our basic developmental needs were not met.

SECOND-GEN. Here, I am going to make myself very vulnerable. Little people, make your judgments. I don't care. I learned to do this with the help of my therapist. Sometimes, I talk to the little child in myself. It is kind of a "sandbox" therapy. I use little Lego pieces, and each one gets another part of me. I have a graffiti child, a helper, ... There is a Lego figure with a scared face. There's a fighter. And then, there is "the little one." Sometimes I just hold her close to me. Sometimes I don't say anything. Sometimes I say, "What do you want to do? Do you want to color today?"

GURUNISCHAN. Or "What do you need to eat? We can eat anything you want."

[*They burst into laughter.*]

SECOND-GEN. People never asked, "Do you want a treat? Are you hungry? Do you want something?" What was wrong with them?

GURUNISCHAN. My God, I know! I am now learning how much I am regulated to a state of hunger. But it is not even just food hunger. This is what it means to reclaim ourselves from deep places of developmental trauma. We are starved for affection, love, and connection. And I don't know how to allow myself those things as I am regulated by insecurity. It's weird to learn it again. It's slow. Like the question, "What do you want to eat today?" I didn't know that such a question activates a mental trigger, resulting in a state of feeling nothing. So, then I'm not hungry.[128]

BOARDING SCHOOLS IN INDIA

Memories from India

Do You Want to Go to India?

We return to Sat Pavan. In the summer of 1981, she was six and had enjoyed singing in the church as a "normal kid." When her father had found a job in Florida, the family returned to "3HO land" but to a friendlier atmosphere than before. In the winter of 1982, a request came to subscribe Sat Pavan to a boarding school in India.

> My mom was against it. Today she still says, "One of the worst things I ever allowed to happen was for you to be sent to India." My father did not want to let me go without her approval.
>
> He said to me, "Do you want to go to India? You know your mom doesn't want it. So, if you can't convince her, you will not be able to go."
>
> I didn't know what it meant. "Do you want to go to India?" Except that it was "Do you want to go to where the Sikh religion comes from? Do you want to go to the land of the gurus? Do you want to go to where the Golden Temple is?"

All of that was very exciting and definitely something I wanted to do. I remember sitting in front of my little altar in my room. I chanted, meditated, and prayed that my parents would let me go to India.

Years later, my mom told me, "I saw you really wanted to go. If I said no, you would be upset. And, later on, you might feel like you missed out on something."

She let me go. I left in February of 1983 when I had just turned eight. It was a marked change in my life. I used to say, "At eight, I became independent from my parents. I became an adult." I never saw that as a negative thing. It wasn't until I started having my own kids that I realized, "What was I thinking? How did my parents want me to do this? I was so young!"

When we arrived in India, we first traveled to Amritsar. We lived in one of the houses connected to the Golden Temple complex. A couple of times a day, we went to the Golden Temple. It was not extremely crowded as it is today. We could go inside anytime. It was bliss. That one month of February was a great time for me. I don't remember being sad, missing my parents, or regretting coming to India. It was everything that I thought India would be.

How Long Is a Year? Two Years?

And then March hit. We left Amritsar and the Golden Temple and traveled to the boarding school in Mussoorie in the region of Uttarakhand. That's way up in the foothills of the Himalayas. When we got there, that's when I cried. That's when I said, "Wait. Am I going to be here now? When am I going to see my parents?" Because, you know, I didn't know what a year meant. I thought I had already been for a year in India. So, when my situation hit me, it was very emotional and hard.

The school term ran from March till the end of October. Once winter arrives in the Himalayan mountains, you get snowed in. It's extremely hard to do anything there. So, the American kids would go somewhere else. In 1983, we went to Punjab. We stayed in historic areas. It was beautiful, and I actually enjoyed it. I loved traveling in India. It was nice, but still, none of us got home. None of us went to see our families.

Some families who had money came over to visit their kids. A few even spent the entire winter program in India with their children. Parents were not encouraged to bring the kids home. "Leave them in India. If you want to see them, fly to India." Maybe there were financial reasons because we were there with 120 kids. But for sure, it was also just set up that way.

In 1984, Indira Gandhi was assassinated by two of her Sikh bodyguards. Anti-Sikh riots followed. Thousands of Sikhs were killed. The Golden Temple was attacked. It was not safe to travel in Punjab. Moreover, they closed the borders to foreigners, so it was decided to send us home during school holidays for safety reasons.

In 1985, I finally saw my parents again after two years. I stayed in the US for three months and flew back to India when school started. I did not feel my parents forced me to go. I never thought it was an option not to go. It was the culture. You were ridiculed if you were from our generation and didn't go to India. You were treated differently by the other kids. If you didn't return to India, it was because your parents were negative, or something was wrong. Every year, I would cry for the entire plane ride over. I probably even cried the first three days. Then I would adjust and deal with being there, looking forward to returning home.

At home, I would get in bed with my parents. I never told anyone. People would make fun of me. The last time we celebrated my birthday was when I was eight. Then I went to India. No more celebration. That's hard for me.

I've talked to other kids of my generation. We're all adults now. Many of us have relationship issues with our parents. It's sad. It started by being separated from them. I used to think I had a good relationship with them. "I can talk to them about everything." But now I know, if I'm fully honest, I didn't do that. We were always told not to talk negatively. So, the idea of sharing scary, harsh, or traumatizing things that happened to me at boarding school was not done!

I've always felt like I needed to protect my parents. My whole life, I felt like I didn't want to tell them anything that would be hard for them to hear. I didn't want them to worry and be upset. I did not want to hurt them.[129]

We Were Like Orphans

Another second-generation adult spoke to Mina Bahadori in an interview about her time at the boarding school in India.

I was eight when I was sent over in the early 1980s. Oh gosh, it was bleak! The school ground was full of gravel. It was a rigid, traditional Sikh Indian boarding school, structured, rigorous, and authoritarian. We were like little orphans, crass and unruly. We didn't ask for what we needed. When we did ask, we didn't get it. We were in autopilot survival mode. From early on, we developed a habit of not asking for help from grownups. If they told us what to do, we just did it. We wouldn't glom on to them. When they were around, we hoped that, at some point, they would move on to another purpose.

The school was modeled after the British system. The Indian teachers applied heavy corporal punishments like a Catholic school in the 1940s. They whacked us on the knuckles with rulers and made us do little punishments such as standing on a chair forever. Some teachers would hit kids on the head with spoons. In a way, it was accepted as the norm. Next to the Indian teachers, a group of American chaperones "looked after" the American kids. They were oppressive and heavy-handed and administered their own discipline separate from the school. It was random. It was aberrant. It was not, "You do this, and as a consequence, this will happen." It was more like bullying. The betrayal of trust by them was bruising at an emotional level. They were cruel in a way that had nothing to do with straight black-and-white discipline.

Mina asked her interviewee if she could talk more about a certain guide who had a reputation for being particularly harsh.

"Right. Nanak Dev. He was so harsh. He was an awful, horrible, terribly cruel sociopath. He set the tone. Other adult guides followed suit. He typically physically attacked boys."

She recounts how, one day, she witnessed him even physically assaulting a twelve-year-old girl. This is what happened: Most children stayed in India during school breaks, because their parents could not afford the trip home. Nanak Dev called those who went home "a bunch of pussies." This girl had just returned from holidays in the US when she and her team lost a soccer game. Nanak Dev made them run laps around the field as punishment for losing. She was running slowly, and someone started bopping her on the back of the head, saying, "Run faster, run faster, run faster." She had said, "I can't run faster," perhaps because she suffered from jetlag or had her period. A bit later, she was beaten up by Nanak Dev in a closed room while other kids were ordered to stand watch outside, making sure nobody went in.

> Kids who deserved his wrath had to carry around a big ten-pound stone. He called it the "Ego Rock," and they had to carry it around for several days. Everywhere they went, they had to take this giant rock. Other guards started doing the same thing, saying, "You're being bad. You need an ego rock." They made a six-year-old girl carry around that heavy thing. She dropped it and broke her toe.

Mina asked, "Wasn't there, at any point, any adult who stepped in and said, 'This is not OK?'"

> If they were there, they were silenced right away. If anything, they were going to get beaten up too. The abuse and violence were so widespread. It was so confusing for us kids. There were adults who knew about it, objected, and said to Nanak Dev, "If you ever do this again, I'll kill you." And then they went back home and did nothing.

I know why he was there. I know why no adult had any power to stop it. We all know why. Because it's a cult. Yogi Bhajan said, "Don't make waves. These kids deserve what they're getting."[130]

Run on Incompetence

Siri hated going to school in the US because he was bullied for his turban and for being a vegetarian. In 1981, when he was fourteen, he was sent to a boarding school in India and stayed there for five years without returning to the US.

I knew Nanak Dev before I left for India. I hung out with him at the ashram in Manhattan Beach in Los Angeles. He was a super fun guy. Super friendly. We would get in his car, and he would drive like a maniac and do all these hard turns that would throw us around in the back seat. That kind of crap that boys like. He was always good for jokes. We would stay up late and watch *The Rat Patrol*, an old British Army World War II TV show. He was this nice guy.

And then he came to India. Nanak Dev came with his wife and kids to be the chaperone for the American boys. She was there for the girls. I had an easier time dealing with him than most other children. I knew the things that would set him off. What you should not do with Nanak Dev was to challenge his authority in public. He couldn't handle that.

Most of us stayed in India when the school break started in the winter. We, the boys, moved to the girls' school for that period. During that holiday, we got to know Nanak Dev because we were dealing with him directly and all the time. There were some firsts for me with him. Everyone who went to India remembers the "Ego Rock." Well, he invented it for me. Behind the girls' school was this hill with old ruins on top. We called that place Hotel California after the cover of the Eagles album. We liked to go up there and mess around. Mussoorie is at the foothills of the Himalayas and has a beautiful alpine outlook. I loved it and was happy in the ever-greens. We enjoyed running around in those hills.

During that winter break, I constantly did what Nanak Dev did not want me to do. I was smart enough not to give him a reason to come on to me, but I was also afraid of him. One day I said something he didn't like. I was good at being passive-aggressive, dropping some comments and infuriating him. He said that I had an ego and that it was massive. So, he went and found a big rock. He said, "Pick it up and write EGO on it." I did that, and then I had to carry it up the hill to the ruins and back down. And I had to do that however many times. And that became "a thing."

I saw Nanak Dev hitting kids with a *gatka* stick on the back of their legs because they were not moving fast enough or not jumping high enough. To me, that doesn't rise to the level of abuse, but I'm not going to take away somebody else calling it abuse. I am not saying it is correct. Often, I knew kids were going to get hit before it happened. I watched them challenge his authority publicly in a disrespectful way. I'm not saying that is an excuse. But for me watching, it was just like, "Oh, no, don't do that . . . oh God . . . ." I appreciate that those kids probably had enough, were fed up, and had a bad day. Or they were particularly sad that day, missing their parents, or God knows what was going through their heads. I'm not accusing anybody of being stupid. I'm just telling you what I saw. It was not cool what he did. There was no morality involved. It was not about good or bad or right or wrong. In our reality, there was a set of rules to live by. If you chose to step outside of those, there were consequences. It was all about survival, knowing your environment, and knowing how to avoid danger.

So yes, Nanak Dev could be hard on us, but he also did things I really appreciate. He recognized our need to work out. He made it possible for us to lift weights. He organized a lot of sports. He got us into *gatka* [a martial art linked to the Sikh tradition] and took us on trips that most normal people don't consider doing. He took us boys from one side of India to the other by train. Those were fantastic adventures we had in all these cities.

One time, half the group had boarded the train with him. The other half was still standing on the platform and could not get on. The train left. And so, there we were, on the platform, a bunch of kids without money, without anything. It was in Benares. We were a thousand miles away from anything we knew. My friend and I started running down the tracks of the train. One boy on the train saw us and hit the brake. Nanak Dev was crazy enough to take us on such adventures. On these tours, we were full-on rock stars. It was bizarre and surreal, a bunch of American kids doing *gatka*. In those days, it was a dead art in India. Very few people did it outside of the classical Nihang community of Punjab. Hundreds of people were crowding and pushing to see us.

So, there were also positive experiences with Nanak Dev. He and his wife had probably been sent there by Yogi Bhajan. They were under resourced. He was the only one responsible for taking care of the boys. Nobody got it worse from Nanak Dev than his own son. We all saw it. It was hard to watch. His biggest flaw to me was how he treated his son. It was brutal. His son was a talented and fantastic kid, one of my first friends in the dharma. That's why I went to their ashram. It was awful, public berating. It wasn't so physical as public and emotional, putting down, insulting. Nanak Dev was such a macho with his big old kicker cowboy boots.

I heard the stories told by the younger kids about the bad treatment they got from Nanak Dev. I will not call them liars. But he is not the only one that I hold accountable. I hold the entire system above him responsible to a much larger degree. The fact that he didn't have any help, that he wasn't qualified, and nobody noticed that. There were people, and I don't need to name names, not just the Siri Singh Sahib. There were layers in between who were officially in charge of the program in India by their titles. They used to come over once in a while and check in. They were clearly not paying attention. And then, ultimately, the Siri Singh Sahib was accountable.

That program in India was not a product of some master plan. That program was run on incompetence, neglect, and sheer dumb luck. There was no plan nor an interest in our well-being. I don't believe somebody was sitting there, pulling the levers: "How do we mess with these kids?"

One of the reasons why these things happened is that we were told we were better. We were superior because we had "the technology," whatever that meant. Because we were living as Sikhs. "The things that will affect the world and everyone else will not touch us. We will be OK no matter what. Just because we live this life." That was put into our heads as kids and the people who were supposed to look after us. They believed in this fucking superiority. We did not need to study modern child development and psychology because we had "the technology." We did not need to consult experts because we had the Siri Singh Sahib. He gave us meditations. "Oh, you have ADHD? Just do this meditation. Are you on the spectrum? Do this yoga, this meditation, take some yogurt." Make up a formula, and it will fix your brain.

The bottom line is that Nanak Dev was not equipped for the job. In the US, he worked in the brass bed factory. He wasn't even good at dealing with his own son. And then you put him in charge of kids far away from their parents? Come on. It is not because you want to be an astrophysicist that you can be it.[131]

You're a Fucking Weakling

On April 16, 2018, a forty-four-year-old man traveled from New York to New Delhi. Thirty-four years before, in March 1984, he had made the same journey for the first time while traveling alone to the school in India. He was ten when he had said goodbye to his parents, his life in the US, and his childhood. We will call him Jasbir, which is a pseudonym.

The next seven years in India were filled with the most unique adventures. He climbed remote mountains in the Himalayas, floated on inner tubes in the Ganges, discovered Rajasthan, and much more. He learned to care for himself and forged bonds with other children, making them feel like family. It was sometimes fun but sometimes a rock-hard time. The memories of the systematic abuse and public humiliation he endured during his childhood in India remained buried in his subconscious, where they marinated for years. The traumas occasionally resurfaced when unpleasant things happened or at trigger moments.

So, in April 2018, one year after "such a moment," Jasbir was heading back to India. In the following days and weeks, he planned to return to the places that largely determined the course of his life. While flying somewhere over the ocean, he jotted down the following in his diary:

> Once a month, I take my ten-year-old self out for breakfast on a Saturday. I take a scrambled egg. He gets a stack of blueberry pancakes. I picture my younger self sitting in the booth across from me, with his turban tied low just above his eyebrows. He wears a stained white kurta pajama, a blue pullover sweater, and Pony Velcro sneakers. He is happily eating his pancakes. At this point, he is complete again. He is safe with me.

Jasbir described the key moments of his 2018 roundtrip in India in his diary. He outlined how it felt to physically reconnect with the bureaucracy, the places, the buildings, the dormitories, the smells, and the sounds. Below, we read how one day, after more than three decades, he walked through the gate of the boarding school in Mussoorie again. He was alone then; he was alone now.

> Over the past six months, I have thought a lot about this moment and how I would feel. In film scenarios, a situation like this, where you return to the place where so many powerful memories belong, often results in a purifying and liberating experience. However, I did not fall to my knees, collapsed, or started crying. Maybe because I had started doing the healing work on my traumas last year. Perhaps because I had cried enough, tons actually. And most of all, probably because I had already tried to process and forgive. Imag-

ine if I had just shown up here without doing all that upfront work. How far would I have crossed the schoolyard before I had wet my trousers?

I would soon see if my healing work paid off. Between the conference hall and the library, on the left side of the square, was the place where I had my first traumatic experience in this school. It was the place where I had met Nanak Dev for the first time.

It was my third day in India. For Nanak Dev, it was his fourth year as the head counselor of the American children. He sat on a concrete bench along the libraries outside wall. It looked out onto the schoolyard. Several American boys were standing around Nanak Dev. As I approached, they made room so I could be brought up to him and look directly at him. He was dressed in the attributes of a traditional *Nihang* Sikh. His dark eyes and angular face were accentuated by a turban in vibrant blue. His black beard was impressive. Despite the homesickness I felt, the familiarity of the beard, turban, and clothes, combined with his charismatic smile and the smell of sandalwood oil, made me feel that everything was going to be alright.

He said, "Jasbir, we have a game that every new child has to play, give me your hand." Smiling, I obeyed. Nanak Dev put his right hand around my knuckles and used his left to hold my forearm. My wrist was in the middle. He began to rotate my hand. "Have you ever had a wrist massage?" These words elicited a laugh from the children. Even though I was only ten, I recognized the malice in what I heard. The hairs on the back of my neck stood up. He looked around with a knowing smile and continued, "I'm going to bend your fingers to your forearm, and your goal is not to cry. OK?" Even though I could not think critically at ten, I understood this. I didn't know anyone here. If I wanted them to like me, I had to make sure I didn't cry. Then they would accept me. I nodded and hoped for the best. He started to flex my wrist. I tensed my body in anticipation. Very quickly, pain shot through my arm, and instinctively I tried to pull away.

"No, no, stay here," Nanak Dev said, looking at me as if he already knew how this would end. He pulled me closer, applying even more pressure. I resisted the urge to cry, breathing out through my open mouth until my lungs emptied. Then, as I breathed in, the pain became sharper, and I felt I had reached my limit. I asked in a trembling voice, "Please, you are hurting me. Can you let go?" He laughed and pushed my fingers closer to my forearm. I couldn't get out from under the pain and felt completely helpless. There was nothing left for me to do but start crying hard. I begged him to let me go. He inexorably kept holding my wrist in this stressed position and pushed even further. The pain became even worse as the sobbing began to race through my body. "Jasbir," he finally said, "you're a fucking weakling." A laugh rolled through the circle of children standing around us. He let go of my arm, hit me on the head, and pushed me away. The pain began to subside, and shame began to creep in. I had failed my first test.

This set the tone for the coming failures and the social ostracism I would feel in the months to come. More physical pain at the hands of this man followed, always followed by crying and public humiliation.

As I looked at this concrete bench thirty-four years later, the memory played through my head without the intense emotions associated with it in the past. I was able to acknowledge and let go of this memory. So far, so good.[132]

Below Par

Investigation into the School Diet

Dr. Alexandra Stein's report on 3HO childhood experiences cited food problems as an example of the extreme levels of neglect in various 3HO settings. Remember, children eating rose petals and drinking water to give themselves a sense of fullness.

In 1982, two medical doctors working for 3HO, Dr. Saram Singh Khalsa and Dr. Alan R. Singh Weiss, went on a two-day school visit to Mussoorie with Yogi Bhajan. Their aim was to investigate food issues that had been reported. Back home, Dr. Alan addressed the parents in a letter. He wrote, "We had heard many disturbing reports of severe deficiencies in the children's diet and the unwillingness of school personnel to remedy this."

The main complaint had been that the diet did not provide adequate protein. However, it appeared that the diet was, on the contrary, filled with protein, mainly in the form of highly nutritious raw milk and milk products. While in the US, the recommended allowances were a minimum of twenty-one servings a week, the school provided twenty-three to thirty protein servings per week. Vitamins and minerals were available in the richly organic vegetables, and calcium in the dairy products.

"The children do not drink much milk. They notice its animal-like aroma . . . and call it 'yak milk.' There is peer pressure not to drink it as it is made fun of."

Dr. Allan concluded that children and parents needed to be educated.

"It was quite sickening to see our adults and children reinforcing each other's negativity," the doctor wrote. He concluded, "The school seemed great, the diet seemed satisfactory to excellent, and the Americans seemed quite negative, but this should change."[133]

Dirty Socks

A 1983 photo, taken by Nanak Dev Singh, was posted on the RishiKnots website in 2009. It shows seven young boys with dirty socks in their mouths. Three wear long dark blue shirts with belts around their waists, the uniform of the gatka martial art from the Sikh tradition. The four younger boys wear graying, rumpled sports outfits. The boys' rishi knots are tied in a thin dark blue or white net. Some look shy and embarrassed, others feign a stern look, and two boys hold a cardboard sign that reads "Dirty Socks."

A comment to the photo mentions that laundry service often did not work for months. And when it did work, clothes got lost or destroyed. Children as young as eight years old needed to purchase their own detergent, buckets, and scrubbing brushes to wash their clothes with cold water in their spare time.

On August 5, 2021, @RishiKnots reposted the picture on their Instagram account. They invited people new to Bhajan's abuse stories to take a closer look at it, to witness the horror and be outraged. While parents were in their flowing, all-white, meditative bliss, kids were being warehoused in a boarding school, alone in India, getting dirty socks shoved into their mouths and being made to pose for a photo shoot. The moderator wrote: "We are the survivors of this brutal and sadistic, and abusive cult. And we say: 'No more light washing. No more excuses! No more erasure!'"

In the comments on this post, a lively discussion ensued. One person suggested that the "enforcers" role should be highlighted. Enforcers were older students executing punishments on behalf of the adult caretakers. Also, the extreme bullying of the younger kids by the older ones needed more attention. For example, lost items would be returned for a bamboo crack across their knuckles or a full day running around for a senior, doing his bidding. Memories are shared of monkey shit being spread on faces, kids being ostracized, etc.

Enforcers

In 1986, Siri was nineteen and in his fifth and final year at Guru Nanak Fifth Centenary School (GNFC) school in Mussoorie.

> GuruNischan (GN). You were given the title "enforcer"?
> Siri. Yes
> GN. By Nanak Dev?
> Siri. Yes.
> GN. So, basically, you were the one giving punishments to other kids?
> Siri. Yes. I don't know how many times I did that. It didn't happen that much. I honestly don't know when it started, why, how I got the title, or why he chose me. I don't know, but I punished some kids. I absolutely did that. And I recruited other kids to help me do it. I definitely put the hurt on some kids. I don't have clear memories of it, which is not me copping out. I have memories of hitting a kid on the sole of his feet a bunch of times because it hurts. I remember put-

ting my knuckles into their sternum and rubbing them really hard because I know it hurts. So yeah, I did that to kids. I absolutely did. I never did it again. That's not me. I've spent my whole life serving humanity as much as I can. I really don't know how it happened. I wish I had an "origin story." And somehow, I'm ashamed to say it, I really took to it. I took to the name. I liked being called out for something, even if it was negative. I don't know why. And the stories have grown. I've heard stories that I had a stick wrapped with barbed wire. That I hit kids with it. Shit. That never happened. I never hit somebody with a barbed wire-wrapped stick. I can promise you that.

GN. I want to say it's OK to not remember because you were a kid.

SIRI. I don't want anybody to think I'm trying to dodge it. There may be people who don't believe me. I can't do anything about that. But you know, I remember a few people I did this to.

GN. And you acknowledge that there's a lot more that you don't remember.

SIRI. Possibly. And this went on for a short time; as far as I remember, it was for one winter break.

GN. Not throughout the school year, you mean.

SIRI. Only during the winter break because I remember the first time. We were in Patna, where Guru Gobind Singh was born. We had taken the trip out there. That's my first memory of being the enforcer. And the last time I remember doing it was that same winter in the Golden Temple complex in Amritsar. I won't name to whom I did it, but I remember it. We were living in the Akal Takht. So that's where I did that. The Akal Takht is the seat of religious authority for all Sikhs worldwide. I mean, it's tragically fucking ironic that that was the place I did that.

GN. And again, you were a teenager. You were put in this position by an adult authority. Especially you, who you have become from your story so far. You first wanted to go to military school rather than India. So, to be put in a position of authority over your peers is not something most people would say no to in your situation.

. . .

SIRI. And what I really wished someone had done, Nanak Dev or the Siri Singh Sahib or anybody in between that chain of command, that chain of authority, I wish they had recognized what was going on. Or they had shown the capacity, the sensitivity, and the kindness to say, "Let's create a culture here. Let's try to say, 'We are family. You are halfway around the world from the people that love you. This is your pseudo-family. So, let's take care of each other.'"

And in a weird way, we did that. But we didn't know how to show it. When I slapped a little kid on the back of the head as he went by, it was my way of saying, "Hey, I like you." I don't know why I thought that was OK. I don't know why any of us thought it was OK. And I make no excuses for it whatsoever. I did it. I was no worse nor better than anybody else. It was the culture we lived in.

[*A bit further into the interview . . .*]

SIRI. To anybody who's listening to this podcast: if I wronged you and I can somehow rectify that, if I can somehow help you with that, or if you need to call me out on something that you think I'm dodging or I didn't own up to, please reach out. Whatever you got to say. I don't care how brutal it is. I can take it. And if that is going to be cathartic for you, I owe you that.[134]

Areas of Concern

In November 1986, the year Siri was talking about, the director of SDFE, the Sikh Dharma Foreign Education program, had visited the school and launched a ten-page report that was shared with the 3HO parents and the Khalsa Council. It listed thirteen areas in which concerns had been raised during the school year. SDFE had communicated those with the principal of the school in India. Below, you find an extract from the section "Physical and Emotional Care of the Children."

. . . the principal has already responded and taken action on some of the points, e.g.:

- dismissing below par personnel,
- enforcing his ban on corporal punishment,
- giving Hari Kaur (qualified nurse from the US) a free hand to make changes in medical care,
- chlorinating drinking water,
- giving blood tests to all food handlers and hostel staff,
- checking hostel staff for head lice,
- attempting to provide hot water daily for bathing (water supply in Mussoorie is sometimes a problem in general),
- making the matrons and supervisors accountable for missing laundry,
- having all students checked for head lice before they enter school in March,
- dismissing the school nurse who was no longer efficient in her job, dismissing two ayahs [housemothers] and a watchman for stealing.

. . .

Overall, the children are healthy, very spirited, and radiant. They have a good sense of independence, connection to and respect for the Siri Singh Sahib and strong, positive peer relationships. Boredom is the challenge for the oldest students. . . .[135]

A Living Hell

Everything Is Rotten

The stories above all relate to GNFC, the first boarding school the 3HO children attended. After the 1988 school year, 3HO kids were no longer welcome in Mussoorie. No one knows exactly why, but chances are that the dispute was over money. This theory is supported by what Bhajan said during a gathering he had in Florida in late 1988 with 3HO youngsters.

A video recording of that meeting shows him sitting relaxed on a white couch in what appears to be a living room. His bleached orange turban is loose and poorly put on. Behind him, a young girl sits by a desk, ready to take notes. She is in all-white 3HO attire with a high-rise turban and veil. Bhajan greets the teenagers as they enter the room. He sends one of his staff out to look for his glasses. He holds some loose papers on which the teens prepared questions for him. The staff member re-enters the room, hands over his glasses, and Bhajan reads the first question aloud:

"How does one relate to their fiancée?"

[*Bhajan looks pleasantly surprised, takes off his glasses, and looks around at his listeners.*]

All right, fiancée is a very fancy line of relationship in which two people are supposed to lie to their utmost, to make each other feel good, and look each other feel good. Actually, the fact of the fiancée is to cross all fences. . . . We engage people that can find out the depth. So, I am not upset how you relate to your fiancée. . . . My only problem is you are all liars, you lie, you are untruthful . . . there is one thing called intelligence, which teenagers refuse to use, and there is one thing called consciousness, which you do not want even to relate to . . .

The tone is set. His words are brutal, and he does not shy away from sexually explicit language. As always, he lacks logic in his reasoning. Cult experts might tell us he confuses on purpose to prepare his followers' minds to be controlled. He reads out more questions and is persistent in the incoherence and brutality of his answers. Despite this, the young lady behind his back diligently takes notes. Her face is serene, as if the brutality does not bother her. As if she only "hears the master speak," meaning that his words are precious and sacred, and she must record them as carefully as possible.

About an hour later, toward the end of the meeting, he enters a shouting mood. With a sharp and somewhat ironic tone, he reads another question.

"In school in India there are punishments."

[*He takes off his glasses and looks around the room.*] Yes, there is. Thank God we are acting so well. Otherwise, according to the Indian corporal thing, if you just do not read your [not understandable words] by memory and you fail, they have a punishment up to 20 canes, and that is admissible. We are fighting very hard not to let your butts go blue. So, we can't do anything legal about it, but we are keeping the pressure and we want you not to be beaten up. But somehow corporal punishment in India exists. It can't be helped. So therefore, don't do certain things for which your butts have to face it.

[*He puts his glasses back on and reads the following sentence.*] "The food is awful."

[*Glasses go off again.*] True! I have no doubt about it. I have absolutely no doubt. Food is Aw-Ful. What is full? We have to get the Awe out of it. So, what we are going to do is, we are going to send them a bunch of recipes. And we are going to set up a program where some of us will go and train the kitchen to cook it that way. So, the kids may not be just all the time eating potatoes.

[*Students laugh.*] We know that. It's not something we feel happy about.

[*He reads the next question in silence and then reads out loud.*] "In India, Indians are..."

[*He looks up.*] You know Indians are, doesn't matter how great they are. They just, they are just for money. They don't understand we are there for religion. [*His glasses are still on his nose. So, he has to bend his head far back to look around the room. He continues with a high-pitched voice.*] They are out for money, and it's a very painful process. [*He looks back to the paper, and with his eyes focused on the paper, he continues commenting.*] I give them so much money, but still, they never stop asking. It's so painful. What to do? That's how they are. Just now I got a letter, "Send us $100,000," bah, bah, bah. You know how much you can give?

[*He returns to the questions the teenagers wrote down and reads out loud.*]

"In India there is punishment . . . treat young children ..."

I know this problem.

"Tons of homework on our holiday, also there is a censorship. Three or four people read our letters before they are ever sent. There is hitting and slapping. The cleanliness of the school is horrible."

Agreed.

"It's a bad way the seniors treat the younger children."

[*He takes off his glasses and looks around in the room. With a smile on his face, he says:*] Let us take this. One thing: everything is rotten, but it's beautiful to live on the hills of Mussoorie. You know what I mean? [*The room stays silent as he keeps looking around.*] And you do eat too much that chocolate. What they call it? Cranberry?

[*The students now call out together:*] Cadbury!

Yes, Cadbury.

[*He shouts now.*] There is not enough supply in the entire town. Number two. Number three: when you fight or do certain things, you mess up lot of furniture in the school. There is a very heavy complaint. They are asking us to pay moneywise all the damage you people do. I understand your competitive nature and your aggressiveness. Why don't you go out and [not understandable verb] some tree? And just try with that? Rather than doing it in the kitchen. You broke up some chairs and all that stuff. We'll pay for it, don't worry. Live freely as much, but don't do that much damage for God's sake!

[*He reads the next question.*]

"Can you please explain the reason why we shouldn't go out and dance at nightclubs? I understand to some extent the influence of the negativity, but if there is a truly going out to dance and not to drink and no drugs or having sex . . ."

[*Yogi Bhajan and the students laugh.*] You are just asking me a beautiful question! . . . You are telling me, "Could I put one candle under my butts, and it won't burn." [*They all laugh.*] That's a good question, I like it. At least somebody is asking not to do drugs, not to have sex, they just want to dance. Come tonight to this room, we will put up a tape.[136]

Whether bills were paid or not paid, in March 1989, the 3HO children were no longer welcome at the GNFC school in Mussoorie. The solution was the construction of a new school in Dehra Dun, also in the Uttarakhand region. The Guru Ram Das Academy (GRD) was built in cooperation with a wealthy Sikh from New Delhi. Everything in GRD would revolve around the ideals of Yogi Bhajan's 3HO Healthy, Happy, Holy vision.

The school year started while the construction was underway. It was one big mess. There was a shortage of food and all sorts of other problems. Classes were organized haphazardly.

What was unique about that time was that Yogi Bhajan chose American supervisors with a military background. The children now also received military training. The Indian students who came to the school were exempted from these exercises.

Diet for Survival

In November 1989, an SDFE newsletter announced that the children would spend their four-week school vacation at or near to the place where Guru Gobind Singh, the last living guru of the Sikhs, had trained his soldiers. The newsletter also informed parents and children of Yogi Bhajan's next decision:

> The Siri Singh Sahib set the diet for the program. There is to be one main meal a day consisting of very well boiled black grams [black chickpeas] with vegetables, accompanied by milk. I am sure it will be tasty.
>
> In addition, there will be two snacks; the leftovers from lunch to be served at dinner and breakfast. He has instructed our staff to have the children eat their meals with their hands (this meal is fairly thick and somewhat dry). It is his wish that they become more in touch with their elemental nature, i.e., survival awareness.[137]

You Do Not Understand

On April 9, 1991, Yogi Bhajan addressed the Khalsa Council on issues parents and children reported concerning the school in India. We reproduce his words here verbatim.

Some people are accusing me, and I am for the school program in India, honorable members; I am not against that program, I am not for that program. I like one thing in that program, it is sending our children to a living hell and making them to survive, so no hell will be hell for them ever. If you want to listen to my words that's all I say. But we never going to tell an Indian cook to stand on a table and cut the potatoes. . . . They don't have the capacity, they don't have the tolerance, they will always sit with their spread legs and put the basket in front and do the job as they do. I tell you today, I never send children in India except for three things. I knew their mathematics will be fine and their spelling and grammar will never be wrong. I didn't send them for science and computers, and I also found out they will be in a living hell, and they will build their personal unity and grit that they shall always survive anywhere in the worst circumstances. I gave them the distance of 12,000 miles, so distance should never bother them. I gave them the capacity to become international without much expenses. You do not understand and value what we have given to our children. When you keep your children here, you will learn it in the hard way, and you will pay for it, and I will be sorry for it . . . .

India school gave us nothing, but it united our children like a rock. There was no facility, there was no water, it was damn cold, food was not tasty. Do you think I do not know? Am I that blind? Who told you that? But what India gave us, we can't create it here. Where will we get the opportunity to send a child 12,000 miles away from us? And I have nothing else but to send them prayers.[138]

No Method to the Madness

No Help and No Plan

We come back once more to Siri. After spending five years at the board-ing school in Mussoorie, he returned to Española. He started working for Akal Security and was regularly assigned as a bodyguard to Yogi Bhajan.

In 1993 or 1994, when Siri was about twenty-five, Yogi Bhajan sent him back to India to look after a hundred children in a newly established school in Amritsar. For some reason, the second 3HO school project, the Guru Ram Das Academy (GRD) in Dehra Dun, ended four years after it started. The new school would be located in the historic home-land of the Punjabi Sikhs. The Punjab region was once again a more peaceful and secure place after the turmoil of the mid-1980s. Therefore, 3HO purchased land near Amritsar. A new school was improvised while the future Miri Piri Academy (MPA) was under construction.

Here we listen to Siri's memories of being a supervisor for the 3HO school kids in India.

> I was trying to take care of a hundred kids. I had no help and no plan. Nobody called me and said, "How's it going? Is everything OK? Do you need anything?" That is not true, some parents would ask me when they came over. But nobody in any authority.
>
> A couple of things happened. I slapped two kids in those two years. I would do it again. I know that's controversial. One of them broke into a servant's quarters. They were poor people. He put all their belongings in the toilet and poured acid on it. Then he went up on the roof and tried to drop bricks on peoples' heads. This kid was out of control. He didn't belong in India. That's the mark of somebody needing professional help beyond what I could do. I slapped him to put the fear of God into him, to keep him in line. Was that the best solution? Probably not. Was it the solution I had?

Yeah. Am I proud that I did it? Nope, but I'll own it because I did it. What that kid did was extreme for those who thought I was an ogre. Literally, he was on the second floor trying to drop bricks on people as they walked by. I don't know how mean you have to be to break into poor people's homes and then pour acid all over their belongings. The other kid dropped his pants and put his bare ass in a teacher's face. He had no shame about it. I slapped him. Again, was that the best way to deal with it? Absolutely not. But I was by myself.

If I didn't maintain such control, there would be dire consequences. Kids would get hurt. I really took it personally that these parents entrusted me with a hundred kids. I was responsible for the safety and well-being of a hundred kids. So, I did the best I could. And the best I could wasn't always good enough. But twenty-five years old, with no training and no help? I had other staff members there. They were all useless. Sweet, friendly, useless.

Those kids didn't ask to be there. They had no choice. They didn't ask for "no laundry service."

"You're trying to make them tougher." That's all bullshit. We can design a program that makes kids tough, where they wear clean clothes and have enough food to eat.

That convinced me even more that there was no method to the madness. There were always excuses for whatever bullshit we were doing that day. "This is what's supposed to happen!" Blah blah blah blah blah. No! I was there. I saw what was happening. I had kids who shouldn't have been there. They had learning disabilities or were on the spectrum and needed professional help that I, nor anybody else there, could give them.

And so, I spent a lot of time focusing on a small number of kids that were "trouble." Not trouble because they were bad kids. But trouble because of whatever they had going on. This program did not serve them. We also had kids who didn't belong there because they were kind, sweet, and gentle, not hard or tough. This program had nothing for them. There was nothing soft, kind, or gentle about this program.

"Get up early. Do lots of physical everything. Clean your room perfectly." Creativity? Art? Not anything like that! "Go sharpen a stick, run out in the field, and spear pigs." That's what "the boys" like.

It was just weird. It was a weird, weird, weird situation, and that's where my relationship with the Siri Singh Sahib started to deteriorate. That's when I stopped hanging out the word. I didn't stop listening to him. Until he died, I would listen to what he had to say. But I would listen with no emotion. I would evaluate it, and basically, I was distrustful of whatever he said.

At the end of those two years, I thought, *I could stay here. I could work at this school, but I'm not doing it like this. I'm not doing it for $500 a month, no income in the summer, nowhere to live.* So, I went to him and said I needed $2,000 a month, which was nothing, but back then, it was something. I could live well on $800 a month in India. I could bank $1,200 a month to buy a house and save money for retirement.

I said, "I'll give you years, and I will come home to something." He didn't even get mad. He said, "I don't think this will work." I smiled, there were no harsh words.[139]

Keeping Feelings Inside

Another survivor who shared his story in an *Uncomfortable Conversation* with GuruNischan said that when he was seven, he had mixed feelings about "going to India." On one hand, he was eager to go, as it all seemed beautiful and exciting. Together with his father, he had visited his elder brother, who was already in India. This reinforced his idea that he had to go.

On the other hand, he also knew terrible things had happened there. In front of the whole school, one of the staff members had physically abused his brother. His parents had telephoned the management in India about it. GuruNischan's guest had witnessed that phone call and did not know what to think about it. He was just seven, after all. In the end, his desire to go won out. So, he left for India when he was eight years old.

This was 1996–1997 when Miri Piri Academy (MPA) in Amritsar was still under construction. In the meantime, an alternative school for the 3HO children was improvised.

They rented houses for us to stay in. In some way, it was awesome as we could do whatever we wanted as a kid. It was like a camp. It's a miracle that just a few incidents happened beyond minor injuries, except for that one time. While climbing on top of a bus, a senior student was hit in the face with a power line. It knocked his teeth out, and he almost fell off the bus. That he was still alive was actually a miracle. The doctors said that if this had hit him anywhere else in the face, it would have fractured his skull, like the teeth are the strongest place to get hit.

We climbed on the top of a bus almost every day. Looking back on it, I realize that my parents may not have exercised their best judgment in sending us there, nor did I. But as a seven-year-old, you don't know what's good for you. So, I was just excited to go to India.

What weighs the most on me is how extremely sad I was when I left home. I cried a lot, missing my parents. As soon as I was done feeling sadness, I knew I would be OK. The rush of endorphins that comes with feeling sad makes you feel better. It just happens naturally. I guessed that was part of life, to feel sad and awful at first and then great after that. It was a theme throughout my first seven or eight years in India.

Every year my mom asked me, "Are you sure you want to go back?"

I always said yes, I wanted to go back, even though I had this pit in my stomach—*I'll miss you.*

And then there was this thought that I shouldn't feel that way. I did not see my brother and all my friends feeling these feelings. So, it will go away.

GuruNischan points out that keeping feelings inside was part of the 3HO ethos. Further on in the interview, this second-generation survivor tells us why he wanted to share his story.

> When I first went to India, I was regularly woken up from my sleep by someone peeing on me, to put it bluntly. Or finding out in the morning that toothpaste was smeared on some of my clothes. I did not know who did it or why they did it. There was no way to tell anyone. To whom and how would I do that? That would only provoke more of the same.
>
> During one of your first *Uncomfortable Conversations*, someone said something that deeply touched me. I forgot who it was. I wish I could remember. He said, "Whether it happened to you, or you did it to someone, or you saw it happen, it's all in your head as pain inflicted on someone. Pain that was caused, that didn't need to be caused. And you know that."
>
> GURUNISCHAN. Yeah, and that does not register only in your mind. Your nervous system holds it too.[140]

A Known Pedophile Sent to India

We return to Siri again. GuruNischan asked if he knew more about the rumors of a pedophile American teacher being sent to Miri Piri Academy in Amritsar. Yes, he did. The abuse happened during the second year Siri worked as a caretaker for the American kids.

> I came home after the school year in India, and I got a call. They said, "Did you know that this teacher was sexually abusing these boys?" They asked me this. It wasn't the Siri Singh Sahib but somebody else who called.
>
> I said, "Do you think I would have kept quiet about that? I'm insulted you're even asking me this." Of course, I did not know. What do you mean? That's an odd question!

"If you think I knew about it, why am I still employed?" I was furious. I called a couple of people, and again I'm not going to drop names, but they said, "Yeah, we knew he was like that. We were afraid it might come out."

GuruNischan. What?!

Siri [*nodding*]. Yeah. So that's what's doubly damning! If you hired a teacher and you've done your due diligence, there's nothing in their background, they seem honorable, and they have no criminal record, how would you know? Then if it happens, you're like, "Oh my God." So, you're out of the field.

But to have somebody say, "Yeah, we were afraid that might happen!?"

GuruNischan. Terrible! It means that it's an "active cover-up," as we've heard about!

Siri [*nods firmly*]. Yeah, I was furious. Years later, they told me, "He was nice to you when you came home. We were afraid you knew."

No, nothing. I had no idea. But apparently, it was a known thing. And nobody bothered to tell me. Forget about official channels. How about somebody called me up and said, "Hey, you didn't hear it from me, but keep an eye out." That might have been something. Somebody believes that I would have looked the other way? Never!

I told you we grew up with these hypocrisies around us. We could not articulate them, but we were taking them in. The other thing I noticed that was becoming more prominent and harder and harder to reconcile was our willful neglect to be professional in everything we did.[141]

The RishiKnots.com website contains more testimonies about excessive bullying and sexual abuse of children in Indian schools by American 3HO guides, staff members, and senior students. This is also reported in Dr. Alexandra Stein's report on 3HO childhood experiences. Unfortunately, many punishments and harms were so normalized that they went unreported. And even when incidents were reported, they were ignored.

Children Are Invited to Speak

On April 25, 2020, three months after the book *Premka* rocked the 3HO–Sikh Dharma world, the Khalsa Council invited second-generation adults to share their stories of growing up in the community. First-generation elders listened as their children talked about the neglect, beatings, slander, abuse, hunger, bullying, and loneliness they experienced. The meeting lasted more than nine hours, some say eleven, without a break. This gathering was emotionally charged and historic. Some survivors had spoken out before but were barely listened to while others spoke for the first time.

For some first-generation members, blinders fell off that day. The side effects of their unconditional and uncritical devotion to Yogi Bhajan became painfully obvious. However, there were and still are deniers who say, "These reporters of harm are just out for compensation."

The day after the Zoom call, the Siri Singh Sahib Corporation sent a message thanking those who shared their stories for their courage to speak out and for enduring the experiences. At the top of the mail was a page-wide banner with a picture of Yogi Bhajan peering into the distance, surveying a globe in bright blue light with a stern, self-assured gaze and the title Siri Singh Sahib Corporation and the organization's emblem underlined with "In God, We Dwell" shining in a white cloud.[142]

Did the person who pressed the send button intentionally add this banner? Or did they use the "standard" template without considering the impact this banner might have on survivors? Did any of the board members or management of the SSSC put a checkmark on this? Did anyone notice the contradiction between the pretended concern for "their kids" and the glorification of the abuser in the banner and the name of the umbrella organization? Is the lack of empathy endemic among leaders of this community? Is this an example of how insensitive and ignorant they are because they have lived in this cult for so long?

Two days after the meeting, the moderator of the RishiKnots website wrote a blog: "To Khalsa Council." The sharp text denounced the lack of organization and support during the Zoom session. RishiKnots questioned whether the leaders understood how much moral courage and commitment it took from second-generation adults to tell their stories. Did the leaders realize that those who testified rendered a service to the Khalsa Council and not vice versa? The blogger mentioned that the 3HO children have been telling their stories for twenty-five years. To retell them is to re-live the pain. It re-traumatizes their bodies and hurts their carefully rebuilt sense of self. RishiKnots invited first-generation adults to look in the mirror and acknowledge their failure to protect their children. The blogger experienced the Zoom call not as restorative but as torturous.

It Was a Brutal, Brutal Place

On April 12, 2022, the Vice documentary *True Believers: Empire of Yoga* was aired in the US. Among those interviewed were three second-generation survivors. This is what they shared about their time in India.
The first one:

> "True believers" of Yogi Bhajan really believed that sending your kids to the schools in India was the absolute best thing you could do for them, and why would you go against that? . . . When I was there, it was very military style, extremely rigid. . . . We were in a constant risk of corporal punishment . . . it was a brutal, brutal place. . . . I do think that the schools were created to make willing servants out of the children. . . . The parents could work harder for the businesses, work harder for the nonprofits, just be more in the hands of the guru. [143]

The second one:

> He [Yogi Bhajan] wasn't even human. He was basically God. . . .
>
> I was six, seven, and eight at the time. We always had to work hard, we always had to clean, and we were put in very tough physical situations. If we complained, we were weak, we were the "problem" child, so you just learned to keep your mouth shut. It was a battle of survival. . . .
>
> Yogi Bhajan separated us, the children, from our parents, so that we'd be reliant on the religion. I think his ultimate goal was that we were reliant on him telling us what to do. We were being groomed to obey everything he said. So, off we went to whichever place he told us to go.[144]

The last testimony comes from Sat Pavan. She had romantic ideas about going to school in India. This is what she says about her India experience in the documentary:

> I was beaten by teachers, and there was a time where the girls in our dorm were caned every single morning. My parents couldn't afford to bring me home [during holidays]. So, I went over [to school in India] at eight. I didn't see my parents until I was eleven. One of the things that was really hard for me to admit to was how I tried to commit suicide twice because I felt alone, and I didn't have parents to mediate, hug me, or make sure I was OK. And so, I felt like, you know, I have to get their attention by ending my life.[145]

Vice also interviewed Tej Steiner. In a trembling voice, he testified about how he and many others sent their children to India.

> There was the idea that this would make them strong and serve them. . . . People had so much trust. Looking back on it, what were we thinking? . . . He [YB] had thousands and thousands of people trusting him. "Oh yeah, you all start sending your kids to India.

These kids will be enlightened. It will be wonderful." All bullshit. It was power. I sent my son away when he was two at the bequest of Yogi Bhajan. We went to pick him up, and he didn't recognize us. Pure, pure child abuse. [*Tej shakes his head and with tears in his eyes continues.*] Sending my kids to India . . . that's a rough one, and I'm working on it. I'm working on it.[146]

SEXUAL ABUSE

When I Was Four . . .

On March 4, 2020, Pamela Dyson, the author of *Premka*, posted the following story on her Facebook page with the comment, "This story was posted previously but was buried in the threads of so much discussion. It is written under a pseudonym because the present situation of the witness does not support her ability to speak out. This young woman is currently in her mid-twenties. She struggles every moment, of every day, with the impact of these events. She shares this in the hope that other young women of her generation will find the courage to speak up. She is eager to have her story shared, so feel free to pass it along."

> When I was four years old, my mom got very sick. She was too sick to supervise me, to know where I was, and keep me safe. Unfortunately, my father took advantage of that. Yogi Bhajan had a small group of people, mostly men, whom he considered very important. They spent almost all day at the estate. Yogi Bhajan would sit in his chair, which looked like a throne. This small group of men,

sometimes one or two women, would sit around him. They were in absolute admiration of him. My father wanted to be part of the group. He realized that I was his ticket in, me and my four-year-old body. Once my mom got sick, he began taking me there every day. I was brought into the room, and almost immediately, Yogi Bhajan called me to come and sit on his lap. I sat there for hours on end, day after day. He was extremely rough with my body. He made it clear that my body was not my own. It was his.

I cannot even describe the long-term effect that it had. I remember I was taken to Yogi Bhajan's bedroom at one point. I was summoned to his bed. My father saw it all happening, let it happen, and left the room. I was alone with Yogi Bhajan in his bed. That is where everything turns black. . . .

I am posting this message because I want people to understand that Yogi Bhajan was willing and able to inflict extreme harm on a four-year-old child. That harm has affected me every day, even as an adult. I have never felt that my body was mine.

Some of you may think this is not abuse. It's not a typical allegation of molestation that is concrete and fully understood. What is concrete is that I sat on Yogi Bhajan's lap for hours. He was extremely rough with me. He squeezed me until I couldn't breathe. He pinched my face so hard it hurt and left marks. There was a TV in the room. It often showed sexually explicit and violent material. They watched it for hours. All the time, I sat on his lap. Sometimes he was sexually aroused. I can't explain the damage that did to me. My father was there. Not only did he not stop it, but he encouraged everything. I was his ticket into the "Inner Circle."

Another thing that harmed me was that Yogi Bhajan forced me to sit on his lap while he shamed and screamed at men, women, husbands, and wives who admired him. Many had joined the ashram to be near him and learn from him. He taunted them so harshly that rarely did anyone leave without sobbing. Grown men and women burst into tears because the man they looked up to had shamed them and torn them apart. . . .

Even though my mom was very sick, I longed to tell her what was happening to me every day when I came home so that she could stop it. But I never told her. Yogi Bhajan and my father threatened they would hurt my mom and me if I told her. . . .

Yogi Bhajan is portrayed as a monument. He is on all the kundalini yoga material that reaches thousands of followers world-wide. The teacher training is based on his quotes and ideas.

I speak out because my truth matters. People need to know the truth about Yogi Bhajan. He was a man, not a monument. In my opinion, he was less than a man. He did not have honor.

I realize that he meant a lot to people. The thought of hurting people I love in this community kept me silent for so long. But I have to tell it now because it has ruined my life and stopped me from moving on, and that is just not OK. I deserve to have a life. I deserve to survive. . . .

Remember, this spiritual group was meant to help people con-nect with God. Yogi Bhajan was supposed to help people achieve that. Maybe he did that for some people. Perhaps he did some good things. Life is not black and white. People are not black and white. So, I will not assert that he did not positively affect this world. That being said, I think it's essential that people know his other side. That he was willing to abuse and use a four-year-old girl.[147]

Getting Ready for Him

You're Turning Out Nicely

One of the second-generation, now adult women, in the Vice documen-tary shared this:

Right around my eighteenth birthday, I was applying to colleges. I was told, "Yogi Bhajan wants you to put off college for a year and work at the Secretariat." And of course, this was considered an honor. I absolutely did not want to do it. I wanted to go to college. But I did it because my parents thought this was a great idea, and if you decided you didn't want to be with him or do whatever he told you to do, you were excommunicated essentially, even if you kept your turban on. . . .

[One day] I was cleaning the house [YB's house] and he said, "Turn around for me," which, I have subsequently learned, was a common thing he did with people. And he touched my boobs, as I finished turning around. I remember, it was almost like sizing me up. And then he said, "You're turning out nicely." You know, like I'm getting ready for him, essentially. . . .

I was being taught how to take care of him at night. I was absolutely being groomed to be one of his concubines, one hundred percent.

INTERVIEWER. Did he ever try to sexually assault you?

SECOND-GEN. He did.[148]

He Is Your Grandfather

Here we pick up the story of Sat Pavan again. The fairy tale of going to school in India turned into a nightmare. In March 1991, she was about to return from India to her parents in Florida. She was sixteen. A new opportunity was created for 3HO children to continue their education at the military school in New Mexico. Arrangements were made with the school: 3HO students could wear 3HO outfits, including a turban, unshaven hair and beard, and other Sikh symbols. Many of Sat Pavan's peers planned to go there instead of returning to India. Sat Pavan found it difficult to decide. Would she follow her peers?

Was that the right choice for me to make for me? My whole life, I had been told what to do. Suddenly, everything I knew was crumbling. I didn't know how to proceed, so I turned to "him." We were always told, "He is the ultimate person in your life. Your parents are fucked up, and people around you are messed up and neurotic. You were sent to India because they didn't know how to raise you. He is the one that loves you. He is your grandfather. He will tell you what is best for you." He loved it that way. His followers turned to him for their marriages or children, for health issues or naming their dog, for buying a house, for an investment, and for coming into new money. That last one, in particular, he was very interested in.

We all had to correspond directly with YB. We wrote him letters. He wrote us back. And so, I let him know that many kids planned to go to this military school. Some would go back to India, but not many. The other option was to attend high school in the United States. We were hammered about how bad high schools in America were. Girls would become prostitutes and boys drug addicts. It was just a horrible thing to do. The movie *Teachers* with Nick Nolte was hot in those days, and YB told everyone to watch it.

"This is what I am saving your children from," he would say.

And then, my parents got a phone call from a staff member of Yogi Bhajan. He wanted me to come to New Mexico to be with him. I thought that was amazing, but I did not know what it meant. He did not say, "Don't go to high school." Just, "Come to New Mexico and be with me."

I remember my mom being a little upset. Privately, of course, because publicly saying you're upset with him about anything was not done.

I thought, *Stop being so attached. It's fine. If YB wants me to be with him, that's a big honor.* She said, "You just got home from India. Why do you have to go now? It is April. Soon, in June, we will all go together for summer solstice. It's just a couple of months away. We have barely gotten any time with you." My father talked to the staff member, who was someone he knew. She told him, "There is nothing to be concerned about. You do not need to worry about money. He's going to take care of her."

It was similar to when I was eight. I told my parents, "You have to let me go." The doctrine was, "Your kids are more enlightened than you are. They know. If they want something, don't stand in their way." So, my parents let me go.

I packed my bags from India. I had my harmonium, the instrument on which I used to play *kirtan* [Sikh prayers], and a sleeping bag. We didn't know what I had to bring. I did not want to take the sleeping bag, but my mom insisted. I would need it for solstice, she said.

Everything Is a Test

When Sat Pavan arrived at the airport in New Mexico, she was picked up by a woman she did not know. Once in the car, Sat Pavan attempted to find common ground with her. She always tried to connect with strangers, so they would start liking her. This would increase the chances that they would be willing to invest in her if needed. It was part of the survival tactics that she had developed over the years. This time her tactic failed. The woman did not respond.

After a two-hour drive, they arrived in Española. They stopped in front of a bunch of trailers that turned out to be the headquarters of Akal Security.

I came from Florida and had never seen such a rural-looking, make-shift commercial building. The woman brought me to one of the trailers. She explained to me how to answer the phone. There were five different lines. The sixth line was Yogi Bhajan's. I had to forget all the other calls if this one rang. I could never make him wait.

I kept on thinking, *What am I doing here?* No one was telling me anything. It was like they thought that I knew what was going on. I said, "So am I supposed to do this today, and then I'm going to see him?"

"Well, he's in California. I don't know when he's going to be back." That was her answer.

"What am I supposed to do here?"

"You are the new receptionist for Akal Security."

I was in a daze that first day, answering phones and trying not to mess up, while in my head, I was trying to figure out what was going on. According to the 3HO doctrine, everything was a test. So, I just had to pass it. My mind went: *How can I deal with it? How can I pass this test?*

How could I make all this work and not complain? Because complaining was not done.

Yogi Bhajan would say, "Where there is love, there's no question."

What Kind of Test Is This?

Sat Pavan was confused. In the office, everyone was in a hurry. "Oh, you are the new receptionist," they said and walked on. Fortunately, some people were friendly and came to say hello. Two people she knew from school in India came by. That felt good. She had no idea what would happen in the evening. Where would she sleep? Where would she stay? When everyone left the office, a woman approached her. She was wearing an Akal Security uniform.

"I usually don't get along with people below five-foot-nine [1 m 75 cm]," she said.

Sat Pavan was five-foot-seven.

"You are going to live with me."

In silence, they drove to her house. It stood on Yogi Bhajan's property. The house was not furnished. There were a few plastic cups and bowls in the cupboards but nothing else. Sat Pavan was led to her bedroom. On the bed was a box spring mattress without linens.

Luckily my mom had been forward-thinking, and I had a sleeping bag and even a towel. "She" went into her room. I heard a click locking the door. I was sitting on my bed. This was the early 1990s. There was no phone, no way to call my parents. I started feeling really emotional and felt like crying. So I thought, *Let me sing. That will give me a sense of protection and safety.* Barely started, the woman banged on the wall, "Shut the fuck up."

I remember sitting there and thinking, *What kind of a test is this? What happened that I karmically brought this on? Is she the good person in this scenario? Am I the bad person? What is going on?*

I spent the next few weeks in a complete daze, leaving me with little recollection of that time. Except for that one time: She invited me to watch a movie. Her room was fully furnished. She told me that she had been a model and an actress. She had been married to a pretty famous musician with whom she had a son. It had been a happy marriage.

"So, what happened?" I asked. "Why aren't you with your husband and son?"

"Because of Yogi Bhajan," she said. "I'm with him now."

Yogi Bhajan was her spiritual teacher, she said. She gave him everything, including her entire bank account. Previously she had lived in Hollywood Hills, but now, she had handed over everything to him. That's why, when she was good, he allowed her to have some money to go shopping.

Her story confused me. But she invited me to watch a movie, so we did. I don't remember the name, but John Malkovich was in it. It played in Turkey or in the Middle East somewhere. There was a lot of nudity and a pretty graphic sex scene. I was shocked. I had never seen anything like this in my life. I looked around the room at the pictures on the wall. I did not want to be there. I did not want to watch that movie and felt uncomfortable with her. But she had so nicely invited me in. I could not go without her permission. When the movie was over, she said, "OK, well then, goodnight."

Two weeks later, Sat Pavan sat outside to have lunch when a woman passed by.

She came up to me and called me by my name. She had known me since I was a little girl in Boston. Hearing that she knew me and my parents made me burst into tears. I felt no connection in the New

Mexican community and was very lonely. Nobody knew who I was or who my parents were. So, I started crying, and she was really nice to me.

The woman listened to Sat Pavan's story. She suggested that Sat Pavan come home with her. She had just given birth and could use a babysitter and help in the household. Sat Pavan would have to sleep on the sofa. The husband would not allow her to enter his space. She would have to wait for him to finish watching television before she could go to sleep. And in the morning, everything had to be tidied up before he entered the room. Sat Pavan happily agreed to these conditions and went to pack her bags. She did not even tell the woman from Hollywood Hills that she was leaving. Her new home was fully furnished and much warmer.

Sat Pavan tried to connect with the husband and learn about him. He had recently inherited money and had climbed the 3HO ranks quickly. He became one of YB's main guides and is, to this day, a big supporter of Yogi Bhajan. After a short while, he told his wife that he did not want Sat Pavan in the house anymore. On a Wednesday, she got the news that she had to leave on Saturday.

"I'm sorry. I hope I'm telling you in time to find another place to stay," the woman had said.

I never told my parents, "I'm homeless in New Mexico. I'm trying to find a place to live. I'm looking for a couch to sleep on." Everything in my mind said, "Don't complain. Don't tell anyone anything bad. It's a test. You will figure out how to survive."

If my parents had known that I was used as free labor in Akal Security and that Yogi Bhajan was not there as he had promised, they would not have allowed me to go. That's what they tell me today, but everybody was told to trust Yogi Bhajan in those days, so they did.

Deep down, I knew I was angry about these experiences in my life, but I never blamed "him". I did not know who to blame and was angry at the community.

Sat Pavan contacted a girl she knew from boarding school in India to ask if she could stay with her. The parents were not enthusiastic about the idea but agreed. Looking back on this period, she finds it crazy that at the age of sixteen, she left a lovely home situation with her parents, who loved her dearly, to go through all this! For what reason?

Yogi Bhajan returned to New Mexico.

He called for me. All of a sudden, I became very important to a lot of people because he was giving me direct attention. My friends' parents brought me over to the ranch where he lived. I got walked into a room that was full of people. Everyone was looking up. All the attention was on me.

"I hear you want to be an actress," he roughly shouted at me.

It was indeed something I had wanted to do my whole life. I am very emotional and passionate, so I think I could have done it.

I said, "Yes."

He started yelling at me. How could I choose such a fucked-up profession?

One of the staff members sitting next to him said, "She's actually really good." She had seen me do a sketch or play in the community. "She has some real talent."

"Oh, shut up," he said.

He started yelling at her. And then he turned to me again, telling me I was going to be the biggest prostitute in the entire world. I was going to be gang raped regularly. It was just mind-blowing to realize that this was my spiritual teacher, my grandfather, who created the entire lifestyle I was raised in. We didn't cuss, nor did we talk about sex. This was the first time I heard such things. What did I do that he did this to me? It was so different from everything I had been taught. They taught me that he was a very enlightened being. Until then, my experiences had seemed to fit that image. But to be screamed at this way? And all the sexual acts being described in vivid ways?

I just cried and cried and stood there in front of everybody. It was as if everyone in this room agreed that this was the norm. This was acceptable except for this one staff member.

She kept interrupting him, saying, "Sir, she is a very innocent girl. I don't think you should talk to her like that." She was close enough to him to do that. I was even shocked about how she talked to him, no one spoke to him as an equal. She said, "Sir, you can tell she's innocent. She's very young. Why are you screaming at her? Why are you cussing at her? Why are you talking about all this stuff with her?"

"Shut the fuck up." He started yelling at her again.

She stood up and said, "I can't take this anymore. If you're not going to stop talking to her like this, I can't be in the room because this makes me angry."

She walked out of the room. I watched her go and thought, *Don't leave!*

That evening I was crying and shaking. Every dream I had ever had about my life was washed away at that moment. My life was going to be horrible. My friend's parents said, "It is an honor what he did to you. You don't understand. He only yells at those he loves the most. The fact that he screams at you means that he really loves you. That he cares about you. To most people, he says nothing. He is so direct with you!"

Sat Pavan was called into the room three days in a row to be yelled at and screamed at. He told her what her life would be like if she did anything she wanted to do.

And then he said, "Or, you can be with me, and I will take care of you. You'll be the wealthiest. You'll be treated like a queen. People will be in awe of your royal appearance and beauty when you walk."

I immediately said, "OK, I'll be with you." It went so fast. He changed his tone and told me what a beautiful actress I would have been, an Academy Award-winning actress. I didn't know what to think about all this. Was he telling me I made the wrong choice? Was this a new test? What did this mean? He was suddenly very sweet, loving, and kind to me, and wanted me to hug him. Afterward, it was like he was done with me. He had broken me. He had won me over.

This is what I see now, I didn't see it then.

Dance with the Governor

An Angel Sent to Hell

Sat Pavan continued working at Akal Security for some time.

One day he called her: "Actress, I'm sending you to Los Angeles. You want to be an actress, so now you should go where all the actresses and actors are. You'll see what it is like. I am sending an angel into hell. You're so innocent, so naive. You're going there, and it will eat you up."

She was given a ticket to Los Angeles. The woman who picked her up at the airport welcomed her by saying, "You're going to be with me. I am in charge of you. Your life is mine now."

She lived in a big house. Sat Pavan's sparsely furnished and make-shift bedroom was set up in the garage. On the first day of her stay, she went into the living room and put the TV on to watch *The Cosby Show*, which she had grown up with. The woman came in and said, "Do we need to watch this? They are so Black!"

I felt like the chill was going down. I thought, *Where am I?* I was supposed to be in a Sikh household. They are supposed to be loving and accepting of everybody. I grew up in India amongst brown people. Was Black bad in this household? It really freaked me out.

I ended up basically being her personal servant for the next eight months. She had a preschool. I had to go and open the school, make all the lunches, and change the diapers . . . I did everything and worked twelve-hour days for fifty dollars a week. She owned me. I couldn't do anything without her permission.

The woman was a tormentor. Sat Pavan did not understand why Yogi Bhajan had chosen precisely this woman for this job, to take up a mother's role with other people's children. Why was he putting such a person in charge of the kindergarten? She had not an iota of maternal instinct in her.

During this period, Yogi Bhajan gave Sat Pavan the directive to do *seva* (selfless service) at his residence. She was taught to clean the living room, his bathroom, the kitchen, etc. Her only option was to do it during her lunch breaks. One day she was doing the dishes in his house.

> I was hunched over the dishes. I felt someone coming up behind me. They put their hands on my chest and pulled me towards them. I jerked the person at first, but when I looked back, I saw it was him. He said, "I'm telling you to stand up straight." He then felt down my body and said, "Be proud of this body. Be proud of these breasts. Be proud of these hips. And be proud of being a woman."
>
> I took it exactly as he said it. "Don't hunch over. Be proud of who you are." I didn't take it as an assault or something negative. There was a reason behind it. I accepted. I saw him as a nonsexual being. I saw him as someone who had given up his family life to serve humanity. It felt weird and uncomfortable, but I didn't see it as threatening. I allowed my mind to quickly make sense of it.

Yogi Bhajan started spending more time with her when she was in his house, coming to talk to her and give her attention.

A Birthday Present at Seventeen

> Yogi Bhajan said, "It's your birthday. I have a present for you."
> I was surprised and wondered what I would get.
> "How are your parents doing?"
> I said, "They are fine."
> "Have you asked them lately how they are doing?"
> "I talked to them yesterday. They're doing fine."
> "I need you to call them and say I asked how they are doing."

I said, "OK," and thought it was strange. I walked back over to the school. The kids were still sleeping. So, I quickly called my mother and asked, "How are you doing?"

"We are doing fine," my mother said.

"I know this sounds strange, but I am supposed to tell you, 'Yogi Bhajan asked me to ask you.'"

She said, "Oh, OK. I guess we're supposed to tell you now. Well, your father and I are planning to get divorced."

My whole world was falling apart. I was standing there, shaking.

This unique birthday gift from Yogi Bhajan cut even deeper when her mother told her this had been coming for a year. Everyone knew about it, including Sat Pavan's younger sister. Yogi Bhajan had instructed her parents not to tell her this since he was now caring for her. And so, they trusted him.

The children woke up, and Sat Pavan had to go to take care of them, but she didn't want to hang up the phone. Her boss started shouting because she was having a private conversation and how unprofessional it was to cry at work!

For the next few months, Sat Pavan was in tears. She felt incredibly lonely and very suicidal. Tears came every time she started talking, or her face would turn red. Three days a week, she went to Yogi Bhajan's class. At the end of the class, he would come to talk to her and give her a lot of attention. As a result, other people started giving her attention too. One day, he asked her to come to him after class. As he walked out, the others told her what an honor it was. Few people were given that honor. The first evening she went, she sat at the table for dinner and was treated like everyone else. The next evening, she had to serve the food. Bhajan let her know that she was on his staff now. In fact, he told her, she had been with him from the first moment she came to New Mexico. He knew everything she had done since then. She was a good girl and had passed the tests.

I just thought, *OK, it's all right. My spiritual teacher does know what's going on. He is on top of everything.* And I was proud of myself. I was holding it together. And so, we sat there in his living room. He turned on the TV, a show was going on, and people were having sex. It was bizarre. I'd never seen anything like it, except that one time with that Hollywood Hills lady. But then it was a film. It wasn't on the same level as this. Immediately I turned red beet and put my head down.

He turned the TV off and said, "You need to look up, look up and watch."

I said, "No, sir. I don't want it. I really don't want to."

He said, "Oh, you are so innocent. You're so naive. You need to watch it because this will help you not be like that."

He put it back on. After a while, he paused it again. He wanted me to describe what I just saw. I said that it was "yucky." I did not want to describe graphic sex to my grandfather, my spiritual teacher. I did not want to sit in the room with him and watch this. I did not want to sit in a room with anybody and watch that.

He wanted me to describe what I saw, how it made me feel, and what I thought sex was. There was a room full of people there. I remember saying, "Why do you ask me? I am a virgin. Everybody else in the room is married. Ask them."

He finally took the pressure off me and asked the other people to describe it. So again, all this was "normalized." He ended up saying that he was in the middle of writing a book about sex with his medical doctor, who was in the room, and this other woman, who was a therapist. This was research.

Not one person in the room set the alarm off that maybe I was too young to watch this. If anything, I was told, "How lucky you are to be one of the selected people to be this close to him and to have these personal experiences with him." This medical doctor and therapist should have known better, no?

This ended up happening regularly. YB was teasing me about how quickly I blushed and said stuff that contradicted everything. He asked me to flirt with him. He would make little faces at me and wanted me to make faces at him being in a room full of people. He was blowing me kisses, and I would blow him kisses. In my mind, it was safe because he was my grandfather who was saving me from everything. He was protecting me.

In retrospect, Sat Pavan wonders why she did not find it strange that he said, "Flirt with me." She had been told all her life flirting was negative. After a while, she knew on which channels and at what times such programs were aired. He threw the remote control at her. She knew that he wanted her to find the program for him. She did her utmost not to blush, not to look serious and not to be startled or show that she was shocked, and to pretend she liked it.

During this period, he started to give me jewelry. Pretty regularly. The first piece was a ring. He put it on my finger and said we were married in a past lifetime. In this lifetime, we were supposed to heal the world together. I remember telling this to my friends and laughing, "What the hell does that mean?" I thought I was not enlightened enough to know what it meant. I was in YB's Inner Circle but also used as a servant. And he gave me all these extras.

Sat Pavan became increasingly engaged as his personal attendant. Her duty was to go to lunch with him, carry his bags, and so on. While she had been used to the very conservative clothes of the community, it changed now that she was accompanying him. She was expected to show up in much tighter and more revealing outfits. She wore see-through miniskirts, skin-tight tops, a full turban, and lots of jewelry. He bought her high heels because he wanted her to look five-foot-nine (1 m 75 cm).

I accepted it all because this was how special people behaved. I was happy to leave the garage. I moved to the estate where his wife lived. I still didn't have my own room and had to sleep in the living room, but I felt like I was in heaven the first night. It was such a step up.

I felt so grateful to him. He was the only one who cared for me, loved me, and wanted only the best for me. I worked as a receptionist in the corporate office overseeing all the other businesses. It was my karma to be a receptionist, he had told me.

A Birthday Present at Eighteen

When I turned eighteen, he was out of town. He called me up and said he wanted to give me a present.

I said, "All I want to do is serve humanity, the Guru, and the Sikh religion."

He said, "No, no, no, no, no, yeah, yeah, yeah, you're doing all that. Besides, what do you want for your birthday?"

And I said, "No, you've given me so much. You've given me a home, a job. You've helped me through all these problems that I went through with my parents."

"OK, OK, yeah, yeah, what do you want? Pick something that you want."

Again, I said, "I don't want anything."

And he said, "How about I take you and buy you a fancy jewelry set. I will take you shopping, and you can get whatever you want. Or I will take you on a trip to Hawaii."

Every time, I would say, "No, sir, you did so much for me."

I could not ask for anything that was greedy. I was supposed to serve selflessly.

Finally, he said, "Do you want a million dollars?"

"No," I said. "I don't need anything from you. I'm so grateful. All I want to do is serve."

He accepted. The staff ended up throwing me this fancy birthday party. He sent me eighteen long-stem white roses.

One day, I got a call from one of the staff ladies. He wanted me to do night duty, she said. The idea of being alone with him at night felt very uncomfortable. I argued with her and asked, "Why can't somebody else do it? I've never done it before."

"Well, you've done all the other duties with him. So now you do the night duty."

"I don't want to."

"He's specifically asking for you. That's a big thing, you know. He's very particular about who he will allow into his bedroom at night. So, this is very special, Sat Pavan."

Everything was always pushed on me: "It is an honor."

So, I said, "OK, it's fine. I'll do it." I really did not know what I was going to be up for.

For her first "night duty," Sat Pavan went early to his house so that one of the secretaries could explain everything. She wore casual clothes and had her hair in a long braid. This was yet another contradiction. He pushed women to cover their hair with a turban, yet he commented on how beautiful her hair was and instructed her to wear it in a braid.

The secretary told her that he slept very little and that if he was asleep, she should put the sheepskin on the floor and get some sleep because she would have to attend to him as soon as he woke.

He was asleep in his chair when she arrived. She sat down and waited. Suddenly he got up and started walking backwards into his bedroom. He got into bed and went to sleep again. Sat Pavan lay down on the floor as suggested and tried to rest. She was too nervous to sleep. Not long after that, he got up, walked to his altar, and sat down. It looked like he was doing his prayers. Sat Pavan just sat there, closed her eyes, and tried to absorb the energy.

Then Yogi Bhajan got up and walked toward his little desk, asking her to get people on the phone for him, pointing to the address book. She looked up the names and dialed the numbers. Then, when someone answered the phone, she would say, "Please hold on. The Siri Singh Sahib wants to speak to you." She would then hand the phone to him.

This went on for a while. Someone would come and relieve her at 7:00 a.m. She was also in charge of preparing Bhajan's breakfast and his tea. She was used to doing that. When she looked at the clock, it was 5:00 a.m. Then, at 6:00 a.m., she would start preparing his breakfast.

When he was done making his phone calls, he was suddenly very energetic and animated. He finally acknowledged me and was in this goofy, kind of happy mood and jumped on his bed like a little child. I smiled and thought, *It wasn't such a bad night. I made it through.*

I had my back to him. I was folding blankets, preparing for me to leave the room, and making sure everything was in order. Then, all of a sudden, he said . . . [*Her voice trembles, and her otherwise lightning-quick talking rhythm slows down.*]

It's hard to talk about this, you know . . . He said, "Come give me a kiss."

I just stood there with my back to him. I froze. Did he just say what I think he said? From this point on, I started conversing with him in my head. "Don't do this," I said in my mind.

He kept saying, "Come over and give me a kiss."

He told me I had never kissed anyone and would show me how to do it.

"Let's kiss like we are in love. Come on, you're my wife, remember?"

I stood there and said, "I'm fine where I am. I'm fine where I am." I kept saying, "I'm OK."

Mentally I was saying to him, "What are you doing? You're better than this. You don't really mean this. You're not really asking me to do this."

Sat Pavan invoked Guru Gobind Singh, who fought against injustice and was seen as a protector of those in need. She kept telling Yogi Bhajan that she felt good where she was while she could not move and was trembling all over her body. He said to her that all his women did this and patted his bed to indicate she should come there.

She said to herself, "Why do you have these negative thoughts about him? He doesn't mean it. He is behaving like a grandfather. He just wants you in bed to give him a hug because he loves you." She trembled, and tears rolled down her face. Her right hand was shaking incessantly.

> After a while, he stopped it, changing the tone of his voice.
> "You're OK. You're fine. Nothing is going to happen. Don't be scared."
> I turned around.
> "Oh baby, why are you so . . . what's wrong with you? Oh no, no, no, everything is fine."
> I walked over, having my eyes on the door. I needed to get out there. He leaned over and kissed me on my forehead as I passed by. I stepped out of the room. I remember walking down the street that morning, trying to make sense of what had just happened.
> I thought, *I will never tell anyone about this ever! Because it is probably nothing. Of course, it is nothing. If I say something, it will make him look so bad. People will think badly of him. I need to protect him.*
> After that, he told me that I needed to come by every evening and give him a hug and a kiss goodnight. Because, he said, I needed to get over my fear of him. I needed to get more comfortable being so close to him. And so, I would go over every evening and give him a hug and kiss goodnight.

He was sixty-four, and she was eighteen. After this incident, she became "his virgin queen." The other women on his staff were considered "damaged goods."

Sometime later, when Yogi Bhajan heard that Sat Pavan had set her sights on a young man, he was not pleased. He told her to stay away from her lover. However, Sat Pavan had been friends with her boyfriend since she was six when they were together at children's camp. They planned to marry in 1994, a year after the incident in YB's bedroom.

> Yogi Bhajan disapproved of our marriage. The day before the celebration, I went to see him. He yelled at me and said I had betrayed him because I had promised to be with him. He didn't want to come

to the wedding and made me feel I was doing the worst thing in the world: doing something for myself. I was confused and cried throughout my wedding day. It caused total confusion.

When people complimented our marriage, saying, "Oh, they're well suited," he would say, "Yeah, I'm very proud of that one. I put that together." He wanted credit whenever there was an opportunity to get credit. Meanwhile, he tormented us from the very beginning of our marriage until the end of his life. He made me feel bad. "You betrayed me. You didn't trust me enough to allow me to make decisions for you. Your big ego wanted to make her own decisions."

After our marriage, YB kept me in Los Angeles and sent my husband to New Mexico. He would not have us live together. We had no money, so we had to get credit cards to fly over and see each other. Even phone calls were expensive. Later, he finally moved us to Oregon, where we've lived together ever since.

He never had peace with our marriage and constantly talked bad about my husband. From his cultural point of view, a woman is damaged once she's no longer a virgin. He created this environment where we constantly felt that our marriage was barely holding on. In YB's mind, our marriage would fall sooner or later, and I would run back to him and be with him. However, he underestimated the power of a love connection that begins at a young age. We could hold that on; it was not easy, but we did.

If I stood up for YB in a way like, "Don't mess with my teacher," he loved that strength. However, if I stood up for my marriage, he said it was ego, me trying to control things, me not trusting him.

And you know what? I needed to hear from others that it was strong of me to stand up for my marriage because I always took it as I was really stubborn and egotistical.

Dance for Me

Even when Sat Pavan was married, Yogi Bhajan considered her "his." He still asked her to dance as he used to do when she was on his staff.

This is another thing I have been dealing with. YB would always say, "You're my actress." He told me that he wanted every man to be in love with me. He said, "Wherever you go, every single man should be completely in love with you." And again, I didn't really know what to think of it. What a weird thing to put on someone, no? Whenever I would travel with him in the evening, he would tell me, "Today, I got this many marriage proposals for you." He informed me how many men he had to turn down who were in love with me. It is only now, understanding narcissism, that I realize it was all about him.

"You are with me. Everybody wants you, but you picked me."

I get it now, but I didn't get it then. I didn't understand those things about men.

After each class, he had me dance on stage for everybody. Other women told me, "You're dancing to seduce everybody." It made me feel uncomfortable. So, one day, I was not dancing with the same abandon I usually did.

He paused me and said, "Why aren't you dancing the way you normally dance?"

I told him all these different women were telling me I was trying to seduce everybody.

He said, "Who are you trying to seduce?"

"No one."

"Who do you think of when you are dancing?"

"God."

"Just keep on dancing," he said.

That wasn't a bad thing. It just created a lot of confusion. What did he want from me? How did other people see me? He would call me late at night and say, "I need you to come over and dance." I love to perform, but I didn't see it for what it was.

One of my biggest fears, when I was first coming forward with my story, was to have that thrown in my face. "You danced for so many years whenever YB asked you to dance. You were so flirty with him. You were always dancing sexy. How can you act like you're a victim of any kind? He didn't do anything wrong. You were the one seducing him."

Even though I was a teenager or in my twenties, I still had that fear and just had to let it go. And you know what? I still dance. I am allowed to dance. I don't need to feel ashamed about that. What is wrong is how he used me in those circumstances.

One time when I was newly married, we were at YB's birthday party. The governor of New Mexico and all these other politicians were there. My husband and I were dancing. Yogi Bhajan came over, glared at my husband, and told him to stop dancing with me. We both pulled over.

"Do you need something?"

He said, "You need to dance with the governor."

So, I had to go and dance with the governor, and my husband was upset.

I said, "Why are you upset? It's not a big deal."

I look back at it now and see how he was emasculating him, saying, "She belongs to me. I need her to impress this politician." My husband was just pushed to the side and sitting there, annoyed and getting glares from YB for being annoyed, like, "How dare you be annoyed? She's mine." He was constantly being told by YB that he was interfering with our relationship and that he was trying to control me. He told me, "Your husband is controlling you. He is against me. He's bad. You need to put him in his place."

It created a lot of turmoil in our marriage for years because of all those interferences that were just weird. Sometimes YB would call me in the middle of the night to tell me he loved me, and then "click," he hung up the phone. These were all total mind games. So many weird things happened.

It Took Thirteen Years

For years and years, the incident that happened during the night service haunted Sat Pavan. Sometimes, the memories would suddenly surface when she was traveling alone in the car. Then, all by herself, she would start shouting, "Why are you doing this to me? If nothing happened, take these memories away from me."

She had been married thirteen years when she first talked about it with her husband.

> I said, "I know that women have made accusations against YB. I know they are lying because I was in the room alone with him, and he tested me, and nothing happened." And then I told him everything that happened in detail. My husband said, "What if you had gotten in bed with him? What if you had given him a kiss? Have you ever thought about that?"
>
> I was angry at him. "Why are you trying to make more out of it than it is?"
>
> When I imagined my own daughter in a similar situation, only then I saw it was not innocent. I imagined her at sixteen or seventeen becoming homeless and being told her dreams would only lead her to prostitution. Or at seventeen, being forced to watch porn regularly and told that all this was just a test. No, I would not want my daughter to go through all this. I could not accept this.
>
> Only after this reflection did I know I had to look at that young girl I was in those days. She should not have gone through all that. A spiritual teacher or a grandfather should not be acting that way. Nobody should be acting that way. From that point onward, the process of trying to understand my life started. Finally, I allowed myself to stop covering it all up. Instead of saying, "Don't get into the negativity," I started saying, "Face it. I can no longer bring this trauma into my life and my kids' lives."

Everyone Has a Story

> In 2020, when I first was figuring out all these things, I started calling people who had been on the staff with me. Even not knowing if anything happened to them, I said, "I need to tell you some things that happened to me, and I need to know what you think."

Of all these people I talked to, and I spoke to many people, there was not one person who did not have a story, and there were so many people who didn't even realize they had a story.

I talked to one friend of mine. She said, "Women are making up stories about our teacher."

I said, "Oh, well, I just wanted to share with you some things I am going through." And I started telling my stories. She just got really quiet. I said, "Are you OK?"

She started crying. She said, "I have similar things that happened to me with him," but she didn't even know she had them. And she was the one who was angry that these weird women were coming forward.

I realize now that when you start sharing something, it joggles other people's memories. I learned that there was not one person on his radar whom he did not take advantage of.

I Was the Community

In May 2022, many second-generation adults called me after I came out with my story. They said it was really helpful as they experienced similar things. Speaking out did help some people in their process of letting things go or healing from them. As I was on YB's staff, he had put me in this position of importance. He presented me as the golden one for the people in my generation. While in reality: I did not go to school, and I did not get anything other than what he decided. I never had a job interview. Everything I've ever done has always been what he or others in the community told me to do.

So, how am I "the golden" of anything? If anything, I am the person that just did everything I was told to do. I am that community I was born and raised in and went through every single of its programs. I lived in it until my mid-forties. So, if you think in any way that I'm not a success, that's on the community. From the outside, it may seem like a strange life, but when it is you, it is normal.

I always tried to help others. I always felt it was a weakness if I admitted I needed help.

YB used to say, "You're so different from all the other second-gen. They should all be like you." I would be with him in the evening, just the two of us. He would say things like, "Why aren't they all coming to me the way you come to me?" When friends were in town, I would ask them to come over and see him. Often, they would say, "Oh no, he's scary," or "I don't want to be around him." However, I remember bringing some second-gen friends to him. Afterward, he said, "Do that more. Bring more of those." Now that everything has come out, I have these questions: If I had known what was going on with myself, could things have evolved differently? Could I have stopped what happened to other people who became part of his harem?

I was the first of my generation to be on his staff and went through everything. I still feel sad about it, like, could this have been prevented?

The other thing is, he would say, "Don't speak ill of your teacher, don't listen to people who speak ill of your teacher, don't think ill of your teacher." I was told that those things get into your head. Every once in a while, somebody [who] would leave the community would get an article in a paper that said 3HO was a cult or something. We didn't even read those things.

I did not even read all the books out there now. Because it is so much a part of me. It is like finally trying to face these things and feeling guilty—*Oh my God, I am going to see him in a bad light!* I used to say to people, "If you are going to say anything bad about him, I am going to walk away." And now I hear people say that to me. They don't believe me, they don't want to listen to me. Some will never figure it out.[149]

The Lawsuits

Attention: The following paragraphs contain explicit sexual violence.

KartaPurkh's Lawsuit

We return to 1975, the early years of the community. Yogi Bhajan was forty-six and had a well-established harem of secretaries by then. Guru Amrit Kaur was one of them. She was twenty-two. That year, she invited her fourteen-year-old sister to the women's camp and even persuaded her to stay after the camp. Bhajan gave the young girl the name Karta-Purkh. In 1985, after ten years of abuse and exploitation, she escaped.

In 1986, KartaPurkh filed a lawsuit against Yogi Bhajan and some of his associates, including her sister.[150] She claimed to be the victim of a thought-reform process. Using yoga, deep meditation, and special diets, Bhajan manipulated her and made her totally dependent on him.

Her file contains charges of physical, emotional, and sexual violence and abuse; exploitation; and intellectual property theft. The last two issues are dealt with in a later chapter.

The voluminous court records give us an insight into her story, starting with her sister's false promises to lure fourteen-year-old KartaPurkh into the women's camp. There would be teachings about "being a woman." Not so. There would be horses to ride. Not so. There would be workshops and lectures on music, martial arts, vegetarian cooking, and raising children. Nothing of the sort. Instead, she had to listen to Bhajan's indoctrinating lectures. They told KartaPurkh it was all for free while this was just another lie. A week after her arrival, the teenager had her first private talk with Bhajan. From then on, he spoke to her almost daily.

An extract from the court case:

> . . . he [Bhajan] would personally instruct the plaintiff [KartaPurkh] and oversee the plaintiff's education if she remained in the group,

studied under Bhajan, and became his follower.... That he, Bhajan, had a quarter of a million followers, and that these followers would assist her in any way in any object she desired. As a specific example, when the plaintiff indicated, she might want to become a lawyer, Bhajan promised that he had followers who were attorneys who would set the plaintiff up in the legal profession once she completed her education and spiritual training. That Bhajan had at that time ten million dollars in his personal fortune, and that he was willing to spend as much as was necessary to fulfill his promises to the plaintiff....

He helped her now because he was convinced that she would be of great value to the community later. He said he was an "avatar," a reincarnation of God.

Despite the harsh conditions at the women's camp, KartaPurkh joined 3HO. She paid Bhajan for her stay, adapted her lifestyle and education plans, and left her birth name behind. Once she was inside, Bhajan prescribed a strict regime of working, chanting, and exhausting yoga practice. She had to pray, meditate, and listen to his lectures for hours. Little time was left to sleep or to reflect on her situation and future. KartaPurkh weakened physically and psychologically. The rules and regime isolated her from friends, family, and outside influences.

Five years after she arrived in 3HO, in 1980, when KartaPurkh was nineteen, had never had sex with a man, Bhajan raped her for the first time. He was fifty-one. The sexual assaults continued regularly after that. Sometimes he was physically assisted by her sister and another woman. They would hold KartaPurkh down so that he could do his thing.

The lawsuit states that besides the so-called medical treatments, brutal beatings, involuntary sexual intercourse, sodomy, and other physical and sexual violence, he also performed bizarre rites, such as urinating on her. As a result of these assaults, KartaPurkh developed severe infections in her bladder, kidneys, and other organs. She had injuries to her rectum and colon, hair loss, nosebleeds, split lips, and bruises all over her body. Her tongue was so swollen that she could not eat solid food for days. Her jaw was dislocated. She contracted herpes simplex and other milder venereal diseases. She had two abortions and was left with permanent scars on her internal genitalia and back from tearing a birthmark. Between June 1978 and February 1985, she was repeatedly mistreated. In addition to pain from physical injury, she suffered from anxiety attacks.

KartaPurkh's self-respect, self-esteem, and self-worth were first undermined and eventually destroyed. She was constantly bullied, ridiculed, threatened, reprimanded, and humiliated publicly and privately. This happened whenever she tried to assert her personal rights or independence. She was made to feel wrong, inferior, and committing sacrilege. Her spiritual bankruptcy was predicted if she even dared to think of deviating from the behavior prescribed by Bhajan. She was constantly pressured to confess her shortcomings and surrender to Bhajan through the group.

She feared resisting Bhajan's sexual attacks, having relationships not approved by him, revealing her experiences to anyone, or trying to escape or leave 3HO. Bhajan had threatened to punish or kill her and her family by physical force or magical or mystical powers. If she escaped, she would end up in the gutter, living as a prostitute, and be rejected by everyone. He told her she would die in a car accident if she left his protection. She was now "useless" to men other than Bhajan. No other man would find her attractive or desirable or want to marry her. In her aura, Bhajan saw that it was her destiny to be sexually abused.

From 1981, when she was twenty, KartaPurkh was permanently watched. Any movement of hers was reported to him. At night he would call her. If she did not answer the phone, he would send a guard. From April 1983, her guards were armed. In July 1984, the guard in front of her house was more relaxed. On March 4, 1985, she escaped and fled to her parents. However, the fear for her life, safety, spiritual damnation, and torment remained.

After KartaPurkh left the cult, Bhajan, her sister Guru Amrit Kaur, and others continued to send her threats. They warned her of the dire consequences if she did not return to the cult or if she told anyone about what had happened. These threatening phone calls continued despite repeated requests to break off contact. As a result of the emotional trauma and psychological injury, she needed extensive psychological counseling and treatment.

All information above comes from her 1986 lawsuit.

He Was Obsessed with Me

After KartaPurkh escaped from 3HO in 1985, she gave an interview to psychologist Stephen Josephs. He had left 3HO a few years earlier. The interview transcript circulated within 3HO in those days, but it seems few people read it.

> I was engaged to be married to a man named David. Yogi Bhajan had arranged it. I was eighteen, and the engagement was going to be formalized when I was nineteen.
>
> That year, the resident secretary of Española left 3HO. Yogi Bhajan was devastated. As soon as he had seen the signs that she was leaving, he started preparing me for her position. The other women of his harem—his so-called staff—lived in Los Angeles. I was the only one who lived in Española. Yogi Bhajan broke off my engagement. . . . He told David it was a huge mistake to show reservations about being a Sikh. No way would he let his daughter—referring to me—marry him because David was uncommitted. Yogi Bhajan made him feel horrible. . . .
>
> My sister invited me to the Florida for winter solstice. I didn't want to go, but she convinced me. She stayed in the same room as YB. Most people know that he doesn't live in the same house as his wife. [She speaks in the present tense because this interview was taken in 1985.] They [Bhajan and his wife] don't get along and are arguing all the time. Instead, Yogi Bhajan travels with these American women from his staff. He calls them his secretaries and they share his bedroom.

I was a very naive girl. My family was moralistic and conservative. We grew up in the country and were not exposed to corruption. I never drank, smoked, or took any drugs, and I firmly believed in remaining a virgin until I was married. Anyway, Yogi Bhajan used the friendship, closeness, and trust I had in him as my spiritual teacher and in my sister, who had it all arranged.

At the ashram in Florida, his usual close group had gathered around him. We were all watching TV in his room, where he and my sister stayed. They had been there for about five days. The show ended, and we all got up to leave.

My sister said, "Wait, I want to talk to you."

I said, "It's late. Can we do it in the morning?"

We went back and forth. In the end, I stayed. I thought she really wanted to discuss something with me. At that time, I had no idea that Yogi Bhajan was sleeping with all those women. I knew what sex was, you see it on TV, but I had no idea he would do anything like that. I really saw him as a messenger of God. He was the herald of the Sikh faith! That is just what I believed. Maybe it was obvious to other adults but not to me. As soon as everyone else left the room, my sister locked the door. Yogi Bhajan announced he was going to have sex with me.

I said, "No, I don't want to. I want to get out of here!" I started crying.

He just grabbed me. My sister was in the room. Anyway, he proceeded to rape me. I suffered. I tried to struggle a lot. He hit me and held me down by my hair. He bit my tongue and lip when I started to resist through my voice. People noticed that for several weeks afterward. They were asking what had happened to me. Yogi Bhajan told some people he had hit me, which is why my lip was cut. It was because he had bitten it. He bit my tongue so badly that it was swollen. I couldn't eat and had to use a straw for five days. I had bruised nipples and a lot of bruising on my thighs. I was very sore. It was just so shocking because I thought he was my God. And my sister totally helped with this. I trusted her!

Gratefully it didn't last long. I mean, he just got in and out and got his whatever. And then I was left with all my bruises, insults, and shame. But I do remember laughing because I had bled so much. A huge puddle of blood. He and Guru Amrit were in a tizzy about it, because it was on the bedcover. Guru Amrit sneaked down to the basement and got some bleach. I don't know if they ever got it out or what. Yogi Bhajan was freaked out that the head of the ashram would notice it.

A lot more beatings, many more bloody noses. I'd get headaches when he hit me in the head so many times. And doing rectal intercourse, having other people hold me down, that sort of thing. But it wasn't as frequent. Because I know he had a hard time even looking at me. He would say that all the time. Yogi Bhajan was obsessed with me. I had a private investigator hired on me.

[*Stephen asks if it is someone from the organization.*]

No. A regular American private investigator. Also, I had a security guard on me for twenty-four hours in the organization. Yogi Bhajan said he had spent $19,000 on a private detective. I thought he was bragging. But then he told me that as I went to the store on such and such a day. I did this and that. So, I knew someone was watching me.

On and off, I entertained the thought of leaving. But I was afraid for my life, and I was scared for my family. I kept hoping it would stop, or at least it would get better.

[*Stephen asks what he specifically said about threatening the lives of her family.*]

After I had been caught talking to a family member, Yogi Bhajan couldn't stand to look at me. Like I had committed adultery. I had broken the relationship. I had betrayed him, and he could no longer trust me. I was just for a fuck. I was always there just for a fuck. It was more explicitly grotesque each time, but it was less frequent. He'd say if he ever caught me communicating with that man or any family member, he would kill all of them and kill me. He said that several times.[151]

When Yogi Bhajan passed away in 2004, KartaPurkh's sister Guru Amrit maintained a leading position in the community. When the abuse revelations came out in 2020, she took a leave of absence and has not given any comments since.

Premka's Lawsuit

At the end of 1984, after sixteen years in the vicinity of Yogi Bhajan, Pamela moved to Hawaii to live with the man she loved. Yogi Bhajan had played many dirty tricks to prevent the so-called number two of his organization, his secretary general, from leaving him, but love won. Pamela enjoyed the calming and healing effects of nature that surrounded the new home that her fiancé had prepared for her.

> Throughout those first months, Yogi Bhajan was calling me on a regular basis, as I continued to hope and expect that he would want me to remain within the embrace of the community that I loved. I couldn't believe that he would want to push me out. However, I soon began to hear some of the ways in which I was being portrayed to his faithful followers and I recognized the pattern. I was being characterized as having fallen to my second chakra and as a traitor to the Guru.
>
> A few months had passed when the yogi called one afternoon to tell me the story of KartaPurkh's departure (i.e., escape). His version of her departure included his cover story. He told me that KartaPurkh was claiming she had been sexually assaulted by him. His defense was to claim that, actually, she had been sexually abused by her own father, therefore, she was emotionally damaged, and that's why she now was falsely claiming that the yogi had abused her.
>
> I was horrified. I knew he had begun to have sex with KartaPurkh. I had seen the bruises, the marks he often left upon his secretaries. By then, she was around twenty years old, and I never imagined it was nonconsensual. I had met her parents—her father

and mother. They had visited the Ranch a few times. Their two daughters, KartaPurkh and Guru Amrit, were both part of the yogi's household.

Now I was shocked that he was making up this horrific story about their father in order to cover himself! It was bad enough that he was portraying me as a fallen woman, a traitor to the Dharma, but to slander the father of KartaPurkh and Guru Amrit? That was beyond the pale for me.

Six months later, Pamela and Siri Brahma celebrated their marriage in Hawaii.

I had told Siri Brahma about my prior relationship with the yogi. I felt I had to tell him before I could expect him to honestly be prepared to marry me. Now that we were married, Siri Brahma grew increasingly irritated with the yogi calling to talk to me. It was about eight weeks after our official marriage when the yogi called again one evening. Siri Brahma was very tense about it, and I expressed my frustration with being in the middle between them. On this occasion, at my encouragement, Siri Brahma got on the phone and proceeded to tell him: "I am getting quite annoyed at the fact that you keep calling and only talking to my wife."

That did it! I'm sure hearing me referred to as "my wife" was the last straw. The yogi lost it totally—he began screaming and cursing and telling Siri Brahma that he had betrayed his teacher, had betrayed his destiny, that he was cursed, and on and on. Shocked at the outburst, Siri Brahma dangled the receiver in the air between us as we looked at one another in disbelief, listening to the yogi raging and screaming and totally losing control. We hung up the phone on our end, and that was the last conversation we had for a number of years. It was actually a relief.

Another six more months passed by.

Over the months, Siri Brahma had been pressuring me to sue Yogi Bhajan. He was adamant that I should be properly compensated, and that Yogi Bhajan had used and abused me over all of my years of service. It was true that I had never been paid for all of my sixteen years of work, nor had I received any formal training to advance my career skills. I had attempted to negotiate some kind of assistance or compensation, but the answer the yogi gave was always the same: "I cannot do that, Premka. It would set a wrong precedent."

I resisted the idea of a lawsuit, but I also knew it would be a way to send a signal to the community about the fact that Yogi Bhajan was, at the very least, deceptive and duplicitous. I also wanted to support KartaPurkh in the event that she was to sue him. I thought that if I filed alongside her, it would be more likely that she would be believed. Again, I still believed in the "myth of Premka"—I thought people would believe me. Sure, I would hope to come out with some financial compensation for my sixteen years of service, but mostly I was motivated by the idea of sending a signal to the community. I wanted to face Yogi Bhajan in open court and force him to speak the truth. If what he was doing, if having physical relations with his staff, was acceptable, then he should stand and claim it!

I had no idea how to reach KartaPurkh. It turned out that both KartaPurkh and I, separately, reached out to Stephen Josephs (former Guru Shabd Singh of Millis, MA). Stephen had left 3HO in 1983. He arranged a meeting for both of us with an attorney named Peter Georgiadis and with a man named Pritham Singh. Pritham Singh was a fierce adversary of YB. He was a former student and one who perceived Yogi Bhajan's dishonesty, his deception, and his flagrant ego. We all met in Massachusetts in 1986.

The basis of my lawsuit[152] remained focused upon the lack of proper compensation for my sixteen years of work. I had been provided with housing and a car to drive, but the lack of any salary, any independent income kept me virtually imprisoned. Dependent. Disempowered. Although the power equation was highly imbalanced and inappropriate between me and YB, I would not claim that I was forced, that I was raped.

KartaPurkh's lawsuit involved extreme violent rape and imprisonment. I was shocked to learn that this was what he had done to her. It was nothing like my own experience, so it was difficult for me to imagine. Nonetheless, our lawsuits would proceed intertwined. I would stand with her. I knew the basic fact was true—Yogi Bhajan had violated her.[153]

Yogi Bhajan on the Lawsuits

It is July 4, 1986.

Women in full 3HO ornament with long fluttering veils chat while waiting for Yogi Bhajan's daily lecture at women's camp in Española. The camera moves slowly past American flags, red-white-and-blue ribbons and balloons decorating the large tent. It then focuses on a white jeep approaching and stopping next to the tent. The chatter dies down as the master gets out of the car along with three female staff members. With papers in hand, the master steps inside and takes a seat at the front. His thin orange turban is carelessly knotted. He gestures to one of his secretaries that he wants to borrow her reading glasses. With frowned eyebrows, he begins to read the document through the huge round glasses. He doesn't look up when a technician installs a microphone right in front of him. Since arriving in the US nearly twenty years ago, Bhajan's beard has grown thinner and grayer, although his mustache and sideburns are still dark. He is fifty-six.

The microphone is ready, but he reads on. On his right wrist shines a silver bracelet, and on the index finger of his left hand he wears a gold ring. His audience waits patiently. After a few minutes, he looks up. The lady at his feet shows him a page from a newspaper. He reads it diagonally and nods.

"Read it," he says while returning her the glasses.

"Hey!" he shouts to his audience. "She's going to read something from the Wall Street Journal."

"She" shows the audience the text printed in a gigantic font and formatted like a poem.

> This just came to me in the mail from Los Angeles. It's a full-page ad, and it's called: The snake that poisons everybody.
>
> "It topples governments, wrecks marriages, ruins careers, busts reputations, causes heartaches, nightmares, indigestion, spawns suspicion, generates grief, dispatches innocent people to cry on their pillows. Even its name hisses. It is called gossip. Office gossip, shop gossip, party gossip, it makes headlines and heartaches. Before you repeat a story, ask yourself, 'Is it true? Is it fair? Is it necessary?' If not, shut up."

She smiles as everyone claps. Approving murmurs rise from the audience. Yogi Bhajan takes the newspaper from her and holds it above his head like it was a trophy. Someone takes a picture. The same woman reads a hymn by Guru Nanak, the first guru of the Sikhs. The text praises the faithfulness and service of women to men.

After this reading, Yogi Bhajan calls a mother and daughter forward. The daughter had a skin problem, he says. The child has been cured thanks to him and the mother, who carefully followed his instructions. The audience claps, and Bhajan looks around with contentment. He straightens his back and continues in a sincere voice.

> By the way, we need your prayers. You will be glad to know that this Friday, the judge returned the case, saying it is too ugly and cannot be accepted. [*The women clap*.] And the complainant is Mukhia Sardarni Sahiba Premka Kaur Khalsa [Premka] and Karta Purakh Kaur Khalsa [KartaPurkh]. And if I tell you one example of the complaint, you shall be shocked. One of the complaints is that Sardarni Guru Amrit Kaur Khalsa and Sardarni Guruki Kaur

Khalsa physically held down at the ground and I perform an act of sodo . . . I don't know what they call it.

> [*The women laugh. Someone calls out, "Sodomy."*]

Yes, sodomy, and then I got up and peed.

The women laugh more modestly now. Yogi Bhajan looks around with big eyes as if to say, "Can you believe that?" He extends his right arm forward with the palm of his hand facing the audience. He stays in this position for a moment, then shakes his head and brings his arm back down. His body language reads, "This is all nonsense."

> That is what it says. There are a series of such charges. And when I remember all this, there is no option [*he raises his right eyebrow*]. The idea is simple. We have only two options. One is to give in to these extremist groups and accept their demands . . . [*he raises both eyebrows*] . . . or to face the charges. And we have accepted to face the charges. There's no other way to go [*he stretches his back and sighs*]. But power of the prayer is the power of the prayer; still, there is no case . . . . and I think now they will submit, will be the fourth time. And there are fifty pages almost, saying that you don't exist. None of you is a Sikh. Everything which is being done and said is fraud. And this is the secretary general!
>
> [*His eyebrows go up in an expression of "You ever heard such a thing?" He stretches his back again and switches to a mocking tone.*] If any fraud was played, I think she is the one. [*He shakes his head as he laughs. Silent laughter rises from the audience.*] But you understand? How dude could do what he did? Life is just a matter of consciousness. It's not something which I and you can do, but just remember one thing in your life and be careful about it. It is the worst risk not to take a risk for the good of others. If you cannot take a risk for the good of others, you are not human. You are worse than an animal because the other life is God in selflessness. The other life is?

The women repeat in a choir, "God in selflessness."

Bhajan effortlessly fills the next forty minutes in his typical mumbo-jumbo gibberish. Then he leads the class in meditation. He shows them how to connect the tips of the little finger and the thumb of their right hand and the tips of the ring finger and thumb of the left hand. The other fingers need to remain stretched. With bent elbows, they should bring their hands next to their shoulders as if taking an oath in court, but then with both hands. As they do so, they have to repeat aloud the following affirmation in a slow but tight rhythm, "I feel better. I am better. And that is my base." After one minute, he asks them to stretch out their arms in front of them with palms touching each other and thumbs interlacing. The arms must point to the left and be slightly higher than parallel with the floor. As they move the arms to the left, the tips of the fingers of the right hand will slide to touch the mounds of the fingers of the left hand. They should keep on looking straight in front of them. A tape is put on with a mesmerizing mantra that they should sing along with, keeping their eyes closed.

The camera at the back of the room slowly moves over the white flock of towering turbans, mostly covered with veils. After a few minutes, elbows begin to bend. Cramped faces try to keep their hands high. Backs are flexed and stretched, shoulders make circular movements, and a brave soul shakes her arms loose for a moment. But there are also statues with blissful Buddha smiles. Some eleven minutes later, Bhajan waves his hand, and the music stops. "Relax," he says. Then, wiping the sweat from his forehead with a handkerchief, he makes a few comments about the weather on this national holiday and says:

> I will ask you one thing in particular, in whichever humble way you know to pray: make prayer, so that we may survive through this period. '84 to '88 is the period of test and trial and strength of triumph. Triumph will only come, the victory will only come with the power of prayer; nothing else can help. As you are all being attacked in your belief, in your existence, and in your identity. Therefore, you don't need to share. I will play my part with your strength and with

your prayer and with my prayer to the Guru to keep our honor afloat, but just remember, it is not we alone; it is our coming generations and our children, grandchildren, and great-grandchildren who have to follow us. They must not feel that we have failed in prayer, and we have fallen. That's why I'll like you to participate with your heart and head bowed in prayer, in strength, in the manner you know best. Thank you very much. May the longtime . . . .

The students sing the song that, according to Bhajan's rules, has to be sung after each yoga class: "May the longtime sun shine upon you. All love surround you. And the pure light that's within you, guide your way home."[154]

The transcribed version of this lecture contains a second part, possibly the recording of that day's evening lecture. Following excerpt of that lecture is an excellent example of the nonsensical drivel that he regularly produced as if he were proclaiming great wisdom and to which his followers continued to sit and listen with earnest faces.

I was asked a question, "How much God is with you, Bhajan?" That was the question I was asked by my teacher one day. In class, out of just like that, we were sitting, he asked everybody and everybody answered ten trillion because there are ten trillion cells in the body and there are seventy-two portions of the body, someone say, seventy-two thousand, some said, seventy-two and it went on and on and finally right in there corner I was and he said, "Bhajan, what do you think, how many Gods are with you, how many, how much God is with you, how much God is with you?"

And I said, "I can say minimum is thirty trillion."

He said, "How you figure it out?"

And I said, "Well, each cell has electron, neutron, and proton, so each cell has three, so ten trillion parts or, ten into three is thirty trillion. It's as simple a mathematics as it could be."

He said, "Well, why you want that much God, isn't that God is one?"

I said, "No sir, God is one, one of His kind. God is not one. God is one of one kind. God is a totality. Negative and positive is God, sin and merit is a God, day and night is a God, holy man and a cruel man is God. Curse and a blessing is God."[155]

So What?

Mani Niall was a teenager when he entered 3HO. He lived in several ashrams and finally ended up in Los Angeles. In 1985, at age 25, he left 3HO–Sikh Dharma. After he left, friends and family in 3HO continued to visit Mani's Bakery and stayed in contact with him. He recalls how insiders reacted to the lawsuits.

I hung out with some friends. The topic of the lawsuits came up. They said things like, "I don't care. The benefits Yogi Bhajan brought into my life outweigh any bad he did."

I also heard that years later from a friend. She said the same, "I don't care."

They were referred to as "the lawsuits." People did not deny them, but they would not look them up or talk about the content. It was just "the lawsuits," and you were pretty much expected to denounce them. People would repeatedly say, "He saved my life. I don't care what else he did. He saved me."

It was not pretty to hear.[156]

Court? No! Let's Go Shopping

Pamela Dyson recounts in a blog[157] how Pritham Singh, a wealthy Sikh who dealt in real estate, had agreed to fund the legal expenses for her and KartaPurkh's court case but finally withdrew. Yogi Bhajan had found a way to financially hurt Pritham by approaching his client base and pressured him via a lawsuit.

Bhajan's inner circle had invented a story to twist the truth around the lawsuits. This time, it was not only for internal use, but it served also in court. The *Albuquerque Journal* reported on it. The Sikh Dharma Brotherhood had filed a claim against Pritham Singh, accusing him of having paid the two ladies, so they would file lawsuits "aimed at discrediting and financially incapacitating" Bhajan and his corporations.

> In court records, Singh [Pritham] denies such motivations. . . . Private security guard [name] stated he overheard Singh tell Bhajan "He had been working for a long time 'to get' him and had found women who agreed to sue Bhajan." Bhajan's lawyers have filed requests for Singh's financial records including requests for documents related to Singh's recent purchase of [names of buildings and] all other properties and corporations in which he has an interest.
>
> Singh's Albuquerque lawyers claim such information is irrelevant. They have asked for a protective order "to prevent taking of depositions whose only purpose is to engage a dragnet inquiry into the defendant's business affairs in order to make him retreat from his financial support of the plaintiffs."[158]

The story of a guard who testified in court "overhearing Pritham talk to Bhajan," reminds me of other stories in which faithful 3HO members were requested to lie to serve "a higher good."

In the end, the cases of KartaPurkh and Pamela were settled out of court.

Gursant Singh, who worked as a driver for Yogi Bhajan and his secretaries in those days, recounts, "We had been told that, while there had been previous allegations by some women of inappropriate behavior from Bhajan, these were without merit and the product of women who really did want to have sex with him but had been spurned."

Like most other 3HO members, Gursant did not read the lawsuit papers while he was in 3HO. In his book, he shares what happened after he read them, which was years after Bhajan died.

> Premka's case was shocking enough but the other—from a very young lady [KartaPurkh] who had been a conspicuous favorite of

Bhajan's—was mind numbing in the extent of the depraved behavior alleged on Yogiji's part. . . .

[Gursant switched to present tense.] What is getting to me about these legal documents is the amount of detail. She was very specific. These didn't seem like some wild accusations that would not stand up under cross-examination.

I want to know more and decide to call Peter Georgiades, the attorney for [KartaPurkh] and Premka Kaur, in Pittsburg. He is very cordial and tells me a lot about the case. He felt absolutely sure that [KartaPurkh] was telling the truth in her complaint or he would not have taken the case. He says that—when she approached him—her whole body was covered with bruises; this was one of the main reasons why he decided to proceed with the case. He mentions that he had tried for several months to depose Yogi Bhajan—in other words, to ask him questions about the case under oath. He had been stymied by the fact that a doctor with the last name of Khalsa had insisted for that entire time that Yogiji was too sick to be deposed.

This strikes a chord in me as, during that entire time, I had been in Yogiji's security detail. He may have been too sick to be deposed but he sure as hell hadn't been too sick to go to *La Scala* for lunch, then to shop in Beverly Hills on an almost daily basis. There was no way to prove it, but I felt like this had been a deliberate obfuscation to keep him from being deposed; hardly the kind of behavior from someone who has nothing to hide.[159]

In 2023, Gursant adds this to the story:

Six times Yogi Bhajan was ordered by the judge to give his deposition. Every time his so-called Khalsa doctors claimed he had heart problems or whatever. . . . Yogi Bhajan could have easily given his deposition. He just didn't want to. As Peter (the attorney of the women) said, "be under the bright lights and having to get his deposition, he refused."

And so, in my mind those deniers of this abuse who say, "Oh Yogi Bhajan doesn't have a say. He's not around to answer these allegations." Well, he had his opportunity back then and six different times he could have given his deposition and given his side of the story about all of these abuses and everything.[160]

We know from testimonies that these court cases from 1986 did not change Yogi Bhajan's behavior. The luring of young girls and his sexual misconduct continued. Women who witnessed the abuse say that as he grew older and his health deteriorated, he had increasing difficulty getting sexually aroused. As a result, he became even more cruel.

Do Not Look at the Cracks

In April 2021, GuruNischan released a podcast telling her own story, letting her anger, sadness, and disappointment flow freely. In the clip below, tears ran down her cheeks.

It was 2018 or 2019, and a student called me.

She said, "I just read these rape papers from [KartaPurkh]. I don't know how you teach anything this man has brought."

I was like, "Huh? What are you talking about?" I hadn't even looked at the rape case from 1986! As woke, reconciled, and healed, and all those things that I thought I was, I hadn't. And I didn't know what to say to her.

She said, "It's right here, on public record!"

I probably asked her to email it to me, but even then, I didn't investigate [nods her head and dries her tears]. It felt like I was as aware as I could be at that time. As soon as all this came out in 2020, I called the student and apologized to her.

I said, "I'm sorry. I didn't listen." It made me realize that we were brought up to be proud and strong because we were so different. We were trained not to look at the cracks. "They're just trying to put cracks in our good thing." It was part of the indoctrination and necessary to support the backbone of our "being so different."

Yet what that also did was prevent critical thinking. It kept us from seeing through a lens outside our little bubble, thinking that this was the magic formula for humanity.[161]

Yogi Bhajan on Rape

Before we listen to Yogi Bhajan, a brief side note: Several sources mention that Yogi Bhajan took a Neuro-Linguistic Programming (NLP) course.[162] A former 3HO member told me YB was instructed on the technique by one of his followers who had attended the NLP training.

NLP became popular in the mid-1970s. Its "reframing techniques" aimed at changing a person's behavior by consciously shifting the context or meaning of words. This pseudoscience was first used in therapeutic settings but it soon attracted the interest of others as well.

Anyone who has listened to Bhajan's lectures knows that he was a master at creating an incomprehensible word salad for minutes on end. English was not Bhajan's native language, but that is no excuse for the confusing and disorienting "gibberish" he loved to use. If you keep listening to it, your mind becomes numb, and you end up in a kind of sleep state. You lose critical judgment, become influenceable, and open to suggestion.

It is April 26, 1978.

A heavy thunderstorm rolls over Ram Das Puri land in the high desert of New Mexico. The master's voice rivals the thunder and rain as he delivers a lecture to the participants of the women's camp in Española. He is forty-nine. Ten years have passed since he arrived in the US. His status as a spiritual leader is now established. Thousands revere and worship him as the sole and undisputed authority within the 3HO–Sikh Dharma community.

Yogi Bhajan spends about an hour preaching about all sorts of things. After a brief silence, he announces, "There is one last point I want to discuss with you. It is about rape." His voice sounds calm and determined. He speaks like a loving and caring grandfather about to share an essential and wise lesson with his children and grandchildren, demanding their attention.

"I have heard a lot of different versions. And some people have asked me a lot of questions. And I never answered that. Today I want to talk to you about it. First of all, nobody can be raped until you do not invite it. Rape is always invited. It never happens."

The rain and thunder have stopped. No sound can be heard in the tent except a light cough here and there, nothing more. Yogi Bhajan raises his voice again. Louder and sharper now, almost shouting. He articulates his words as if he wants to nail them into his listeners' brains.

"A person who is raped is always providing subconsciously the environments and the arrangements. If you do not provide the circumstances and the arrangements, it is impossible."

Another silence follows. A woman sitting near him coughs. There is no video, only a voice recording of this lecture, so we cannot perceive the audience's body language. How many women present have ever been raped? By him? Maybe last night? What about KartaPurkh? Is she present? If so, how does this resonate with her? She is not raped by him yet. That will happen in a year. The silence is deafening as Yogi Bhajan begins to speak again.

> There was a certain question asked: "Suppose a woman is going with a chaperone of a male. And that man is attacked and gets unconscious. What this woman should do?"
>
> When did I tell you to depend on the chaperone? I have always told you to depend on yourself. Learn self-defense.

How do the attendees perceive his rapid transition from "Rape is always invited" to "Learn self-defense?" How does his plea for "self-defense" land with those who have been abused by him?

I will tell you the story of a woman of 3HO. She was going some-where to buy something in the market. She came out, and these three hooligans stopped her. They started mocking at her. One person had, what do they call it? Those karate people, that stick which has a chain in between.

[*A student calls out, "Nunchaku."*]

Yes, that's it. That hits bad you know. He started playing with that. This woman was fully trained. When she found out the way is blocked, within the spur of the moment, those three were, with that flying thing, on the ground, and she walked over them.

[*A faint laughter can be heard.*]

One said out of the cry, "Tell me, you angel of a death, what is your name?"

She said, "Sat Nam."

Because she trained herself. She knew how to have a self-defense. She loved to live with dignity and divinity. She loved to live with herself, perseverance to the idea of preserving herself. She was not afraid of those three negative guys. She knew it: she can cut them out and make them plus I say to you all, if you have the right to live, then you must have the right to learn to live with grace. And learn it now without wasting any day. You have lived as chicks. I know that. But now you must live like eagles. Negativity should totally die when it comes under your claws. And you can fly to the heights of the height with your feathers and with your grace.

You are not born to be raped. You are not born to be misused. And you must not fall under those claws of people who do not know how to live. You must understand our philosophy is very well explained in the song of the Khalsa. Learn perfectly how to create environments of self-defense. Obey the rules of dignity and self-defense. And qualify yourself for the self-defense. Because you must understand when one is raped, life does not become very sweet thereafter, in spite of the fact you may not be physically hurt. But it gives you such a mental injury and it gives you such a deep spiritual scar that it takes very long time to come out of it. Therefore, it is your right and very legal right to learn self-defense.

From this point onwards, the lecture continues with his typical babbling. He confuses everything and everyone. Your brain melts if you try to find logic in his thought patterns. And when there is a moment when you think you have understood where he is going, he takes a turn back into the jungle.

Here is a brief summary of the remainder of Bhajan's lecture that day: People who worship guns never abuse them. Having a pure consciousness is essential. Also, practically: keep your surroundings clean. Plant trees, hedges, and flowers, as these attract birds. He was lucky enough this morning to see white doves flying around in his garden. He advises everyone to also be clean and careful when eating. They are fortunate they don't live in Hong Kong, where in a 10 by 15 room, fifteen families live. Most children die there because the adults crush their children at night while they are sleeping. They are suffocated under the weight. Oh yes, these are standard types of deaths and very common in that part of the world. Someone once had asked him something about Hong Kong. He had answered with a question, "If the Chinese ever find God, what would they do?" Nobody had given an answer. He had said, "They will prepare him and eat him."

There is laughter. It's as if his earlier statement, "Rape is always invited," has been forgotten.[163]

Ten years later, in 1989, Bhajan said:

Thank God, to the grace of God that woman has that tolerance, and she goes through. But the funny part of it is there are some women who get stimulated by being beaten. That 30 percent of women . . . like to get beaten and it stimulates them. Thirty percent women, 20 percent women get abused and it stimulates them, and 30 percent women are those who provoke violence and like to enjoy it, it stimulates them. So, it is not a one-way traffic that men are all dirty and

women are good, or women are bad, and men are good. Man, basically has to be understood that he has 16 percent less tolerance and
that's enough.[164]

The library of Yogi Bhajan's teachings made available by KRI, the
Kundalini Research Institute, contains more than three thousand items.
Over four decades, they were captured on video or voice recording and
were transcribed. More than once, Bhajan attempted to open his followers' eyes. In July 1988, for example, he said:

I came here and I didn't give you anything, it's all fraud. You think
I'm a good teacher and all that. It's not true. It's a total lie. I'm not
a good teacher. I'm not a good man, I am not a God man. I don't
believe in all this nonsense. I believe very sincerely that God made
me a man and that's all I am. Big and small, and these titles and the
whole thing is all debauchery. I live with it because that keeps you
going. Not it doesn't keep me going. It serves me no purpose. But I
do believe I have given you identity and whenever you are in your
identity you are strong, when you are not you are weak. This is my
experiment; this is what I have learnt.[165]

An Independent Investigation

Attention: The following paragraphs contain explicit sexual violence.

Defenders vs. Supporters

In the first months of 2020, after *Premka* was published, new abuse
stories surfaced almost daily. The dams of the Healthy-Happy-Holy
image gave way, and the mud flew in all directions. The Siri Singh Sahib
Corporation (SSSC), the organization that oversees all for-profit and
nonprofit entities, had no choice but to act. In mid-February 2020,
they commissioned the Buddhist-inspired organization An Olive

Branch—AOB for short—to conduct an independent investigation. The AOB team had expertise in investigating ethical issues in the context of spiritual activities. Over two months, the AOB team contacted nearly three hundred people to examine allegations of Yogi Bhajan's sexual misconduct. Half of these were reporters of harm or persons who witnessed abuse. The other half were followers of Bhajan, who wanted to mount his defense.

In late July 2020, the seventy-two-page AOB report was published on the website of the SSSC Office of Ethics and Professional Standards.[166] It reported twenty-four charges of sexual assault and abuse, thirty charges of sexual harassment, and thirty-four complaints of unethical behavior.

> We acknowledge that it is likely that not all individuals who had been harmed by Yogi Bhajan came forward to participate in this investigation. There are various reasons they may not have done so. These include the possibility that they left the community long ago, have moved on from their experiences, and do not wish to revisit the traumatic experience from years ago. . . .
>
> Despite the painful and humiliating experiences, many women maintained a relationship with Bhajan. The reasons they gave were obedience to their spiritual teacher, a desire to protect his reputation, a sense of being unique, and wanting to please him.
>
> . . . although some of the Reporters of harm may appear to have remained willingly in sexual relationships with Yogi Bhajan for several years, the student's consent cannot be assumed because of the power differential between a spiritual teacher and their students.

The report illustrates the stark contrast between the testimonies of Bhajan's supporters and those reporting harm. Here is one example from a supporter:

> His [Yogi Bhajan's] whole mission was to elevate his students, to elevate women, elevate our future generations, to make us

invincible by accessing the Source energy that is within all and building a conscious and graceful life in the Sikh tradition. There is no way that he would ever do something with the intention to harm another. He loved us so much that he was willing to be misunderstood in order to help us.

And an example from a reporter of harm:

He [Yogi Bhajan] bit my tongue. He sucked on my tongue, and it turned blue. I cried, but he would not let go until he finished. A staff member noticed my tongue was blue. The woman said, "Where'd you get the blue tongue?" but she knew what it meant. It happened to her too. I was sleep deprived for ten years. It got to the point where I dreaded and loathed private time. He would bite me on my neck, ears, and cheeks, and I cried. He bit my privates. He showed no remorse for hurting me. I took pain pills like candy. [Before Yogi Bhajan's kidney transplant], he would "go at me" for hours, biting, gripping, pinching—like he was trying to get his life force back.

Unfortunately, the AOB report only dealt with Bhajan's sexual abuse of women. The numerous other malpractices and crimes, such as atrocities in Indian schools, the homophobic culture, exploitation, fraud, life threats, and so on, were not looked at. The AOB team forwarded the "other" complaints they received to Ethics and Professional Standards (EPS), the team that reports to the SSSC. How many "other" complaints there were, and what happened to them, was never made public.

Numbers in the AOB Report

Twelve people reported that Yogi Bhajan's had sex with them repeatedly over several years. Several named other women—women who did not participate in the AOB investigation and with whom Yogi Bhajan would have had sex.

Six women reported that he directed them to shave off their pubic hair, while a Sikh rule says you cannot cut your hair.

Eleven women reported that Bhajan directed them to have sex with other women. Seven women claimed they were forced by him to have sex with multiple partners. Sometimes he was involved, sometimes not.

Three reporters said that Yogi Bhajan raped them or penetrated their anus. All those were nonconsensual sexual acts.

One female reporter was directed by Yogi Bhajan to have sex with a young man, specifically to engage in anal sex.

Eight persons reported that Yogi Bhajan injured them during sex. If women had bruises or bite marks, they stayed home, saying they were sick or had to attend to personal matters. They covered their injuries with clothes or kept their mouths shut. While most interviewees did not remember seeing bruises or bites, seven reporters said they saw those marks of physical injury on the women serving Yogi Bhajan.

Nine persons reported unwanted touching of intimate parts in interactions with Yogi Bhajan. The incidents occurred outside of sexual intercourse; some happened in public.

Seven women indicated unwanted touching of their breasts by Yogi Bhajan. Two of them were minors at the time. One was fifteen, the other one seventeen. Three reporters said they witnessed Yogi Bhajan inappropriately touching women's breasts. Two of his accusers were directed to touch his genitals.

Four women reported situations where he proposed sexual acts, inviting them to step in bed with him, etc.

Three women reported that he had them describe their sexual experiences with others.

Two minors and one adult woman were unwittingly exposed to pornography at his hands. Four persons observed Yogi Bhajan and others watching pornography. Supporters of Yogi Bhajan said he showed porn to inform people about how the world views women. They also testified that Yogi Bhajan did not want certain secretaries to know that he was watching porn.

Seventeen people complained about his sexually offensive language. He used the word "fuck" and called people a "whore," a "prostitute," or other unsavory names.

From the testimonies, the AOB team distilled 115 environmental factors that could facilitate sexual and other types of misconduct. Below are the outlines and key insights from that research:

- Eleven individuals explained why most people in the community did not know about Yogi Bhajan's sexual misconduct. They said that he kept secrets and kept people in the dark about many aspects of his life and the organizations he operated.
- Without being questioned about this topic, fourteen Reporters voluntarily stated that 3HO/Sikh Dharma was a cult, or they felt they had been in a cult.
- Seven Reporters said they understood that Yogi Bhajan was God or had been raised to see him that way. This view led them to compromise their own agency in service of someone they saw as all-powerful.
- Nine Reporters commented that they were inhibited from speaking out by Yogi Bhajan because they feared the consequences of doing so. They had observed that those who did speak out were usually shunned, shamed, or driven from the community.
- Thirty-two Reporters provided accounts of Yogi Bhajan exercising damaging control over their major life decisions—decisions about their education, marriage, children, and procreation. Additionally, four other Reporters witnessed Yogi Bhajan's control of others' life decisions.[167]

Supporters Saw Nothing

Many supporters of Yogi Bhajan do not believe the allegations because they never observed inappropriate behavior. To them, everything he did was in the best interest of the students. "Such a holy person cannot do such things."

The AOB team reported:

It is possible that these Supporters simply were not aware of the various methods that Yogi Bhajan employed to manipulate the behavior of those in close association with him. As noted by one Reporter, most members of the community were oblivious to what was going on behind the scenes. A relatively small number of people had more access to the inner workings of 3HO/Sikh Dharma than the vast majority of Yogi Bhajan's students had. And even those who had access were not able to see the whole picture or to easily extricate themselves from his influence.

Conclusion

The conclusion of the AOB report is straightforward.

. . . based on reports of harm from thirty-six people, the investigation concludes that it is more likely than not that Yogi Bhajan engaged in several types of sexual misconduct and abused his power as a spiritual leader.

The specific sexual misconduct included various forms of sexual battery, sexual assault, and sexual harassment as well as conduct judged to be unethical according to the Sikh vows and inconsistent with Yogi Bhajan's own teachings.

We also conclude that by behaving in such a way, he abused the power entrusted to him as a spiritual leader. . . .

In response to the AOB report, the deniers ordered their own "independent" report. In the Thompson Report, published at fairinvestigation.com, a former lawyer and qualified private investigator listed several arguments why An Olive Branch was not qualified for the work they did. She questions their abilities and points out flaws in the AOB report.

While the AOB report is difficult to read because of the cruel practices it describes, the Thompson Report is a reader's nightmare because of the legal jargon that abounds in it.

She Caught His Eye

George Craig McMillian, also known as Kirantana Singh—we will call him Kir—was twenty-three in 1971 when he joined 3HO. He embraced Sikhism and became a popular performer of *kirtan*, devotional songs. Kir was one of Yogi Bhajan's first bodyguards. He slept by the master's bedroom door at the ashram on Preuss Road in Los Angeles.

After a while, Kir was sent to an ashram in Northern California, where he met a young woman, Kirn Jot. Every morning they sat together during sadhana. They fell in love. One day, Bhajan came to the ashram, and she caught his eye. He took her to Los Angeles. She was paired with a young Punjabi man known as a devout Sikh. He was a nice man, but Kir was devastated by the engagement news and left for Hawaii to go surfing.

A year later, Yogi Bhajan visited Hawaii. He sent out his minions to look for his former bodyguard. They found him. Yogi Bhajan received the lost son with open arms, much to the dismay of YB's entourage. The yogi asked Kir to return with him to Los Angeles. His job would be to guard the ashram, lead sadhanas, train novice teachers, and work in the Golden Temple restaurant during the day. Kir loved challenges, and after such a long isolation and all the surfing, he could do with a change. He accepted.

> In Los Angeles, I lived at the ashram. As a guard, it's your job to see what is going on and be curious about everything. So, I suspected that he was having sexual affairs with his secretaries. But I didn't really see it as my business. The way I looked at it was that it was part of his culture. Every rich Maharaj has concubines. And they

were all adults. So, I knew, but I did not want to know. I was just doing my job.

The first time it really hit me was at a Tantric course in San Diego. Someone had threatened Yogi Bhajan and tried to attack him. The guy was in love with one of YB's secretaries. We stopped him, but Yogi Bhajan was shaken up by the event. That night I kept watch at his door. That was the first time I heard him putting the make on one of his secretaries. There was a serious discussion about it. He tried to harass her, and I didn't want to hear that. But there was no denying it. I started praying. Out of that came the best song I ever wrote. It was crazy. The song became popular and is on an album from 1975. Every time I listened to it, I felt this strange twinge because I kept thinking about the night I wrote it. That night was my first awakening to all that. From then on, I knew that something was "off" at Preuss Road. I started watching and guarding with different eyes and thought about leaving. But then tragedy happened.

Kirn Jot's assigned husband was killed in a car accident. Because he had been a devout Punjabi Sikh, Yogi Bhajan's wife wanted his ashes to be returned to India. Kir was asked to accompany her. It was his first trip to India, and he became very ill. In Amritsar, Yogi Bhajan's wife left him in the care of her father-in-law. According to Kir, "Papaji" was a beautiful, quiet, and serene retired medical doctor. They became good friends. Papaji brought Kir to the Golden Temple. Despite his illness, Kir went for forty nights in a row to clean the floors of the temple. During the day, he had high fevers, but at night, they miraculously disappeared. Kir lost thirty pounds. After forty-two days, he left Amritsar for Dharamsala to meet the Dalai Lama and study with him.

A few weeks later, a group of American Sikhs, including Kirn Jot, came to India for a celebration. Kir returned to Punjab to join them. And so, Kir and Kirn Jot met and fell in love again. Someone in the community had seen this, and the lovers were immediately separated.

Kirn Jot was sent to Los Angeles to live with Yogi Bhajan, and Kir was sent to Española to run a program with drug addicts, a story that will be told in a later chapter. After some time, Kir found himself back in Los Angeles. At night, he served in the gurdwara, where he read from the holy book.

I would start reading and Kirn Jot would show up sitting at the back. Before I finished, she would leave, so we never talked. I couldn't stand it and made an appointment with Yogi Bhajan. He and four of his secretaries were there in his room, all nice and cordial. I asked him permission to marry Kirn Jot. Panic exploded. Yogi Bhajan looked away and went down some dark hole. The secretaries started talking nonsense. It was as if a knife had stuck right into my heart. Finally, one of them stumbled on her words and said they would speak to me about this in a few days.

One evening between the two back gates, Kirn Jot caught me. I hadn't talked to her since India. She was tearful and said, "You can never ask that again." I was about to ask why but she stopped me, put her head down, and walked away. I went hollow. That was it for me, I left 3HO. I met a wonderful woman, whom I married. She was not a 3HO person, but we practiced Kundalini Yoga together.

A few months later, Kirn Jot publicly accused Yogi Bhajan of raping her. In front of the whole *sangat*, she was ridiculed and shamed. Yogi Bhajan himself was the most vicious and crude in the ridicule. Nobody in Los Angeles stood up for her. I believe it was 1975, but I am not sure about that. As far as I know, she was the first woman to leave for those reasons. At that time, I didn't know. She told me all this later.

About a year after she last spoke to me at the gate, Kirn Jot called me. We met at a small apartment. She was scared that I would ridicule her the way other people had done and make her feel ashamed. Me, her best friend! She slowly started telling the whole story. How he forced himself on her and raped her. How he was trying to get her into other sexual relationships with the other secretaries.

She was broken and totally on her own now, crashing at people's houses, confused, brave, but very scared. She said she came to me because she knew I would not break my marriage vows, even if we loved each other. She trusted me. She wept. I held her firmly, afraid of what I felt. And then we went our separate ways. I never saw her again.

This meeting wrecked my marriage. I was still in love with Kirn Jot and felt broken. Our marriage lasted for another seven years. After that, I just couldn't function. I lost my sexual energy. We're still good friends.

Over many years, 3HO people continued to call it all lies: Kirn Jot made it up and tricked me. That was horrible. I returned to my extraordinary Tibetan Tantra masters to study and heal slowly. I found my own unique path. Years later, I heard that Kirn Jot had died from ovarian cancer.[168]

HOMOPHOBIA, POWER, AND EMOTIONAL ABUSE

No Man Is Born Faggot

No Son of Guru Gobind Singh is Gay

Guru Gobind Singh (1666–1708) was the tenth guru of the Sikhs, the last human guru. He completed the *Guru Granth Sahib*, and from that moment onwards, the holy book was considered the eternal Guru. Yogi Bhajan asked his Western Sikhs to regard Guru Gobind Singh as their father and to behave like his sons and daughters.

Meeri was born in the Phoenix ashram in 1975. We previously read how he was sent to a random family in Española at the age of four, raised himself, and cleaned bathrooms at this young age. Forty years later, he is GuruNischan's guest in an *Uncomfortable Conversations Podcast*. His carefully trimmed beard is slightly graying, and his half-length black hair is combed back tightly. A thin necklace glistens under the open collar of his ochre shirt. A large brown dog is lounging on a mat beside him. Every now and then, the quiet and seemingly contented animal gets up to assume an even more comfortable pose or to parade behind Meeri's back.

Meeri spent his early school years in the US. Later he was sent to India, and like most 3HO kids, he stayed there until he graduated. He deliberately does not talk about his time in India in this interview because others already did. He wants to address the homophobic behavior of Yogi Bhajan.

When Meeri returned from India in 1993, he was eighteen. He was forming his identity as a young adult and trying to understand himself. In a newspaper, he saw an article addressing people under twenty-one who had questions related to their sexuality. He drew a circle around it because he wanted to revisit it later. His mother found the newspaper, saw his note, and confronted him with it. Pointing to the article, she asked, "Is there anything you need to tell me?"

He replied that he was indeed questioning and having doubts. All the people around him were getting married, and he didn't even have a girlfriend. He explicitly said he wanted to keep this private as he was still figuring things out. He was exploring.

The next day when I came home, my mother told me she had arranged an appointment between me and Yogi Bhajan. This issue was way too big for me to deal with. His guidance was needed. So, I was carted off to Yogi Bhajan's private headquarters on the ranch in Española.

I was eighteen, had never kissed a person, and was entirely like a goody-two-shoes. I was dressed all in white, my head tightly wrapped in a nice turban. I had all my *banis* [Sikh symbols] on. I wanted to look good for my meeting with the master. I walked into the room. A group of posh-looking people was sitting there, in posh-looking clothes and with lots of jewelry on them. Yogi Bhajan sat on a throne. Someone was massaging his feet. Another was combing his hair.

The question he bellowed out in his big voice was, "Oh Meeri Peeri, I heard you want to get fucked in the ass?"

I just clammed up and zoomed out of my body. I looked at myself from the outside and said to myself, "Say something!" So, I said,

"No, sir, I want to be happy. I want to be truthful. Living truth. I don't want to live in a lie."

I heard him respond, "Well, you can't. No son of Gobind Singh is going to be gay."

I repeated, "I just want to be happy and live in truth. I don't want to have secrets."

It went back and forth; I was still out of my body and felt like a robot.

Meeri had seen a lot of hypocrisy within 3HO. For example, he knew that one of the community leaders was married with children, even though he was homosexual. This frightened the young man. He did not want to become like this. Later he discovered more 3HO members were in similar situations. Yogi Bhajan forced homosexuals into arranged marriages with heterosexuals. Meeri did not want to follow that path.

Growing up, Yogi Bhajan was like a godlike figure to me. We were told he was a bridge to God and now he told me that "I want to get fucked in the ass" while I never kissed somebody. That was huge. I kept repeating that I wanted to live the truth.

Now, it took me a little while to find out what the truth was.

I was a lot in YB's vicinity, in his living room at the ranch, following his yoga classes, and during the gurdwara services. In those days, he spent much time in Española instead of in Los Angeles, where his other headquarters were. That's when I did these telepathic exercises, during which I tried to get him to hear my thoughts.

Even before I interacted with him personally, when I was younger, I connected with him on what they call the "etheric level." I am sure other yoga students can relate to this. I talked to Yogi Bhajan in my dreams, and he spoke to me. In that setting, my interactions with him were loving. He was like a grandfather wizard. He was light.

But in the physical setting, it was different. Then he cussed, he was brash, and he was a bully.

I was in India for eight years, so I understand Punjabi. One day I listened to this phone conversation. I heard him say in Punjabi, "If you fuck with me, I have connections to have your dead body float down the river."

At one point, I spent a whole summer at the ranch because I was babysitting Yogi Bhajan's grandchildren. It was interesting to have this personal and physical close-up with him. So, whenever I was around him, I played these mind games. I tried different internalized tones. I made fun of him. I told him he had no balls to see if that would catch his attention. But it didn't. I tried these bombastic things to challenge him to the limit. I wanted him to blink or signal that he heard what I was sending him telepathically. But he didn't.

It culminated in a specific moment when I sat in front of him and said (mentally), "Well, this is your last chance. I'm getting out of here and cutting my hair right now."

He didn't even look at me. He just kept talking. I got up, walked out of the room, took off my turban, braided my hair, cut it, put on my turban, and went back into the room. Nobody batted an eyelash.

Over time Yogi Bhajan said, in front of his company, "Oh Meeri, you're really becoming such a beautiful son of Guru Gobind Singh."

And I answered, "You can't see me." I even had the guts to say, "I don't trust you."

That's when he lost it. He slapped me hard in the face. My turban flew off, and everybody saw that I had cut hair. That happened when I had already decided to leave. I was just waiting for an opportunity to get out.

What makes me so angry is that everybody around me knew about my situation when I was eighteen. There was no support. It was a small community, and there was a lot of gossips. Everybody knew everybody's business. None of the older people in the community said to me, "Listen, I understand where you're coming from. I'm going to support you."

Hearing today that KRI is coming up with stupid statements in support of BIPOC and LGBTQ is so disingenuous. The best thing I heard was, "I love you even though you are gay." That was the best thing I could expect.

I did a lot of therapy to work through the shame and the guilt. I internalized many things because Yogi Bhajan told me personally that I would never be happy and that I would come home in a coffin. Really abusive things he said to me. But there is also the impact of society's view of me. How I swallowed it all and kept it inside of me. I said to myself, "I am little. I am less than."

GuruNischan acknowledges what he is saying. She emphasizes how the internalized shame is reinforced by the silence that was so loud. By not speaking out, the community was telling the mentally and physically abused children that they were wrong. Meeri nods affirmatively.

"Silence" was the loudest voice in the room. Talking about it in 2020 is cathartic, but it is also scary. Especially with 3HO as it stands now. It feels like you are screaming in the wind. No one is listening, really. The report of An Olive Branch, they just take it in and let it dissipate. I asked my mom how they were dealing with it. [Meeri's family is still in 3HO.] She said, "It's really a tough time for us." Her current husband does not even want to hear about it. It makes him physically ill. Other family members tell me these people who talk badly about Yogi Bhajan just want money. "None of the claims are verified." [169]

Meeri and GuruNischan conclude that the current 3HO support for BIPOC and LGBTQ is no more than a veneer and not enough to heal the deep and painful wounds of the past.

Closeted to Ourselves

We briefly met Mani Niall when he told us about 3HO members who ignored the lawsuits. His first contact with 3HO was when his sister married into it. He was twelve. At fifteen, he went to live in an ashram and moved between ashrams several times. Then in 1979, when he was eighteen, he landed in Los Angeles working for the Golden Temple restaurant and later opening Mani's Bakery.

GuruNischan calls him Uncle Mani because they are related by marriage, as are many people within 3HO. Mani wants to participate in the *Uncomfortable Conversations Podcast* to testify about how gay people were treated in 3HO's early years.

There were many of us, but we didn't know. We were in our own form of denial. A lesbian woman said some time ago that most of her friends in the early days were gay. I said, "Yeah, most of mine were too." But none of us knew it. There was this whole gay mafia, but we were closeted even to ourselves. We did not have the self-awareness that we were gay. I can say that "I knew it" since I was in seventh grade, but I had put it in a deep corner of my being.

One day we had a meeting with Yogi Bhajan with our restaurant team. He was doing his usual thing: being harsh to this person and friendly to this person. So, I went into this meeting as "Mister Open-Hearted."

And suddenly, out of the blue, he says to me, "So, do you want to be gay? You can do it, but you can't do it here. Well, you will be very good at it."

The floor was taken from under me. My grounding, my everything was fucking gone, just history! And you know what? I denied it, as gay as possible.

And then, there was this other meeting. My wife at that time was there too. She was afraid of him. I was more relaxed. He was my teacher, and he was awesome. He ripped me a new one. The first time he was not confrontational, he had said, "You can be gay. Just don't do it here." This time he blasted it out at me and totally validated all her fears.

He sent me to good old Hari Jiwan Singh [one of Yogi Bhajan's henchmen]. Hari Jiwan grilled me on my sex life and my masturbatory fantasies. Had I ever had sex with a girl in tenth grade before I got into 3HO? He went right for the jugular, and he would not stop. I just sat there answering his questions because my teacher wanted me to. And it was gross. It was debilitating, demeaning, and just not pleasant, but I did it. I answered all those questions. I'm sure he went to Yogi Bhajan and said, "This guy is gay."

I've heard from other people over the years that he called me a "fag" and said very, very, very derogatory, vivid, descriptive, bizarre sexual things about me. For what reason? I don't know. Several people tell me they heard him vividly querying them, "Did they see me do this? Did they see me . . ." What was his problem?[170]

How to Come Out of It

On several occasions, Yogi Bhajan made inappropriate and harsh statements about gay people. He did this while several of his secretaries testified that he forced them to have sex with each other, sometimes in front of his eyes.

As early as December 1974, during a lecture at the winter solstice event, he said:

What do you think of people who considers themselves as gay? They have lost happiness temporarily. Gay and a lesbian, I don't put it down, but I want you immediately to come out of it. Because it's a, it's a misconnection in the polarity relationship. I know those who are gay, I interviewed one of their, I have a "Yogi Bhajan show" in Los Angeles and I got chief of the gay center on my interview. He was the most clever person I have ever interviewed. He will say "your worship, your holiness," you know what he reminded me through this? Mean men be holy don't ask me any weird question, so what should I do?

Those who call themselves gay or lesbians are those who unfortunately could not have right kind of experience in relationship. And you know sometimes you have a kind of relationship somewhere and you want to stick to it. But the best way if a gay wants to come out of it all he has to tell himself it's a matter of the past. I am not this. I am not this. In forty days, he can totally cure himself, and Los Angeles many have now normal relationships. But they are now so many, you know, one day they may have a president like that what am I going to do?[171]

The audience laughed.

Six years later, in 1980, at the women's camp in Española, he said, "There is a very common saying and I like to translate that for you, no man is born faggot, it is the mother who made him."[172]

In July 1988, Bhajan told a story of a woman he was counseling and with whom he had a conflict. She had gone to the barber shop and had cut her hair and made her son and husband cut their hair too. Bhajan said:

She walks around there with a great pride. But do you see a woman who is a mother and who has this kind of venom and this kind of clutch control system what she is producing? And how that child will ever grow to be a full-fledged normal male? Gays don't come from the Earth and bounce back from the heaven and come back as gay. This is not true. Parents make them. Parents affect children very deeply and undermine their future and prosperity extremely well.[173]

You and You, Get Married

Former 3HO members say that Yogi Bhajan arranged over five hundred marriages. Peter Blachly, the musician, remembers how it went in

August 1971, at the end of a ten-day Tantric Yoga course at his ashram in Washington, DC. That was shortly after Peter had experienced his first Tantric Yoga at the summer solstice event at Paonia.

> Towards the end of the ninth day, he asked several of the Ashram members—both from our own Ashram and from other cities—to stand up. He looked the group over for a few seconds, then started matching men and women up in couples. All the rest of us looked on and cheered. This was great fun! Within a few minutes, Yogiji had "engaged" three new couples—men and women who had never even met before—and announced that they would get married the next day. We believed that was a master who could see our auras and read our destinies. No one was better qualified to make spiritually appropriate matches. The chosen couples looked at each other and gulped.
>
> A similar match-up, but on a much larger scale, had just occurred in Paonia. About a dozen couples had left Paonia in brand new marriages.[174]

The AOB report mentioned that girls of nineteen years old were put into arranged marriages with men who were twenty-two to twenty-three years older. They were like gifts to people with money or to boost new business relationships. "We were like tokens," one woman said. Someone else testified in the AOB report that Bhajan used forced marriages to manipulate his students. Couples who were ill-suited for each other would be more loyal to him. "You had to circle your whole life around Yogi Bhajan. When he said, 'Sneeze,' you sneezed. When he said, 'Get divorced,' you did it. It was all a loyalty requirement."[175]

Miscarriage? Your Own Fault

It was a hot summer day on July 22, 1983, at the women's camp in the high desert of Española. The participants had gathered to listen to Yogi Bhajan. There is no video, only a voice recording available of this lecture.

YB. Hey! How many girls lost pregnancy?

[*The students mutter something.*]

Oh, that's all? Not many. Well. This year is a nonpregnant year, kind of. And now, somebody tells you the summer was hot, that's why you couldn't . . .

[*Again, the students are telling him things we cannot hear.*]

In Sahara, people give birth every month, you know.

[*The students laugh.*]

It's pretty hot. . . . This is a problem I am seeing among our teachers and students. So many hotchpotches are being said and done . . . Somebody was saying because there are exercises going on, therefore, people are losing pregnancy. Now how many people lose pregnancy because of exercise in the whole United States? Now, who is going to believe this?

[*Something is happening that we cannot see. The students are laughing. A bang follows.*]

Yeah, this is psychological that you want to be beaten up and insulted. That's what I was teaching: people want to be raped. Nobody rapes anybody. People want to be beaten up. A lot of people I have seen, they need sex after being beaten up. Yeah, that's the one simple thing. They provoke their husband, boyfriends, and whatever it is to the point that there is always a fight. A terrible fight, and the reconciliation of that fight is sex. They enjoy it.

There are a lot of things in us for which sometimes we are aware, and we do this, and sometimes we are not. But summer was not hot enough to cause pregnancy, miscarriage. Summers are never hot enough, and no summer dries up the hormones.

[*The students laugh.*]

Somebody should tell her. What's her name? Avtar Kaur? Give her my message. You know why most miscarriages happen? Give me your opinion.

[*Students answer all at once: emotional, hormones, . . .*]

Mostly, mostly it is the uterus and the strength of the uterus. But the strength of the uterus depends on your nervous system too. And a lot of diseases are because of stress. And Avtar Kaur is insecure about her career. Her career got her the abortion. If she wants to hear the truth, ask the damn person to feel it and understand and stand up truthfully and let me discuss with her.

[*It seems Avtar has been spotted in the audience. Bhajan calls out to her.*]

Stand up, Avtar Kaur. Let me tear you apart. Are you not a behavior bitch to yourself? And did you, were [you] not honestly insecure about this pregnancy, and you never wanted this child? What about your career? How much you thought about it? How much you stress yourself?

AVTAR. I didn't feel like I cared about it . . .

[*We can only hear her voice from afar, very faintly.*]

YB. Consciously or subconsciously? Child is not a game, baby. Child don't come to those who use child as escape. Child comes to those who, as a mother, wants them. Motherhood is not a profession. It's a total indulgence and total sacrifice. You hear from me. You think you can manipulate everything? One thing you can never manipulate is pregnancy. If God let you manipulate pregnancy, then the entire kingdom of God will fall apart. Now tell, tell me truthfully how you receive pregnancy? In your own words, loud and clear. Once. One chance to be honest.

AVTAR. I prayed for . . . [*Yogi Bhajan interrupts her and yells.*]

YB. Prayed for? I don't want to hear! I am not up to these gimmicks. Talk to me professionally! I'm reading your aura. Don't lie to me! Stand up to me, dumb! Put your hands together down. Stand as a human being. No. Not folding of the hands. Nothing. Stand straight. Now confront.

AVTAR. I wanted to have a child. . .

YB. You wanted to have a child. That is true. Everybody knows that. Otherwise, you would not have spread your legs. Come on.

[*The students laugh.*]

YB. Come on now. Let us debate it out at the level you are at. Come on.

AVTAR. I don't want to tell . . .

YB. I don't want you to tell me anything. I will fix you. Come on. This is one day I want to clean you out "confrontingly." I am sick of it. You wanted a child. Then what?

AVTAR. And I thought everything was fine.

YB. And you got it, right? And then, what you started thinking? Come on.

AVTAR. I thought it was perfect . . .

YB. Perfect, ah, ha, hey, hey, wait a minute, N O P, that won't work.

The rough and senseless dialogue continued for a while.[176]
A woman who was there witnessing the whole thing wrote in 2020:

He had her stand up and blasted her right when she returned from the hospital. He was basically saying that it was all her fault. He was being abnormally abusive to a woman who had just had a miscarriage. The thing that makes me really sad is that I never really told anybody that I witnessed this. And I didn't stand up for her as a woman and a sister. We all should have stood up for her. Nobody stood up for her because we would all be in his trance. It's very, very sad.[177]

Avtar Kaur was the 3HO spiritual name of Tara Brach, a psychologist, writer, and leading teacher of meditation, emotional healing, and spiritual awakening. At a workshop she organized in 2019, she recounted what had happened to her that day in 1983. She shared what Yogi Bhajan's brutal attack right after her miscarriage had brought about in her. She used this old 3HO memory to introduce a reflection on "fear thinking." On the day of the incident, Tara had been a devoted member of the 3HO–Sikh Dharma community for eight years. She had hoped to find a spiritual awakening there.

I was twenty-eight. I was at a gathering of our spiritual community [3HO]. Two days before, I had had a miscarriage. It was very hot outside, and we had been doing a lot of exercise. I was worried that maybe the heat of the desert had caused it. That was mentioned to the spiritual teacher. In a gathering of a couple hundred people, Yogi Bhajan had me stand up. In front of everybody, he basically blamed me for losing the child.

He said, "You were willing to have sex, but your ego just wanted to work. You're selfish. You didn't really care about having a child. That killed the child."

As you can hear, that's abuse. Over the next few days, I was devastated because this was my community, and this was my teacher. I spent hours in this little gurdwara, a one-person Sikh temple. I was meditating and praying. It came down to "Do I believe his condemnation of my personal badness?" And remember, in the hierarchy, he had a lot of power. He was a male. He was at the top of the hierarchy—a lot of authority. What he said tapped into my already existing identity of "bad self." My shame around being a driven person, self-centered, egocentric, and ambitious, and all the things I didn't like myself for.

So, I was like, "Well, wait a minute. Is it true? Am I bad?"

I meditated a lot, and the process that really turned me towards healing was this: from all the swirls of "I'm bad," "Am I bad?" or "How could this happen? He wouldn't have done it if there wasn't something wrong with me," I made kind of a U-turn. I said, "OK. Stop the thinking."

I went to my heart. I knew that all I could do was to be with the waves. I had to go under the thoughts, to the waves of hurt and grief, around betrayal, anger, and shame. So, the process was: to drop the "fear thinking" and just go directly into the rawness of the waves. In that presence, a quality of self-compassion and tenderness emerged that became so filled with light. So full. It was so tender and big that I realized this was who I was. That was more true than any of the stories either of us, he or I, were telling me about myself. So, the after-the-RAIN was that I just stayed a long time in that presence.

RAIN is an acronym Tara Brach uses in her teachings to indicate a four-step process: Recognize difficult emotions. Allow them to be there. Investigate them with curiosity. And finally: Nurture them with love.

> I kept saying to myself, "This is it. Just rest in this. Just rest in this."
>
> Forgiveness became possible because it was just as limiting to stay in the abuse-victim story as it was to anything else. It wasn't because "Oh, he deserves to be forgiven." It was just for the freedom of my own heart.
>
> And now I can look at him and see a being that's very mixed (he's not alive anymore), but him being driven by his own demons and whatever. So, I left the community and warned others because I didn't want anyone treated that way. So, it was ultimately empowering and, at the time, devastating. I share it because it had everything to do with the seeds of genuine trust.
>
> Not that I won't cause harm and haven't caused harm, but that compassionate presence, that openness, wakefulness, and tenderness are more the truth of who I am than any of the waves.[178]

Power Was His Game

We have already looked at various stories from Siri's life. But what about his love life?

After five years of schooling in India, Siri returned to the US and began working for Akal Security. This was before Yogi Bhajan sent him back to India to care for a hundred children.

> I lived in Española when I was twenty-two. I dated a woman who lived in another city. In Española, an eighteen-year-old girl had a crush on me. Her name was Jiwan. The Siri Singh Sahib had engaged her when she was ten to someone she did not want to marry. One night, temptation got the better of me. I made out with her. People found out. The Siri Singh Sahib said, "That's it. You marry Jiwan."

My girlfriend had to marry someone else. I was shell-shocked, ashamed, and disappointed in my own behavior. I called my girlfriend.

She said, "Well, this is how it must be. I'm going to marry this guy. You marry that girl."

Yogi Bhajan had gotten hold of my girlfriend for days. He told her stories about all the women I had slept with. All lies. Those stories broke her down. Jiwan was happy because she got what she wanted. She was eighteen, so I am not judging her harshly for that. My girlfriend and the other guy got married. That was done.

Siri did not want to marry Jiwan. He kept saying "No" every time they asked him. Because they kept insisting, he finally did it. Yogi Bhajan forced him to do something that every fiber of his being resisted. It broke him. He felt worthless.

My life was not my own. My desires were not my own. My wants were not my own. I saw it as my lot in life. I did not love my wife. I went into marriage like, "Well, fine, I have to marry you. That does not mean that I have to like it. Don't call me your husband. I'm not calling you my wife. 'You want dinner?' 'No, I'll make my own if I want some.'" I was so shitty to Jiwan, she didn't deserve it, as it was not her fault.

If only someone in my childhood had told me, "Own every decision you make. If somebody tells you to do something, evaluate it. Then decide and look at it as your decision." How different would it have been if I had said, "All right, sir. I hear what you say, and I agree with that." How powerful is it to say, "I agree with that, I will do this, and I own this." But it was different, it was about "You obey."

And so, you know what? FUCK him. I can forgive him. That's for my healing so I can move on. I'm forgiving for selfish reasons. But it was not cool. I was not the only one he did that to. And it wasn't just over marriages, who you slept with, your business, or whatever else.

POWER was his game. MANIPULATION was his game. . . .

Several years into the marriage, I had an affair. That got found out. The Siri Singh Sahib called the young woman into his living room, saying, "You choose him, or you choose me. If you choose him, I'll never speak to you again, and neither will your family."

He isolated her on the ranch and started raping her a year later. I found out about that six years ago. I threw up. Do you think I don't bear some fucking responsibility for what happened to her? Do you think I don't carry some guilt for that?

I'll tell you something else. My parents divorced when I was five. When I was seventeen, my dad started coming around. My parents began talking and wanted to get back together. They were eighth-grade sweethearts. My dad missed her. He was never a Sikh but had a lot of Sikh friends. He met the Siri Singh Sahib.

He said, "I have no problem with the religion, but I'm not wearing the uniform."

The Siri Singh Sahib told my mom not to get back together with my dad. That was kind of shitty too. Who knows what would have happened. I'm not saying that they would have lived happily ever after. But what kid doesn't want their parents to get back together? It's like, "Who are you to mess with free will? Who are you to take that away?"[179]

EXPLOITATION, FRAUD, DRUGS, WEAPONS, AND MURDER

Doing Business in a Cult

It Was All His Thing

SatHanuman was born in New England. In his early twenties, he discovered Kundalini Yoga, and in 1972 he joined a 3HO ashram. He worked for the Golden Temple restaurant in Washington from five in the morning to eleven at night. At the end of his shift, he cleaned up so that everything looked spotless and would pass inspection. Then he slept for three hours, took a cold shower, did yoga, and started preparing vegetables and playing waiter again. "That was called teacher training," he says as he laughs from beneath his nicely fitted burgundy turban that matches his shirt and contrasts with his thin white long beard while being interviewed by GuruNischan.

His first marriage was an arranged marriage. He and his family moved from ashram to ashram, sometimes on their own initiative but often at the request of ashram leaders or Bhajan.

SatHanuman's first commercial success was in 1975. He had been sent to Boston to work for the Golden Temple Emporium. The store was in an expensive neighborhood right across the street from Harvard University and sold a lot of junk, such as shells and plants. When he arrived in the shop, he looked around, found fifteen pairs of Birkenstocks in the back room and started selling those. Out of that first initiative grew a quality shoe company. It went from one store making $100 a day in 1976 to $5,000 a day just a few years later. The shop was community-owned, and SatHanuman earned $200 a week. He was promised a management position but never got it.

His talent as a salesman was soon recognized inside and outside the community. He became a regional sales manager. By building trust and good relationships, his success grew. In the early years, the sales managers in 3HO worked as independent salespeople. Thirty percent of their commission went directly to Yogi Bhajan. SatHanuman's business contacts told him he would be better off investing this money to expand his business, but he was loyal to his teacher.

In 1992, after almost twenty years of marriage, SatHanuman divorced his first wife. He married his current wife, with whom he had a perfect business partnership. By that time, the business model of the 3HO companies had to change due to legal issues. In 1993, holding companies were established, and from then on, salespeople became employees.

SatHanuman juggles strange-sounding names of 3HO products, companies, and holdings and recounts anecdote after anecdote about the frequent changes in the structure of the 3HO business wing. Calling his exposé during this interview a roller coaster is too weak an expression.

He relates that the Siri Singh Sahib had another title yet to be mentioned: the Chief Management Authority, a title reflecting his aspiration to conquer the world with his companies. With Yogi Tea, he has certainly achieved that goal.

"But above all," says SatHanuman, "it was all HIS thing."

He would take it to the level that satisfied HIS needs. The rest of us—we were paid dirt wages. A true business leader should give his people a fair salary and provide abilities to grow. Like in other companies, let people come up for review and give them a raise. Do you know how many reviews I got in sixteen years? One. They may have done it for people they hired who were not part of 3HO but not with us. While we did the pioneering work.

I'll give you one example of how we made a business grow. Clif Bar hired us in 1996. They had four bars. The existing monthly commission on the East Coast was $5,000. When my wife and I left in 2002, the monthly commission was between $75,000 and $100,000. When you have all those eggs in your basket, you're not paying the people who pioneered all that? And we had forty companies we represented, among which were big companies like Annie's Homegrown Pasta, Kettle Chips, and Organic Valley family farms. This last one started with a hundred farms, and we helped them grow to two thousand farms.

So, the businesses were thriving, and we were paid dirt wages. We brought in $200,000 in commissions per month, saw it all going to KIIT [the Khalsa International Industries and Trades company, kiit.com], and we were paid . . .

[*He doesn't say how much, but he shakes his head to make clear it was not a fair amount.*] Moreover, between 1986 and the mid-1990s, we had no insurance, no retirement plan, nothing. After that, they realized they had to treat us like Golden Temple and Yogi Tea employees.

GuruNischan. Because there are employment laws, right?

SatHanuman. Yes, they were legitimately a business that had to go by the law. By real laws. [*They both laugh.*]

SatHanuman talks about the incompetence of business management in the same way as Siri described the lack of professionalism in the school program in India and the flaws in the operational management of Akal Security. "Things were not set up to work properly," Siri had said. SatHanuman confirms this.

I just kept trying to plug holes, but they didn't want me to do any-thing above a certain level because they knew I would stand up for things and challenge matters if they weren't right.

My wife and I left in 2002. Not even a year later, the holding company we worked for folded. Their biggest egg, Clif Bar, left them after seven years. If you take out that trust factor, you can only "do smoke and mirror" for so long.

When SatHanuman started his own business, his former 3HO bosses had made certain that none of his past business partners would want to work with him. That was painful, as he had built good relation-ships with them over the years. He had to start all over again, from scratch.

Now I see that YB was using everybody. He was a master at manip-ulating. Keeping circles, within circles, within circles, within cir-cles, . . . So, this guy over here didn't know what this guy over there was doing and da-da-da. He was really good at that. He had that energy that he could . . . [*SatHanuman gestures with his arms in front of him, indicating that Yogi Bhajan could rule over them all.*]

Looking back now, we say, "Who would even listen to that?" . . .

Let me tell you what happened when my grandmother first saw him. She came to a lecture together with my mother. My mother thought Yogi Bhajan was pretty neat.

My grandmother said, "No, no, he's not. He's a con man."

She was on to him, in her eighties, and I was in my twenties.

I was like, "Grandma, come on."

SatHanuman's blinders fell off in March 2020 when his eldest daughter Sat Pavan, yes, that Sat Pavan, told him what had happened to her. Until then, he had defended the Siri Singh Sahib. He had forgiven Yogi Bhajan's shortcomings because of his many good deeds.

Now his daughter had made him realize the abuse was far greater than he had ever realized. A friend advised SatHanuman to listen to different episodes of the *Uncomfortable Conversations Podcast* of GuruNischan. So, he began to listen to the stories of second-generation adults and others. He contacted peers with whom he had lived in various ashrams. Some, like him, started seeing and recognizing the huge discrepancy between Yogi Bhajan's words and actions. But others continued to deny it and went after those who told the stories in a not-very-nice way, as SatHanuman calls it.

> It was the devotion that kept us so blinded. Back in 1972, I was at a three-day weekend intensive at the Orlando ashram. We were chanting to Guru Ram Das.[180] The person leading the chant with his guitar turned to me and said, "Everybody here thinks we are chanting to Guru Ram Das. I think we are really praying to Yogi Bhajan." In other words, he IS the Guru. I put that in the back of my mind. Remember, he always said, "I am not a guru. I am the teacher."
>
> I've spoken to other people who have come to this realization. In those days, who thought that we were in a cult? Who thought that? People who left probably, like Premka and others who left. But the rest of us who kept going weren't thinking that way.
>
> I wasn't thinking that way before March 2020. I was thinking in terms of the legacy of this great teacher. I mean, he has a Highway in New Mexico named after him. A hundred percent of Congress honored him when he died. He was this great yogi, right?[181]

Happy Worker Bees

At one point, the 2022 Vice documentary shows an image of at least a hundred people dressed in white, standing close together on a large field. With their arms stretched above their heads, they bend their upper bodies forward and backward at a hasty pace, chanting a hurried *Sa Ta Na Ma Sa Ta Na Ma*. Yogi Bhajan sits on a throne and surveys his dis-orderly moving crowd. The Vice reporter says: "By 1984, summer sol-stice celebrations at Ram Das Puri in New Mexico are in full swing. It's been fourteen years since Yogi Bhajan first arrived in the US, and 3HO is now running more than a hundred ashrams worldwide. But as its influence grows, so does the need for money to sustain the ashrams and their recruitment drive."

It then shows a map of cities around the world where ashrams are located.

"Businesses could be set up quickly because there were many worker bees available worldwide," says Tej Steiner. "Happy worker bees," he adds. Yogi Tea became the number-one herbal tea in the United States in three years.

"That was us," says Pamela in the documentary. "That was the people. The entrepreneurial spirit of all of us."[182]

Dirty Security Business

GuruTej Singh was a devoted student of YB who had studied martial arts, among other things. In 1980, he started the company Akal Security in Santa Fe.[183] As it became successful over the years, Yogi Bhajan stepped in and took control from GuruTej. Bhajan had a bigger vision and used his political savvy and connections to win big government contracts. For many years, Akal Security guarded US courthouses, large government buildings, Homeland Security buildings, embassies, airports, and immigrant detention centers.

On August 27, 2018, Philip Tanzer wrote the well-documented article on issues with Akal Security. He reported that Akal earned $113 million in 2017, mostly from federal contracts.

One topic Tanzer looked at, was Akal's involvement in the child separation policy applied to refugees at the southern border of the US with Mexico.[184] ICE, the Immigration and Customs Enforcement agency, worked for the Trump administration that introduced a zero-tolerance immigration policy in the spring of 2018. It was a hot topic in the media. Akal Security had worked with ICE for twenty years, so questions were raised about their involvement in executing Trump's policy.

Many yogis shuddered at the idea that their spiritual practice was partly funded by dirty money. Under the lead of a Kundalini Yoga teacher from Los Angeles, concerned community members started asking questions at the Siri Singh Sahib Corporation (SSSC) overseeing all profits and nonprofits. Instead of getting more clarity, more questions arose. Informative YouTube videos were created[185] and a petition was launched in July 2018 titled "Tell Akal to Sever Ties with ICE."[186] The petitions' goals were: "to immediately divest from all ICE contracts and subcontracts" and "to establish a system of full transparency by which members of the community can evaluate our funding sources."

More than a year later, on August 21, 2019, the SSSC released a statement—no longer traceable today—announcing they would no longer bid on federal ICE contracts. The petition organizers responded with following statement on their website:

> After more than a year of relentless effort of the part of petition organizers and advocates, we are pleased to read the statement. . . . While we remain troubled by any ongoing connection between our community and human detention, we acknowledge the meaningful action steps outlined in the statement. . . . we believe maintaining any link to ICE keeps us complicit in the injustice of the prison-industrial complex and family separation. We continue to pursue the goals of our petition. . . .[187]

Tanzer pointed out in his article, that this SSSC statement meant little, as Akal Security had worked as a subcontractor on these projects since 2001.

Directly or indirectly, Akal monitored ICE detention centers in several states since 2002, and they executed deportation strategies. Through these ICE detention centers, Akal was also able to save thousands, if not millions of dollars, by using detainees as a pool of cheap labor. Tanzer copies in his article, an Akal Voluntary Work Program Agreement for one of their detention centers. From the five-page-long standard ICE agreement,[188] they copied and adapted two paragraphs to create the

Akal agreement. They even had the guts to put a link to the ICE document at the bottom, as if this concoction was the official version. The less-than-half-a-page Akal agreement read:

> Detainees that participate in the volunteer work program will not be permitted to work in excess of 8 hours daily or 40 hours weekly.
>
> Detainees that participate in the volunteer work program are required to work according to an assigned work schedule and to participate in all work-related training. Unexcused absence from work or unsatisfactory work performance could result in removal from the voluntary work program. Detainees must adhere to all safety regulations and to all medical and grooming standards associated with the work assignment. Compensation shall be $1.00 per day.

The text in the standard ICE agreement reads: "at least $1.00 (USD) per day."

In addition to the disgusting profits made through detention centers, Tanzer cites lawsuits filed by Akal employees in 2016, 2017, and 2019 for alleged violations of law related to minimum wage and overtime pay. Many more irregularities related to Akal Security are denounced in this revealing article.

Stealing of Intellectual Property

In 1986, KartaPurkh sued Bhajan not only for sexual abuse but also for exploitation and theft of intellectual property. Her lawsuit claimed that she worked thousands of hours for Bhajan's organizations and businesses for a salary far below the legal minimum with no compensation for overtime, and she missed out on ten years of education and career opportunities.

In addition to that, she developed a line of natural hair and skin products for the Oriental Beauty Secrets division of Khalsa Sunshine, a 3HO company. Yogi Bhajan promised her a ten percent ownership interest in that division and a seat on the board in return for her cosmetics formulas. To protect herself financially, she went to see the chief legal officer (chancellor) of the 3HO Foundation, who drew up and signed documents that assured KartaPurkh all would be fine. In October 1983, she handed over her formulas. Marketing began in 1984 and continued for at least a few more years. She was never given a stake in Oriental Beauty Secrets or a board seat. Instead, Bhajan kept her formulas, got all the profits, and KartaPurkh was left with nothing.

When she realized that in December 1984, she protested vehemently to a legal officer of the 3HO Foundation. She presented the agreements signed by Yogi Bhajan and the assistant chancellor. These turned out to be false. Bhajan and the chancellor knew this.

And there was more. On Yogi Bhajan's request, she developed recipes for candy bars. Next to a salary and an expense allowance, she was to get a share in Golden Temple Bakery and a fee for each candy bar sold. In fact, she received $300 a month for a year's travel expenses. That was it.

The third business fraud involved her biscuit recipes for Nanak Cookie Company. If her recipes were successful, she would become a partner in the company and receive a percentage of the profits. The biscuits, Lemon Up, Ginger Zam, Paradise Pistachio, and Raisin Oats, were developed, produced, and sold. She had been working on them for seven months, and there was no pay.[189]

Tax Evasion

It was mentioned before how the presence of the religious nonprofit Sikh Dharma International kept prying eyes at bay and allowed other entities linked to the 3HO–Sikh Dharma community to take advantage of the beneficial tax schemes. Pamela Dyson shared, "Yogi Bhajan had a letter go out suggesting to people that they put their houses and their ashrams in the organization's name. This was useful for cheating with property taxes and the like. And all would be secured for the future generations."

KartaPurkh's court case alleges that the chancellor's office of the Siri Singh Sahib Corporation mailed instructions to all affiliated companies on what they needed to do to obtain tax-free status. Private properties were put in the organization's name, so they could use them tax-free, and Bhajan would ultimately control everything.

Generous Donations

In addition to income from his profit-making companies, Yogi Bhajan collected money in many other ways. Tej Steiner attested, "We were always donating money to him. And he received tremendous funds for the yoga he taught and from personal donations. Yogi Bhajan was fascinated with wealth. He traveled, and there was always private luxury around. Most of us were hippies. We loved simplicity."[190]

In 1985, the *Santa Fe Journal* published an article about people who had left 3HO. One interviewee claimed to have donated $90,000. Another gave $30,000 for the construction of the gurdwara in Española. Yogi Bhajan had led them to believe that all the land and property belonged to the community. In fact, they came into the private hands of the yogi.[191]

And then, there is the story of how the 150 acres (61 hectares) of land, named Ram Das Puri, came into Bhajan's hands. For a long time, a myth circulated, it went like this: according to the native people of the land, the Hopi elders, people in white clothes would come. They were the saviors of the world. The elders believed that Yogi Bhajan and his followers were those people. They had arrived![192]

We know by now that Gigi, formerly Guru Gun Kaur, who bought the land, "donated" it to the community. In 1977, Gigi received a $1.3 million inheritance from an uncle. When Yogi Bhajan heard this, he started influencing Gigi behind her husband's back. One day, Bhajan invited Gigi over, showed her a map and asked her to choose between a piece of land in Colorado or "this land here." He pointed to a plot of land near Española. She chose the latter.

Gigi's mother tried to stop her daughter from spending her inheritance money this way. She wanted Gigi to be declared mentally ill and hospitalized. She went to court to do that, and several hearings were organized, but her daughter never showed up. On October 7, 1977, an article in *The New Mexican Journal* read: "The mother blamed the 3HO organization for the alleged mental illness of her daughter. 'I believe that because of the undue influence this 3HO organization has had upon her, there has been a tremendous and drastic change in her personality. . . .'"[193]

Two days later, *The New Mexican* printed an update titled, "Sought Sikh Woman 'in India.'" Gigi's lawyer, G.T.S. Khalsa, a 3HO member, had told the judge, "She's on tour with 125 Americans to the Sikh temples of India. They're expected back sometime in November." He added that to his knowledge, Gigi never contributed to the 3HO organization as the mother had claimed. Instead, she "made the donation to the 'Siri Singh Sahib of the Sikh Dharma Brotherhood,' the Corporation Sole of Yogi Bhajan, rather than the 3HO organization. . . . 'It's the same as if she had contributed to the Catholic Church,' said Khalsa."

The judge closed the case. No investigation was possible because Gigi was absent.[194]

On June 22, 2022, Gigi explained to GuruNischan that she had been in India when the first hearing was held. On her way home, her husband had been waiting for her at a stopover in New York.

> He said, "We can't go home. Your mother is trying to deprogram you."
>
> I didn't believe it was true until last year [2021]. My niece and I hadn't talked to each other for probably thirty-five years. She told me that her father, my brother, was involved in an attempt to "deprogram" me.
>
> Anyway, on my return from India, I was not allowed to go home. The next day, my husband put me on a plane to London. I was pretty shattered because, after India, you want to come home and decompress in your own space. Instead, I had to go to an ashram in London. I didn't know anybody there and had to stay for eight months.[195]

Ram Das Puri was the name Yogi Bhajan gave to the land, "Puri" being his birth name. To this day, it is the central meeting place for the international 3HO–Sikh Dharma family. Gigi never received any return, payments, or income from the millions of dollars 3HO generated from Ram Das Puri. Gigi has been homeless and living out of her van for several years.[196]

Fraud—Fraud—Fraud

Organized Crime Family

This is the story of Guru Bir Singh and Gur Siri Kaur as they shared it with GuruNischan. For simplicity reasons, we decided earlier in this book to call them Bir and Gur. They informed us about the zeitgeist of the 1960s and 1970s and why moving into an ashram in those days felt so good.

Bir and Gur met in college, where they did yoga together. In 1974, they went to live in the Honolulu ashram, where Yogi Bhajan gave them their spiritual names. A year later, they married and had two children. After seven years in Hawaii, they moved to Los Angeles and later to Northern California, where they lived when this story hit them. Bir and Gur were faithful members of the 3HO–Sikh Dharma community for eighteen years. Bir recounts:

> In April 1992, we were in Los Angeles to meet the 3HO family. I saw the Siri Singh Sahib talking to Kirpal Singh. A bit later, Kirpal came to see me. He said he was reorganizing a business he was running for Yogi Bhajan and asked me if I could help them out for about a week. Everybody was in good moods and spirits in Los Angeles. I had no idea that would be the last time I would speak to my spiritual teacher of eighteen years. I had no clue, really.
>
> We returned home to Northern California. A few days later, I was in my office. Gur was there too. Suddenly, I saw a bunch of

detectives and the assistant district attorney, the ADA, of California coming through my office door. They made sure that my wife was separated from me, and we were cornered so we couldn't run out of the door. We had no clue what was going on. I told the ADA that none of this made sense to me. The funny thing is that the office phone rang. But, of course, they were not letting me pick it up or move. The answering machine picked it up. It was Kirpal Singh who left an interesting message while five detectives and the assistant district attorney were listening. They unplugged the answering machine and took it with them.

I didn't know what this was about. I asked the ADA if I needed an attorney because I couldn't figure out where the questioning was going. It got more intense, more intense.

So, long story short, I went to the office of my corporate attorney.

He looked at my face and said, "Oh my God, Bir, what's going on?"

I said, "I don't know."

I told him the little I knew, that I had five detectives and the ADA in my office.

"Are you being arrested?" he asked.

I said, "I don't know, but they're right behind me."

He got on the phone and called a criminal attorney. The detectives walked into his office and said, "Yes, he's under arrest." They handcuffed me. They talked on the phone to the man who would become my attorney. So, they took me to jail, and that's how it all started.

That night, on the local news, breaking news on television, was my case. "This man is arrested." I forgot what they said I was arrested for because I didn't know what I was arrested for. [*Bir points to his wife sitting next to him.*] She didn't know what I was arrested for. We were only hearing it from the newspapers and the television. In the morning, my picture was on the front page. So, we had to read the story to try to get an idea or a glimpse. That kind of messed things up a little bit. My business closed, my wife's employer terminated her contract, and our kids were bullied at school. So, it kind of went downhill really fast.

I called my spiritual teacher [Yogi Bhajan], who always told us, "Look, if there's ever a problem, do not walk but run over here. I will be there for you."

Well, there was a problem, so I called him.

They said, "He's not talking to you. He's not taking your call."

I sent letters, telegrams, FedEx, anything I could, but I've never talked to him since then. A year later, I tried again and was told, "He doesn't want you to scream and yell at him." I wasn't going to scream and yell at him!

There was an awful lot at the beginning that I didn't know. I was a little naive about what the heck was going on, not knowing at that time that he and Kirpal knew something was going on with their "business," which was the Canadian Lottery scam.

Somehow, they thought, "Well, let's stick Bir in the middle. Let's go stick him in this and see what happens."

GuruNischan asks Gur how it was for her. What happened to her?

First of all, I want to say that the raid was highly traumatic. It was a shock. We didn't see it coming. We had no clue that somebody was coming to arrest my husband. I call it a raid because that's what it was. As my husband said, our office was infiltrated, and we were separated. We were both drilled with tape recorders on. They were trying to get information and get proof of what had come down the pike.

Honestly, we were as innocent as could be. We had no clue what they were talking about. We thought we were doing a favor to our spiritual teacher. That was all we knew. Once my husband was arrested and taken to jail, I knew that the truth would have to prevail. So, I was holding that within myself, "Somehow, the truth is going to come out eventually."

One of the things I did was I dressed myself up in street clothes, which were just regular clothes. I took off my turban, combed my hair down, and curled it. I took off all other Sikh uniform stuff, which was unusual for me then. I dressed in a professional suit with an attaché to look like an American corporate person. I went down to the county courthouse, entered, and showed my ID as if I belonged there. By the way, I had no clue what I was doing. I was just determined to figure out what this case was about. I was very focused and one-pointed. I had a tremendous amount of faith that there would be some revelations to prove my husband was innocent. I wasn't going to be a bystander. I was going to be a participant in ensuring he was proven innocent. My children were young. Our whole life was at stake here.

So, I went down to the courthouse, swung open the doors, and walked right to the back where all the files were. Just acting as if I had done it a million times when honestly, I was using my intuition to figure out where those files would be. I went through all the different case files and finally found my husband's case. On the cover was his name and what he was being charged with. It was a mindblower, like fraud and embezzlement and all these things. I opened the folder and out poured letters, like twenty to thirty letters. Various people in the dharma had written letters! They stated that my husband was the ringleader of this fraud. These were the people we raised our children with, we went to worship with them! People we trusted. We pretty much grew up together, you know. Some letters came from Yogi Bhajan's inner circle, but many came from just ordinary 3HO people. Later I heard that Yogi Bhajan had gone to the women's camp. He had ordered these women to write these letters saying my husband was the mastermind of this Canadian Lottery scam, and Kirpal was duped by him!

It was just one more layer of trauma. We had just gone through the trauma of the raid, and now this! The very community we had devoted our lives to was writing these letters!

I thought, *Oh my gosh, now he's got people saying that they know firsthand that he had committed these crimes.* The ante on his chances of being sent to federal prison was just raised. His imprisonment was supposed to be between eight and ten years of his life. I was in shock reading those letters. I had no way to copy them. We didn't have cell phones back then. So, I took notes to get as much information as I could. With all this information, my husband's attorney figured out what was happening. Until then, nobody had told us what was going on.

Yogi Bhajan wouldn't speak to us. After having free reign for almost twenty years, we could walk in anytime and talk with him without an appointment. That's the relationship we thought we had with him. And now, all of a sudden, persona non grata.

The attorney was grateful because this info gave him something to go on. He could start building a case that proved that my husband was innocent. Yes. That was "my day" when I played detective and was in disguise. I said, there is no way I'm letting my husband take the fall for whatever this thing is. For the pure heart he had and the great guy he was. And my children, he was my children's father. I couldn't let anything happen.

[*Bir takes over here.*]

My attorney called the police. They let me out on my own recognizance. My wife and I went to see him. It was two days after my arrest. He kept asking me if I knew who Gurujot Singh was and what my business with him was.

I told him, "Well, I could identify him. I could point him out in a crowd, but I've never really talked to him. My attorney had never met me. He did not know me, so he questioned me several times. And then, he turned his computer towards us. On his screen was Gurujot's arrest and the whole thing about the drug smuggling incident. He still didn't know me from Adam or what my involvement was, but he got on top of everything. Later the ADA told me he was the best attorney in the county I could have gotten.

When we were still in his office, he asked, "Do you have any pets?"

We said, "We've got two German shepherds."

"Well, here's what I'm going to tell you. The police are probably going to raid your house, looking for evidence. It will be either one or two o'clock in the morning. They're most likely going to shoot your dogs. So just be prepared. They will tap your phone."

We were scared to death. My God, we never heard of anything like this. A few days before, our life was going on as it had been for eighteen years.

So, we go home. Gur picks up the phone, and she hears somebody on the other end saying, "Yeah, so connect the red wire to the green wire, and the yellow wire to the blue wire."

She literally picked up the phone while the police were tapping our lines!

GUR. That's how primitive it was back then.

BIR. I found out later that this just happened after the Rodney King incident in Los Angeles.[197] Consequently, the FBI all went down to Los Angeles. In our case, I was the first to be arrested. They wanted to incarcerate me and then transfer everything down to Los Angeles. So, I would be the one in jail.

The FBI told Northern California, "We're a little busy right now, in the middle of this Rodney King thing, so you keep him up there. And we will eventually transfer our guy up there too."

Everything happened so fast. Yogi Bajan left immediately for New Mexico, not to return to Los Angeles for years. Kirpal was arrested at a bank. He was taking 600,000-plus dollars out of the bank. My attorney told me I was arrested for grand theft for running the Canadian Lottery scam.

Five months went by. They let me know that the charges against me would be dropped. But I had to agree to sit down in a meeting with the detectives and ADA. They figured out that Kirpal and Yogi Bhajan knew what they were doing. I just got stuck in it. I had no money; I had no knowledge. Was I guilty of being really stupid? Yes,

I was. But when I saw the Siri Singh Sahib talking to Kirpal Singh, I blindly trusted all of that. I had no idea that this was going on.

The ADA made it clear to me that this organization had an element of organized crime in its businesses. It looked no different to them than the organized crime family in Chicago. She appraised me of different businesses they had investigated for five months and what they had concluded. They also explained that there were two unsolved murders of members of 3HO and the Sikh Dharma Brotherhood. She gave me a little bit of information on that. After laying out this organized crime element of "the family," she said, "Everything in our investigation takes us one handshake away from Yogi Bhajan. Can you close that gap? Would you please cooperate and close that gap?"

I told her, "I can't." I really wasn't involved in that part of the family. I wasn't privy to that circle.

She said it was interesting that certain members, especially those involved in the business end, saw the yoga as a sideshow. And then, they saw that certain people on Preuss road (Los Angeles ashram) seemed to wear lovely silk clothing. They drove very nice cars, Mercedes, and Lexus. They slept in brass beds. While others on Preuss road wore whatever they could sew themselves. They slept on the floor. They drove whatever they could afford. She just couldn't believe it. She was trying to draw her version of what she called a cult.

So, they said, they figured out I was guilty of "being a dummy." I didn't see it coming and should have known better. But honestly, I trusted my teacher of eighteen years.

Gur goes on to talk about their difficult time during those five months. Their life was over. They were rejected not only by their immediate community but also by the whole Sikh Dharma community. They had no friends left, and their families did not know what to think. It was all horrible. Everything had changed.

Bir had to go to court one more time. The words "sect," "sect leader," and "sect members" were heard multiple times during the session. For Bir and Gur, the bubble had burst. They had no more illusions. They could not get in touch with anyone in the Los Angeles community.

Except . . .

BIR. I only got one call. That was from Ram Das Singh, the attorney of the organization. It was in the early stages. He only wanted to know from me, "What does the FBI know?"

Well, shit, I didn't know what the FBI knew!

So, now, after five months, we were back in court. When my case was opened, the ADA [also prosecutor] of California stood up.

She said to the judge, "Your honor, I wish to dismiss all charges against Guru Bir Singh in the interest of justice."

The judge was just floored. When the gavel came down, all charges against me were dismissed in the interest of justice. Kirpal was sentenced to San Quentin state prison. But everything in our life was shattered. We hugged each other, stuffed the few things we had in a U-Haul trailer, and drove away.

My attorney said, "I've never had a client, let alone a family, that doesn't know who they are, where they're going, who they are going to be, and what they're going to do when they get there." We just left, and eighteen years were over like that. We said this is graduation. We graduated from elementary, middle, and high school and from university. So why wouldn't we graduate from this? We didn't have a clue who, what, when, or where the rest of our world was going to go.

GUR. There are a few things we did with quite a bit of intention. One was that we decided, we are not victims! We were ready to do our inner work. Get clear within ourselves of who we are birthing now. What is our life about now? Who are we? We took our children, went to counseling, and did many proactive things for our inner growth. Deep inside, amid the devastation, while being let down by the family, our community, and spiritual teacher, we knew that our relationship with the creator could not be impacted by other people.

That was our North Star, our intention in everything as we moved forward.

I also knew that once everything gets taken away, something really magnificent will take its place. That was the way that I chose to look at it. Not to say that we weren't devastated. We weren't grieving. We weren't wholly impacted.

BIR. We always knew where to bow our heads. And honestly, spirit, source energy, whatever you want to call that one creator, was always there as long as we listened to that silent voice. We just got real humble real fast. We listened as we were guided, having no idea where we were going and what we would do. When we looked back at it just a few years ago, we saw it was totally divine.

There is no right, no wrong, nobody is right, nobody is wrong. Everybody's path is different, but there's only one creator. That same creator who breathes in me breathes in all my brothers and sisters and everyone else.

GUR. I would like to share one more thing. My career has been in hospices, working with people who are dying. I've met quite a few people who died and came back from death. They are no longer afraid because they understand the universe.

That's how I feel about what we went through. When everything has been taken away from you, and you don't know what's going to happen, once you've had that happen, you realize that what comes next is even more amazing. You no longer fear loss, letting go or change. That's my message to people. When you're holding on for dear life, you're creating resistance. So, you are resisting what you're being birthed into and what's coming next, and the possibilities. There's no need to be afraid. All is perfect. The universe is always taking care of us. Whether we understand it or know it, or not.

BIR. What was amazing was that people started coming closer to me as soon as I took the uniform off. I wasn't used to that. That was new. It was wonderful.

Related to our 3HO graduation story, we don't have any axe to grind. We don't need to call anybody out. We don't have any ill feelings toward anybody. We've had a beautiful opportunity to work through a lot of that. We're certainly here to be part of the solution and not part of the problem.

We totally trust the creator. We must pay attention, listen, and go "through our hearts" instead of "to our heads." Love is there, no matter what. It's there for the taking. We just have to let it in.[198]

Drug Program Fraud

We return to Kirantana, Kir, the former bodyguard of Yogi Bhajan, who was separated time after time from Kirn Jot, the woman he loved. After her husband's death, they met again in India, and the love spark ignited once more, but Yogi Bhajan did not allow it. Consequently, Kirn Jot was sent to Los Angeles, and Kir tells us what happened to him.

I was sent to Española to take over the drug rehabilitation program. It had been in operation for a couple of years. I soon discovered it was a big mess that had been dumped on me. I had eight young men out in a house in the desert with no supplies, help, or program. It was a government-granted program well into the six figures category. They had received all that money because they had about six teachers, plus Yogi Bhajan, listed as active teachers of the program. So, on paper, to get the grant, we had a fantastic program.

I never saw any of those teachers, or Yogi Bhajan, the whole time I was there. Turned out they were just present on paper, and all the money was taken by Yogi Bhajan and the ashram to buy land and Peruvian Paso horses. The money to run the program was gone long before I arrived.

To make more money, they gave up the house in the desert. We moved to the Gold House on the ashram property, and three more clients came. We were kept isolated from any of the people in the ashram. I was told to put the guys on work crews, chain gangs for doing the dirty work around the ashram, like cleaning irrigation ditches. I was given a helper. We spent most of the time in Española begging for throw-away produce from the markets to feed these guys. The ashram dropped off flour every week to make chapatis [Indian bread], and that was it.

I cared about these young boys, and I was furious. I kept looking for Yogi Bhajan or Wahe Guru Singh, the head of the ashram. I wanted to talk to them. Everyone stayed away, everyone.

Finally, the government grant inspector made a surprise visit. He was furious and immediately shut the program down. Some of the boys had to be sent back to jail before they could find other programs. These young boys had come to the House of Guru Ram[199] for help, and this is what happened to them?

I came looking for Yogi Bhajan, but he knew my anger and ran. Word spread through the ashram that I had had something to do with the program's shutdown. During an ashram meeting, tempers went over the top. I started blurting out the details of what the program had turned into. The ashram guards began coming at me from across the room. Pandemonium ensued. I was ready for them, but just before a riot started, other guards jumped on those guards, and we were separated.

I chased Yogi Bhajan to Los Angeles. They wouldn't let me see him. So, I parked in front of his ashram at my old guard job. Finally, we met and went at it eyeball to eyeball for five hours straight. It was epic. Exhausted, he finally said, "The money is gone. Why are you freaking out? It's gone." Then someone came in to massage him. He lay there, had no concern for those boys, the reputation of the ashram, or the fact that he and everybody involved, including me, could have been put in jail for fraud. The money was gone. In his mind, that was that.[200]

No Karma over the Phone

On the website GurmukhYoga, Gursant has been sharing stories of malpractices within 3HO since 2009. We copy here one of the remarkable narratives posted there by an anonymous woman.

I was twenty-four. Yogi Bhajan had sent me to work for a telemarketing business. Harijiwan, one of his henchmen, had started it up in Española. It was 1989 or 1990. I went down there and saw the operation. My neighbors were on the phones calling themselves things like Mary Smith and Bob Thomas because customers had too much trouble with the Sikh names. I let it pass. I got a job in the packing room, preparing shipments of typewriter ribbon. It suited me fine. I'd come in for a few hours after work to make extra money.

After a few weeks, I asked about a sales job because it supposedly paid better. The boss gave me a script to read: "Hi, my name is . . . . I work for your copier company. We just revised the owner's manuals and want to send a new one out to you. But our computers are down, so I don't know your specific model number. Can you please look and read it off to me so that I can send you the correct manual?"

According to the model number given, the people in the boiler room could tell what brand it was. They would wait two to three weeks, and then a different person would call back and pretend to represent the company their machine was from.

"Hi, I'm from Xerox/Canon/Sharp/. . . and I want to send you your toner . . ."

Unless their "customers" were wide awake or had formerly experienced a similar fraud, they would unsuspectingly cooperate in preparing the delivery, resulting in an invoice many times higher than they would receive from their regular supplier for the same goods.

I started on a Friday and did my shift of four hours. They gave me a stack of cards with numbers to call, mostly charities, because charities are often staffed by volunteers. These naive people are likely to give up the information. The Salvation Army. The Navaho Children's Milk Fund. Organizations that cannot bear the cost of being ripped off.

This felt wrong, but they told me, "The Siri Singh Sahib knows about it, and he says it's OK." However, the longer I did it, the worse I felt. One girl on the phone started crying.

She said, "I really want to help you because I can tell by your voice that you're honest, but I gave out information once to someone over the phone, and then we got this huge bill. My boss said he would fire me if I ever did it again. I'm sorry, I'm so sorry!"

Sometime later, an old man said, "Young lady, you sound like a good girl, and you know what you're doing is wrong. Stop before you imperil your mortal soul."

I felt like throwing up. By that time, I was crying so hard I couldn't go on. I gave my stack of completed cards to the boss. He was flabbergasted. The average success rate was 15 percent, but I got an 80 percent. He wanted me to come back on Monday. I told him I caught myself wishing the people on the other side would hang up. He said that wasn't good. He asked me to think about it over the weekend. He really wanted me back.

From there, I drove to the video shop in Española to return a movie. Everyone I looked at, I wondered, "Could I con them? Could I get them to believe a lie?" I had never looked at people in that light before. After only four hours of lying, I saw people not as fellow human beings but as potential marks. I thought like a predator. I had broken my Sikh vow "to earn my living honestly by the sweat of my brow." Inside, I felt filthy and defiled. No one had done this to me. I did it to myself. I cried all night. The next day, I reached out for help. Someone referred me to one of the Sikh ministers around. When I talked to him, he defended the phone room activity. It was just a business. I had been self-employed before, for many years. I argued with him about business ethics. He seemed not to believe in that.

Desperate, I called Bhai Sahib Guru Liv Singh for spiritual advice. I had had a conversation with him before I took my Sikh vows. At that time, he said that I was not "Amritdari material" (not

fit to become an initiated Sikh). I did it anyway. I told Guru Liv
Singh that I had broken my vows by lying on the phone to cheat
people out of their money. He said it was OK. Sometimes people
had to do what was necessary to earn their living. So, he kept making excuses as to why lying to make money was not bad. I told him
that phone sex would be more honest work for me because at least
the customers would know what they were getting. "If telling lies
isn't breaking my vow to earn my living, honestly, I'm going to go
out, eat a steak, smoke a joint, and get laid!"

"You can't do that!" he sputtered, "That would be wrong!"

I pointed out his inconsistency. I asked him why lying was OK
when the vow says you have to be honest. He confessed money was
tight, and he thought of working there himself. Holy sh*t! I asked
him if he believed God and Guru would take care of him? He was
a Bhai Sahib [a respected title in the 3HO Sikh community]. Where
was his faith? I told him that he needed spiritual guidance more
than I did.

That Sunday, I saw him after gurdwara. He asked me what I had
decided. I said that, if necessary, I would sell my body on the street
before lying on the phone again. I reminded him that I was not
"Amritdari material." He went pale and couldn't look me in the eye.

My housemates got back in town, and I told them how torn up
I was about having broken my Sikh vows. They said that it was OK
because "The Siri Singh Sahib says there's no karma if you lie over
the phone because your aura isn't touching the other person's aura."

WTF????? We got into a massive argument about it, and someone screamed in my face, "IF YOU THINK THE SIRI SINGH
SAHIB'S WRONG, THEN YOU'RE WRONG!"

I called a law enforcement agency anonymously. I asked whether
certain hypothetical operations of a hypothetical phone room were
legal or illegal. The man told me it was so illegal that if they ever
busted such an operation, all the employees would be led out in

handcuffs. I had no intention of reporting the phone room, but I was terrified that someone else might. So I shared this information with one of my neighbors, a mother of small children, and begged her to stop working there for her children's sake, if not for her own.

Then I went and got a *hukam*[201] to ask the Guru for guidance on working in the phone room. This is the only time ever I read a sentence in which the Guru threatened with fire and brimstone. The *hukam* sounded like this: "The thief thinks he can hide his actions from God, but God sees everything. When his time comes, Death's myrmidon takes him to hell, where he is chained to a pillar of fire for eternity. But if he truly repents, he will be forgiven."

I copied it, typed it up, sent one copy to Yogi Bhajan, and stuck another copy to the front door of the phone room. All hell broke loose on my head! Someone had reported that I had called a law enforcement agency. They went on the warpath against me. One of the ministers called me and warned me not to threaten anyone's business. I told him that I wasn't threatening anyone's business because it was not a business. It was a con game.

Harijiwan, the toner business's boss, said my problem was that I was clinging to Western Judeo–Christian ethics. Those rules did not apply to Sikhs. "Thou shalt not steal" and "Thou shalt not lie" were part of the Judeo–Christian code. Sikhs were not bound by that ethical code. I argued that Sikhism is moral in its own right, entirely against lying and stealing. He wouldn't listen.

He told me smugly that this came from the Siri Singh Sahib. If I disagreed with the Siri Singh Sahib, I wasn't a Sikh (this was the second time I heard that). At that point, I lost my temper. I jumped out of my chair, leaned across the desk, and shouted into his face, "How DARE you tell me I'm not a Sikh! Apologize right now!"

He literally flew backward in his chair and stuttered apologies at me. I was surprised at how scared he was. It felt so satisfying, but after that, my goose, as they say, was cooked.[202]

The above story is about the boiler room in Española, New Mexico, and dates from 1989 or 1990. On Yogi Bhajan's request, Gursant also worked for this fraudulent business. He wrote about it:

> Yogi Bhajan would frequently visit the office and always leave us with this cryptic statement: "Remember, there's no karma on the telephone!" I took it as God's truth and put my consciousness under wraps. . . .
>
> In the late nineties when I worked with Harijiwan Singh, who was later dubbed "The Toner Bandit," we would change the name of the company every couple of weeks from names like Central Office Supply to Central Distribution, etc. When we racked up huge phone bills, we would just change from AT&T to MCI or Sprint and then put the account under the new company name in order to avoid paying the bills. No one could track us. I was a genius with that type of stuff.
>
> I certainly had my doubts about the morality of the whole thing, but I was so good at it, I figured it was meant to be.[203]

In August 2000, the *Rocky Mountain News* from Denver, Colorado, printed an article titled "Toner Bandit Gets Prison Term." Victims had sued Harijiwan and his accomplice Kirpal for fraud. The fake invoices had been prepared in California and printed in Colorado. Kirpal had opened a distribution center in Aurora. The scam ran from 1995 to 1996, the newspaper said. More than a thousand victims were involved in the Colorado case, and more than $300,000 were extorted through fraudulent invoices. Harijiwan was given twenty-four months in prison and had to pay clients over $150,000. He ended up serving eighteen months. And Kirpal was sentenced to six months and fined $5,000.[204]

In 2023, toner bandit Harijiwan's band White Sun won a Grammy award in the "New Age, Ambient, or Chant" category for the second time.[205]

Gemstone Fraud

Gemstones and jewels—Yogi Bhajan loved them. Gursant recounts the story of the gemstone fraud in a post on his website.[206] He remembers driving Bhajan to Jerry's in Beverly Hills while on security duty. Usually, Hari Jiwan, who ran the gemstone businesses, accompanied him.

This is not Harijiwan the toner-bandit, but Hari Jiwan in two words. It is said that this gem man and Gurujot were Yogi Bhajan's top lieutenants. They were his nearest and dearest accomplices, his right and left arm, both swindlers.

In Española, Bhajan's personal gems were kept in a small room in the ranch with cupboards that stretched the length of the walls. When Marina, the Italian woman who arrived at Bhajan's court in 1999, first saw those drawers full of jewels and gemstones, it made her dizzy. When she was massaging Bhajan's feet, and visitors came along, he would often ask his secretaries to bring out a few drawers to show them off and impress.

In the earlier days in Los Angeles, the gems were in a bank in Beverly Hills. Three times a week, a secretary would say to Gursant, "Let's go get the crown jewels," and he would drive her to the bank. From the numerous safe deposit boxes, she would choose the gems and jewels with which Yogi Bhajan would adorn himself for the next few days. They were selected according to the astrological situation of each day. The first time Gursant saw the outrageous number of gem-laden trays, he was shocked.[207]

While he was part of the inner circle, Gursant was also involved in different scams.

We had started off trying to be Healthy, Happy, Holy. Now money became the priority. Even though our morning *sadhana* (spiritual practice) from 4:00 to 7:00 a.m. was still considered the most important part of our day, we salesman were excused at 5:00 a.m. to take advantage of cheaper calling rates to the East Coast where school offices were open at 8:00 a.m. [He is referring to the toner fraud "business" here.] The whole emphasis of saving the world through our yoga and Yogiji's teachings shifted to "make money, make LOTS of money." And, if the methodology was unethical at best and nauseating to anyone with the slightest sense of morality, well it was OK, provided you were sending your *dasvand* (tithe) to Yogiji. . . .

I was quite open about everything I did. People didn't like that. Bhajan's devotees, especially the secretaries, preferred to maintain a certain sheen of "goodness"—as long as certain things are not spoken about, they are OK. But these things, like my gambling, were never "officially" OK. That means my lifestyle was never officially sanctioned and I was supposed to hide who I really was. Meanwhile, our spiritual teacher completely approved of what I was doing. I couldn't wrap my mind around that, and I caught hell for it.

Because I refused to lie about the scams I did, the lawsuits I started, the gambling, the used car racket I had going on, or any of the rest of it, "the squares" always took a distinct dislike to me. But why should I lie? This is who I am. My father would have been proud of each and every deal I made, each and every dollar I earned.

Whereas Yogiji's other students, despite how they made their money through scamming people, always liked to play it straight. They jumped when Yogiji said jump and made a career out of covering his tracks as well as their own. While Hari Jiwan Singh was pulling a phone sales scam selling supposed "crown jewels" to lonely old people, he was beefing up his image as Yogiji's personal yoga-teaching assistant at Summer Solstice. And while Toner Bandit Harijiwan Singh was secretly running the invoice scam with me, he was becoming certified as a "Kundalini Yoga and Gong Master"—the go-to guy for anyone seeking true enlightenment. The hypocrisy![208]

In June 1997, the Federal Trade Commission (FTC) filed charges of gemstone fraud against three of Hari Jiwan's telemarketing companies. One of them was called the Sweet Song Corporation. The court case says they routinely misrepresented the risk, value, appreciation, and liquidity of the gemstones they sold. They falsely claimed that consumers would realize tremendous profits and promised clients could easily liquidate the gemstone portfolios after eighteen months. After the sale, however, all contact was broken, and they refused to liquidate the stones after eighteen months.

In 1998, Hari Jiwan was convicted. He paid a bail of $100,000. He agreed to a monetary judgment that required the company to forfeit most of its assets.[209]

Faulty Loans

In 1993, Khalsa Financial Services, of which Gurujot was the chairman, was convicted of fraudulent activities.[210] Customers were led to believe that their money was invested in time deposits, while it was used to make secret loans to Bhajan's companies. In addition, problems in accounting and record keeping were discovered. Gurujot lost his registration as an investment adviser. He and the company's vice president were banned from working with brokers, stockbrokers, investment companies, or advisers.

Drugs and Weapons from Thailand

We all heard about the DEA [Drug Enforcement Administration] breaking into the Virginia ashram, pointing guns at people lying face down on the floor. In this pot [marijuana] smuggling case, Gurujot was arrested and put in jail. His partner fled to Canada. In a drama like that: the DEA breaks into your ashram, and a guy goes to jail . . . How much more proof do you need that some shit is happening?[211]

On February 19, 1988, a lawsuit was filed against Gurujot Singh, the leader of the Virginia ashram, and his son-in-law.[212] The court case reads like the screenplay of a movie about drug smuggling. Three major drug shipments from Thailand to the United States are described in detail. One in 1983, another in 1984–1985, and another in 1987, each transporting tons of marijuana. The money amounts ranged from a few hundreds of thousands of dollars to $2 million. Gurujot also ordered an M79 grenade launcher, an M2 .50-caliber machine gun, and pistols with silencers. The case mentions frozen Swiss bank accounts and requests to launder millions of dollars. Undercover agents were called in to catch Gurujot and his partner. He was arrested and jailed, and his partner fled to Canada.

The lawsuit stated Gurujot was the leader of a recognized religious organization. "Each member of his Sikh community had offered to put up their home as surety for his appearances." Gurujot had access to millions of dollars in cash and was familiar with money laundering techniques. Evidence showed he had used one of his companies, Khalsa Financial Services, as part of his illegal drug activities.[213]

Behave or I'll Kill You

Yogi Bhajan told Tej Steiner to be wary of his devotees who had guns. Siri had to threaten people for the master. Meeri had overheard him tell people on the phone he could let their dead bodies float on the river. And KartaPurkh's court case claimed that Yogi Bhajan threatened to kill her and her family if she spoke out. Her lawsuit lists other examples of Bhajan's extortion and threats of physical violence to influence affairs to illustrate that this was a standard modus operandi of YB. The following two cases are described in KartaPurkh's court case.

Steven Epstein from Texas was a follower of Bhajan who had invested a lot of money and time in Bhajan's companies. He never received the promised compensation, nor did he receive the agreed-upon legal documents confirming the transactions. In 1985, Epstein's wife demanded

that Bhajan and the involved companies behave and act more professionally. She planned to divorce her husband if things were not put in
order. Bhajan responded by threatening Steven Epstein with death if he
ever "stopped working for him." And Epstein's wife would suffer
Bhajan's revenge if she tried to divorce her husband. He would file
harassing lawsuits so she would "never have peace." He would hire psy-
chologists to testify that she was an unfit mother. He would ensure she
was denied custody of her children and do whatever it took to put her
on the street with nothing.

Another case is that of Brook Webb. In 1984, he and three other
people were involved in a Bhajan-controlled landscaping company in
Tucson, Arizona. They were dissatisfied with how the 3HO ashram
leader ran the business. Webb and the others threatened to resign and
leave the company, taking several clients with them. Bhajan flew to
Tucson, confronted Webb, and threatened to kill him if he left the
company.[214]

Dead Body in a Trunk

In the story of Bir and Gur, the California ADA mentioned two unsolved
3HO murders.[215] Perhaps one of those was this one, documented on the
site of Wacko World of Yogi Bhajan in 2002.[216] The first newspaper
article is from September 1986.

> Victim Found in Car Trunk.
>
> Eugene (AP)—The body of a man was found in the trunk of a
> rental car at Mahlon Sweet Airport late Saturday afternoon, touch-
> ing off a homicide investigation that continued Sunday.
>
> Eugene police have not determined the identity of the man, who
> was clad in a yellow shirt and blue jeans and wearing a pager, by late
> Sunday.
>
> Authorities said they did not know how he died. An autopsy was
> scheduled for Monday.

The car, with the body still in the trunk, was towed at dusk from the airport to an undisclosed location for further investigation.

The body was found shortly after 4 pm by an unnamed employee of Budget Rent-A-Car . . . an employee of a cab and limousine service who saw the body later said: "He looked like he had been dragged somewhere. He had bruises on him . . .

As copies on the site of Wacko World of Yogi Bhajan show, the Eugene newspaper followed up on the case in the next days and weeks interviewing people and citing court documents. The victim was identified as thirty-one-year-old Peter Hutchings, a cocaine dealer who "was reportedly in Eugene negotiating drug deals" five days before he was murdered. This was when he was last seen alive and the day when the rental car was noticed for the first time at the Mahlon airport parking lot. The detective working on the case had said, "We've talked to enough people who are substantiating rumors—that he was a drug dealer. . . . [The murder] appears to be drug connected, but why he was killed, we don't have a motive." Hutchings was known to be a former Eugene resident who moved to Hawaii about six months before his death, the paper said.

One month after the body was found, an acquaintance of Hutchings was arrested "on charges of possession of marijuana and cocaine." He knew the victim as a major cocaine dealer from whom he bought stuff to resell. Hutchings used the man's apartment in Eugene to complete his drug deals. The acquaintance declared Hutchings "had a [local] drug connection," and he had seen him "with cash 'in six digits' from drug transactions."

That fateful day, the acquaintance had overheard a dope-oriented conversation that Hutchings had about going "somewhere in two hours to get something and meet four hours later to bring that to someone else." According to the court case, the same day, Hutchings "also made a 45-minute call to a friend in Salem who apparently was involved in Sikh religion, as was Hutchings."

Hutchings was indeed a 3HO member. His spiritual name was Guru Preet Singh. According to information from an anonymous source on the Wacko World of Yogi Bhajan, he was a former drug dealer trying to go straight by becoming a Sikh, and with the support of 3HO technology. Gurujot was going to help Guru Preet in setting up a business. Still, first, they had to raise capital by selling some drugs. The victim's last 45-minute call is alleged to have been to Gurujot, who was at the Salem ashram.

The site cites an anonymous ex-3HO member who claims to have met the victim on a vacation with 3HO friends not long before the murder. According to this source, Guru Preet, who had appeared extremely frightened, had said he would be killed. Suspecting he was back in the drug business, the ex-3HO member had tried to convince him that going to jail was better than living in fear. Guru Preet answered, "Why are you telling ME this?"

Similar stories are told by other ex-3HO members who prefer to stay anonymous due to the delicacy of the matter. They confirm that Guru Preet knew what was going to happen to him. During a sailboat trip with 3HO friends, he was extremely nervous and told someone, "This guy and this guy are going to kill me." The names he allegedly mentioned were well-known leaders from the 3HO community.

The story goes that Guru Preet Singh mismanaged a marijuana delivery at the port in Oakland, which later led to the arrest of Gurujot Singh in the Virginia ashram mentioned before. No information on the investigation's further course is available, so it seems that this murder was never resolved.

UNDER THE GUISE OF HEALING

Sat Nam Rasayan Island

at Nam Rasayan (SNR) is a meditative healing technique linked to Kundalini Yoga as taught by Yogi Bhajan. It is said that Yogi Bhajan practiced it, even if he rarely spoke about it. One of Yogi Bhajan's devoted disciples, Guru Dev Singh, had noticed his master's healing work and in 1978, Yogi Bhajan began teaching him using the ancient method of "teaching through silence". In 1988, the student got a mission: to teach SNR openly, which had never been done before. Guru Dev moved to Rome where he started the International School of Sat Nam Rasayan.

SNR communities appeared in major cities around the world. Yet, SNR always remained smaller in scale than 3HO–Sikh Dharma. That did not prevent Guru Dev from being one of the star teachers and VIP guests at major 3HO yoga events. His workshops were very popular. As he gained more followers, the SNR master began to copy Bhajan's behavior. Devotees, confidants, and servants formed his inner circle. They constantly swarmed around him. His entourage breathed an air of secrecy, specialness, and superiority like that of his master. According to his followers, Guru Dev had a softer character and looser style. He was kinder, less strict, and more accessible—but unfortunately, no less abusive.

After the death of Yogi Bhajan in 2004, the SNR organization became fully independent of 3HO–Sikh Dharma. Guru Dev ensured he was the only master of his SNR kingdom. The homepage of the international SNR community, www.satnamrasayan.it, displays large banners with an often-smiling Guru Dev, calling him "a great man of moral stature and compassion."[217]

Forgive Me

He Called Me "Princesa"

My first encounter with abuse in the Kundalini Yoga world happened in the SNR realm. In 2011, I had followed an SNR training in Germany. I loved the practice and wanted to share it in my home country. In January 2012, I organized a Sat Nam Rasayan course in Belgium. Two teachers were planning to take turns teaching monthly weekend sessions. One of them was Hari Singh, a Mexican, like Guru Dev. He lived with his wife and children in Amsterdam. Insiders had told me that Hari was called the spiritual son and protégé of Guru Dev.

During a break in the very first session led by Hari, a student had shared with him that she was involved in a painful and difficult divorce. At the end of that day, Hari called her forward and asked her to share her e-mail address so he could send her a meditation that would be good for her. One year later, this is what she told me:

> It wasn't long before our emails became more and more laced with temptation. A few days later, a box of Hari Tea was delivered home. He started calling me "Princesa" and called himself a bandido. Later that week, he visited me at home and brought presents for the children. I felt overwhelmed and flattered by the way he approached

me. I admit I said "yes," but the initiative was his. He was impressed by me and needed to see me again. His marriage was in bad shape, and they would split up. He kept calling and Skyping me, even when he was in Mexico. Over the following weeks and months, we kept seeing each other.

After a while, I happened to hear that Hari had other girlfriends. Everyone knew but me. When I asked him about it, he became quiet. I started feeling guilty about his wife. I asked him how he could do that to her. He repeated that they had grown apart.

I stopped the relationship. It was hard to understand how naive I had been to believe his stories about how great I was. He was just a man who abused his status as a teacher to charm me and get what he wanted. I had been so overwhelmed and only began to think clearly afterward. I had even imagined he wanted to choose me as his next partner.

She shared this in March 2013, after the second session of our second year of training. She had called me, as I was the course facilitator. Her intention was to tell me that she wanted to stop the training "for a personal reason." When I heard her say "for a personal reason" in a broken voice, alarm bells started ringing. I had seen the flirtatious behavior of Hari toward the young and beautiful, to which she belonged. I had noticed that she and Hari seemed to get along well during the previous year but that she avoided him this year. I sighed and realized I should have talked to Hari about his playboy conduct. It had bothered me, and it had been a subject of gossip among the older students from the start, but I had not reacted because I thought he was a good teacher. I chose the easy way . . .

I said to her, "If there is something that could be helpful to the others, you might want to share."

She was quiet for a moment. Then she said, "I'm embarrassed to talk about it. And I don't want to talk behind Hari's back, but on the other hand, I'm so angry with him." She kept silent for a while. "You know what?" she said in a determined voice. "I'm tired of taking his responsibility on my shoulders. He asks me not to talk about it, but I'm sick and tired of hiding."

And then, she shared her story.

I was furious with Hari. He knew about the vulnerable situation she was in. I was not looking forward to informing the SNR leadership because I had experienced the hierarchical, patriarchal, and extremely old-school structure of the SNR organization on less delicate issues. On earlier occasions, it had been made clear to me that I should know my place; my role was to serve and be obedient. The lower ranks were not expected to have personal opinions, comments, or suggestions. Full stop. However, I had no choice. Appropriate action was needed as Hari taught not only in Belgium but in many different locations.

Fateh Singh was my contact for organizational matters. It was tricky because he also worked for Hari Tea, so Hari Singh was his boss. I asked for a meeting related to the SNR code of ethics at the annual *surjhee* event, a meditation event with Guru Dev that started a few days later in the Netherlands. I had copied both our teachers to the mail. Hari immediately replied by email, only to me. How could I send such a message to Fateh? He and I had worked well together, hadn't we? He had shown me great appreciation, love, care, and respect. He reminded me that not long ago, I told him that I respected his work. He would never share our private communications with Fateh. What was my problem? Could I please call him so we could put all this behind us?

I called him. He was agitated. Immediately, he called the student by name. He talked about his relationship with her as if it was the most normal thing in the world. As if I had known it all along. His biggest concern was that I would talk to Fateh. I should NOT do that. I had to understand that the young lady had played a big part in all this. He was not the only one to blame. I mentioned the power differential between a teacher and a student, her vulnerable situation because of her divorce, and that he knew about it. He calmed down a bit. A few minutes later, he said he had made a mistake. He asked me to keep it between us for now. We would talk at the surjhee event. The next day, Fateh called me. I told him Hari asked me to work it out with him.

At a surjhee meditation event, the Kundalini Surjhee mantra is repeated 11,000 times over three days. I was in a light trance when Hari tapped me on the shoulder. Like a zombie, I followed him out of the hall into the garden. Hari reiterated that the relationship had been with the student's consent. I reminded him about the power imbalance. He agreed again that he had crossed boundaries. Like a child, he promised he would never do it again. There was a lot of pathos. I used this opportunity to give him feedback on how he obviously paid more attention to the beautiful young female students. To my surprise, he agreed and thanked me for pointing this out. He would work on this. I remember this conversation as completely absurd. Hari almost bowed to me, which made me feel like his grandmother.

He said, "In Mexico, family members cover for each other."

"This is not Mexico, Hari."

"But I treat you like my sister."

"I am the organizer of a course in which you teach."

He asked me to forgive him for this mistake and to protect him. He requested a second chance. I gave it. Yes, this was the stupidest thing I could have done.

A Second Case

When Hari was almost on his knees in front of me at the surjhee event, he knew he had had sex with another student six months earlier, in September 2012. After a two-day workshop in Antwerp, individual healing sessions with him were organized. His last "patient" that evening was a student from our training who had just broken up with her boyfriend and felt sick and depressed. While Hari knew this, he let the healing evolve into intimacy. She had asked him if this was OK, and Hari had convinced her it was. So, she spent the night with him, and they had sex. Hari asked her not to talk to anyone. The secrecy did not feel right, and she wondered where her loyalty to him came from.

A few months later, the two women met at a women's circle. They shared their stories with each other and with the facilitator. They felt it was time to break the silence and decided to inform me. I recalled Hari's words at the surjhee event as she shared her story. I realized how he had deliberately deceived me. This time, I called Fateh directly and asked him to inform Guru Dev Singh and let us know what they planned to do to acknowledge the damage done, repair the harm, and prevent Hari from continuing to seduce and abuse students. (I had no idea in those days that Guru Dev equally had sex with his students and abused them.)

After I had spoken to Fateh, I called Hari. Again, he was apologetic and repeated his mantra of keeping silent toward the outside world.

"It depends on how you and Guru Dev respond to this," I replied. "What is your plan? Are you considering therapy?"

He kept silent.

As president of the Belgian Federation of Kundalini Yoga in those days, I reported the issue to the US Ethics and Professional Services team working for the SSSC. The head of EPS told me she could not do anything as SNR was a separate organization. She supported our approach to request acknowledgment, reparations, and actions to avoid this from happening again. She informed one of the SNR trainers in the US.

In December 2013, both women wrote letters to Guru Dev. Their accompanying mail said:

> We see our own role. But we also know that it is a teacher's responsibility to maintain a pure relationship with his students, not to get involved in flirtations and have sex with them.
>
> We ask that Hari looks deeply into his behavior and stops using female students for his own needs. It is time for an open discussion about the teacher–student relationship in the SNR training so that this misconduct can stop. Thank you for reading about our experiences and doing what needs to be done.

I have no clue what the SNR leadership did with these letters. In any case, recognition of the damage done never occurred. Guru Dev removed Hari from the training in Belgium and assigned a replacement teacher. When I shared my concern that without appropriate actions, Hari might continue his abuse during training sessions in other countries, Fateh replied: "As the course organizer and school representative, please don't extend the discussion beyond the persons directly involved. Please work out your personal questions with me, Hari, or Guru Dev. Your personal process is different from [names of the two women]. Please don't intermingle it. Please follow the flow and Guru Dev's suggestions and serve the school and the students in a neutral way."

Mid-February 2014, a new training year started. The teacher for the first session did not show up and was unreachable. I tried to contact Fateh but could not reach him either. The next day I found a message from Fateh in my mailbox.

> Thank you for your message from today.
>
> Please accept my apologies as I was not keeping track of the start date [of our training]. I was traveling all week and was going to write you this weekend.
>
> Due to the ongoing polarization and the most recent circumstances, we concluded in review with Guru Dev Singh that we have to allow some space for the situation in Belgium and we cannot conduct the training right now as projected.
>
> Could you please inform the students accordingly? We would be happy to welcome those who are interested to begin or to continue to study Sat Nam Rasayan in Amsterdam, Paris, Germany, or at any Sat Nam Rasayan retreats or events.
>
> We are grateful for the service you have rendered to the students of Sat Nam Rasayan in the past years in organizing the workshops and the training. Our prayers are with you for the years to come.
>
> Please do not hesitate to contact me if you have any questions.
>
> Thank you so much.
>
> Best regards, Fateh Singh

I called a Dutch friend who had been present at a Sat Nam Rasayan meeting in Amsterdam with Guru Dev a few weeks before. As my mother had been taken to the hospital, I had not participated. My friend told me that, when the Belgian situation was discussed during that meeting, Guru Dev had asked, "How can we stop that woman?"

"That woman" was me.

Guru Dev's decision had been that: all SNR activities in Belgium had to be canceled. I was ex-communicated, and Belgium was a "no-go" zone for the next two years.

Being thrown out was a relief, but I was furious. They canceled the 2014 course, and no one, absolutely no one, had the decency to tell me so that I could have informed the students. My Dutch friend felt embarrassed. They had instructed him not to contact me. He was afraid, he said. SNR was a big part of his life. He could not go against Guru Dev's will. I felt sorry for him.

But where were the teachers? They also knew that the training had been canceled. How little respect can you have for those who fill your pockets so lavishly? Where was the teacher from Hamburg? I considered him a friend! I knew it was also a painful affair for him, as his financial income for 2014 depended heavily on our training. Teachers went home with a few thousand euros per session. Besides the training income, they cached good money from the individual healing sessions before and after classes.[218]

What Hari Did Is Peanuts

Eight years later, in September 2020, I was asked to share the Belgian 2013 SNR abuse case on the private Facebook group Beyond the Cage. I posted our story; some people were shocked, and others were not.

I received a message from Marina from Italy. "What Hari did is peanuts compared to what Guru Dev did," she wrote. That explains it all, I thought. Our first phone call lasted more than two hours. Marina overloaded me with juicy, funny, and horrific stories about Guru Dev and Yogi Bhajan. It was dizzying.

"Why don't you write all this down," I said. "These stories should come into the open."

"I would love to do that, but my English isn't good enough. And I shouldn't write in Italian because nobody here in Italy wants to listen to me. They say I am crazy. Because that's what Yogi Bhajan told them after I left Española. They are all deniers, still worshiping Yogi Bhajan and Guru Dev." She kept quiet for a moment. "But you know what? I want to have it on paper while Guru Dev is still alive. I hear that he is getting weaker every day. He won't live long anymore."

"Write it down in Italian, and I will make sure it gets translated into English," I heard myself say.

Marina started typing her story on her mobile phone. I looked for a translator but soon realized that it would be costly, and worse, take ages to finish. So, I decided to translate it myself using online translators. Marina sent me her text messages. I translated, she reviewed, and we called each other on Sunday afternoons. She gave me more info, I adapted, and she checked again. It took us more than four months to finish the first part of her story. Finally, in early March 2021, the first part was ready. Here is a summary of her story, a good example of how confusing it is for students when they are seduced into sexual contact with their teacher and how damaging it can be.

In 1990, Guru Dev Singh came to Italy to teach Sat Nam Rasayan. I was thirty-two, and Guru Dev was forty-two. I was part of his first group of students in Bologna. I was seduced by the healing practice and by the teacher. There was much less of a power dynamic in the relationship between him and his students than I had experienced with other teachers in the Kundalini Yoga world. He was not authoritarian, did not insist so much on following the Sikh system, and did not intimidate in the way Yogi Bhajan did. That made him seductive and more approachable.

Soon I found out that I was interesting material for him. Looking back on it now, it is possible that I was a little in love with him, but not that much. And other students were also charmed by him, as often happens in a student-teacher relationship or therapeutic setting. . . . Immediately after my divorce, in early 1996, my relationship with Guru Dev changed. The day after the fateful first time I had sex with him, he informed me that:

1. I was not the only one with whom he did his Tantric practices.
2. Our sexual relationship was necessary because my self-esteem had collapsed after my husband approached my daughter. (That was why I divorced him.)
3. Our relationship had to remain secret. First of all, for my daughter's sake, but also because the consequences of talking about it were unpredictable.
4. It would be good for me to have a new partner.

Guru Dev skillfully put me in touch with a friend from Rome who was also one of his students. I understood my situation with the master was ambiguous and wrong. Guru Dev was married, and according to the Sikh religion, which he strictly adhered to, marriage was a sacred bond. He did not think of polygamy. Therefore, I thought it was right to end our relationship. I decided to give it a try. The "recommended" man must have thought the same, and we started dating, which was not unpleasant. Having someone for myself was quite nice. I tried to find peace with the idea that the time for sexual adventures with the healing master was over.

When I saw Guru Dev again, I discovered he was planning to continue his experiments with sexual energy with me. It stunned me, and I was angry about it, but the truth was, at the same time, I wanted it to continue. I liked that he wanted me. And more than anything else, I wanted to know more about this complex healing technique he was beginning to teach me. This was confusingly intertwined with my feelings and desires, my anger, and his indifference.

He knew. He knew everything. At least, that is how I saw it then. And I was so eager to learn. That's why I wanted him. I wanted to master this healing technique that used energy flow between people, especially the sexual energy that enhanced the healer's abilities.

I molded all the details of what was going on to match what I wanted them to be.

Meanwhile, my relationship with my eldest daughter Olivia became increasingly disastrous. She lived with her boyfriend most of the time and rarely came home. She did not talk to me and looked at me with contempt. I could not reach her, understand her, or let her understand me. She did not want to have anything to do with me. I was disappointed in her. I didn't understand why she allowed herself to behave like that toward me, to be so disrespectful. I didn't know how to handle the situation.

I needed a therapist who could help us. Guru Dev was my teacher, my friend, and the best therapist I could think of. He was my idol. He offered his help. Olivia loved going to him for treatment whenever he came to Bologna. And so, he started giving her SNR sessions every month. Then he took her with him when he traveled with his family to the US, India, etc. At first, she went with him voluntarily. A little later, she started using marijuana and drinking regularly, even alone. Before, she used drugs and alcohol occasionally, but only in a social context, as young people do. But now she was using it on her own. The relationship with her boyfriend ended. She was living at home again. Things were getting worse between her and me. And she no longer wanted to go to the sessions with Guru Dev.

When I told Guru Dev about my daughter and her reluctance to come to the sessions, he reassured me. He said she was very twisted. What had happened with my ex-husband had destroyed her and our relationship. He was working on fixing it. I had to curb my doubts and stop worrying because he was fixing the situation. . . .[219]

When Marina and I finished putting the first part of her story on paper, Marina asked her oldest daughter permission to publish it. Olivia read the text and agreed to it. On March 9, 2021, we posted Marina's story on the private Facebook group Beyond the Cage.

Olivia was inspired by her mother's coming out. She recognized she was also ready to bring her story into the open, preferably when Guru Dev was still alive. She first shared her story in a Zoom call with just a few people she trusted. After that, on March 25, 2021, Olivia had her two-hour interview with GuruNischan.

Guru Dev Singh's Obsession

It Was Very Confusing

Olivia was sixteen when her stepfather gave her psychedelics and tried to kiss her. Marina got home just in time to prevent further abuse. A divorce followed. Marina mentioned that her relationship with her daughter had been complicated since that incident and that she had sought Guru Dev's help. Olivia had known Guru Dev from her childhood. Her mother took her to Guru Dev's workshops in Italy and at the European Yoga Festival in France. He was like a father figure to her, someone she trusted. Going to see him once a month for a healing session was not so bad for her.

However, in the summer of 1996, that changed. Exactly one year after her stepfather assaulted her, Guru Dev started abusing Olivia. She was seventeen. He was forty-seven. GuruNischan asks Olivia how counseling and healing turned into abuse.

> It was, above all, very, very confusing. On the day of the first abuse, I felt very much frozen. I did not understand what was happening. During treatment, he started touching all over my body. I don't know how informal I can go here, but he was fondling my right breast, for example. I went completely into a "freeze" state. He would explain to me it was part of the healing. Energetically, whatever place he was touching would have an opening on my neck, or it would release something somewhere else. He was brain-framing

me. I was in shock and did not know what to do. That was it. That's what was happening.

While I was still in shock, he proceeded to let me know things like, "You and I have known each other for lifetimes. I remember you, meeting you under the wisdom tree. Finally, we've met each other in this lifetime. Age is not important under those circumstances. You and I are finally back together. We can continue to do our work."

And there I was, in shock, listening to this dude I thought was some sort of parental guide to me. Someone I completely trusted with everything. I believed he was someone who knew the truth. So, I asked myself, *Is this true?* Because I couldn't even read my own feelings at the time.

I wanted to leave, but he had pinned me down. He started to instill his programming. He said he recognized me the first time he saw me on the sadhana field at the yoga festival. That was the first time that I was there. I was thirteen years old. I realized that he had started grooming me back then! And indeed, every time I would meet him at his classes, there would be these little moments when he would call me, "Oh princesa!" or "Oh linda!' He knew where I was coming from. My self-image and my self-concept were very low. I didn't have a father figure to protect, nourish, and guide me. He knew that he could do almost whatever he wanted.

I remember walking into his classes. Before all his students, he would pay extra attention to me and make me feel good. Which felt GOOD! Because I always felt like shit. I felt that I was unheard, didn't really matter, and that whatever I spoke was not valued. And there he was. A person that is validating me in whatever way he did. Those were the years I built up such trust in this person.

And so, during that long shock time on that day, I wasn't sure what to do with the information he gave me. I absorbed it. Also, he told me something else that messed me up completely. He said, "We have been lovers for many lifetimes. You and I cannot be lovers in this lifetime because it's not allowed."

He said that while he was putting his hands all over my body, kissing me and things like that. And then, he also told me that this must remain completely secret. Completely secret! Because I was the only one. Because I was the special one. Somewhat chosen, blah blah blah blah . . . And that if I told anyone, he would tell everyone that I was crazy.

So basically, I was choked right there. [*Olivia makes a movement like cutting her head off.*] He put a massive framing in my head. I don't like using "brainwashing." It would have been nice if it was "washing." But no, it was a "frame."

And there I was, dealing with such a magnitude of a situation, with my seventeen-year-old really shitty tools to deal with it. *What am I going to do? This man is married, has children, and sees tons of people. I'm a seventeen-year-old kid. And somehow, this person is telling me all these things. So, what am I going to do???*

So, I left. I was confused, and I remained confused. For the initial time, I went along with his leadership. "OK, finally, we see each other." He was putting it under the fake name of healing. He said that we were healing something. That we were healing my situation.

And it was even more confusing than that.

Intercourse probably happened twice over a year. He always held it back. I don't even know why. I have no idea what his motives were. There was, for sure, plenty of foreplay. He would undress himself sometimes. Most of the time, there was no intercourse, but he was definitely doing anything else.

You know, he would always "stage" a situation. Like, he would "use the elements" to protect our space. Or whatever he thought might protect our space. And then the things would happen.

GuruNischan. So he was using healing language to frame an atmosphere that allowed him to do whatever.

Olivia. Yes, that's correct. So that confused the shit out of me. I was following his lead, thinking that he knew. That he was seeing a bigger picture than I did. Until!

Until I started to question things. I remember vividly one time I asked him, "Look, man. You are every weekend in a different town. Are you truly telling me I'm the only one?"

That question had popped up in my head several times.

He answered me with a question, "Do you really believe me to be that person?"

And obviously, I was like, "Oh well, no, of course not."

And then, what he does, like second moments later, he just puts me on his knees. He pulls down my pants and starts spanking me, telling me he is "resetting my nervous system."

I was just so humiliated! From then on, the question marks kept avalanching in my head. "What is going on with this human being?"

GuruNischan. I'm disgusted.

Olivia. I know. That's what I'm left with. Disgust is all that I'm left with from those experiences. Jesus Christ!

What Face to Put On?

In April 1997, Olivia turned eighteen. She was on her way via New Delhi to Rishikesh in India with Guru Dev, his wife, his children, and his assistant. Every year Yogi Bhajan and Guru Dev Singh traveled with their entourage to Rishikesh in India for the *Reman* event. During that gathering, they would recite a verse from the holy book that leads to wisdom 11,000 times.

That was the shittiest, most awkward time I have ever had, along with all the others. I thought, Why does he put me in this sad, sad role? Having this affair while his wife was there, and his assistant, and his kids? And why the fuck are we going to the Golden Temple to clean it! What are we cleaning? It was terrible. Anyway. During those trips, my "private healing sessions" with Guru Dev continued.

I remember that we were in a hotel room in New Delhi. Everybody else was sitting at the dinner table waiting for us. And he just took me, you know. He put me on all fours and had sex with me. Right there and then. He slept with his wife and one of his kids in this hotel room. I did not have time to say, "No, back off."

And then, moments later, I had to sit down with everybody at the dinner table, and what kind of face was I supposed to put on? I was feeling like the worst crap I've ever felt.

After that, I think, all things really started to crumble down for me. I was very reluctant to go and meet him. I was very disturbed and unstable. I was using substances. I don't know, probably I did that to not feel all the great conflict and pain that I was experiencing. [220]

I No Longer Existed

One day while Olivia was at home with her mother, the bomb burst, and she threw everything out. Below, Marina describes how she experienced that moment.

In the springtime of 1998, my relationship with the partner Guru Dev had recommended to me ended. It did not work out. We remained friends. It gnawed at me, but I got over it quickly. I still had my privileged and secret relationship with the chief, who personally took care of my grown-up daughter. I could not do that. After all, she was a teenager, and you know how they are. My youngest daughter was always with me. I told myself that sooner or later, both would be well-balanced human beings, ready to fully develop their spiritual potential. Thanks to me, they grew up in the safest and most protected place you could imagine in the world. I created a much better situation for them than my mother had done for me.

At the beginning of the summer, the conflicts with my oldest daughter were intense. She was totally out of my control. I had not heard from Guru Dev since the end of May. Every now and then, I called "the friend" because I was homesick.

One afternoon my daughter confronted me. She asked if I truly believed that Guru Dev was that "pearl of a man" I was promoting? Did I really think he was a model of integrity and faithful to the sacred Sikh principles? That he was not cheating on his wife?

While thinking of something which could cover up possible gossip, I asked her with whom she thought Guru Dev was cheating on his wife. I was ready for any answer, but when she replied, "with me, for example," my heart missed a beat, time disappeared into a void, and I fell into nothingness.

And then she threw it all on me: the mornings when I gave her money for *brioche e cappuccio* to take to the house where he and I had slept together at night. The place where he was waiting for her for the treatment. I had *forced* her to go. The trip to India. I had sent her because of her crisis at school and the use of marijuana. He insisted that she would go because she was so depressed that she might commit suicide. He knew her "committing suicide" was the easiest button to push with me. I had confided to him that seeing my oldest daughter die had always been my greatest nightmare. Ever since she was born, I had had that fear for her. God knows why. With the younger one, I never had that.

He used this lever, "She is suicidal," every time we saw each other and when I asked him about her and why her relationship with me was getting worse and worse. My fear made me shake, so I pushed her to go. He told me she slept at the hostel with his assistant in India. He and his family stayed in a five-star hotel because his status demanded that. Status was not important to him but fundamental and necessary to define his position within the community. Now I see how the people he chose to be in his entourage were determined by the money in their bank accounts or by significant economic self-sufficiency, excluding me.

Olivia told me that every morning, Guru Dev, who was forty-eight in those days, would come to the hostel for the "healing." Then he would send his assistant away and sneak up on my eighteen-year-old daughter to have sex with her.

She did not want it, but he was obsessed, she said. I asked her if his assistant knew.

"She knows everything, but it is convenient for her to pretend she does not know."

I was annihilated, frozen. I no longer existed. Guru Dev was my master, teacher, friend, and lover. And his assistant was my friend from before, before Kundalini Yoga entered my life, before Guru Dev. I looked at my daughter, the house, and the objects on the table. Everything was foreign to me. My breathing had become very shallow, and I suddenly felt drained.

She was waiting for a reaction, but I no longer existed. So, she went to her room and closed the door. I also went upstairs. I wanted something to say to her, but nothing was inside. My brain was like water. My heart was gone. I went to bed and got so cold that I started to pull out the winter duvets from the closet. I put them all on top of me. But still, I was frozen. My teeth chattered, and I had no thoughts. I was in shock.

After I don't know how long, my daughter left. She left the house. As she passed by, Olivia told me she didn't know if she would be back for the night. I didn't have the strength to stop her. To hug her or to tell her that I was there for her. I didn't have the strength to cry, not with her, not on my own.

I don't know how long after she left, I picked up the phone and called him. I could only say, "Why? Why her? Why so?" He answered that he was in a healing session. He called me back after ten minutes. I don't remember what he said precisely at that time. My memory gets confused with the thousands of other times he made excuses, came up with motives, reasons, and strategies, etcetera, etcetera.

Three days later, my daughter arrived back home. She was pretty much out of herself. She told me that she was going to Favignana [a Sicilian island] to see a friend. She said she needed to leave and didn't want to be with me. And I was not able to do anything but watch her go away.

Guru Dev phoned me again. He did that because he wanted to keep me under his control. The situation was critical for him. I was a loose cannon, just as much as my daughter was. He had to ensure that I kept silent and didn't disclose a thing.[221]

And indeed, Guru Dev kept things under control. He ensured that Marina and Olivia's stories were never taken seriously within the community. Mother and daughter never received any formal acknowledgment of the damage done. That is why it felt so right for them to disclose their stories in March 2021 while he was still alive and in an era in which people were more willing to listen.

The End

After I had posted Hari's abuse story on Beyond the Cage on September 23, 2020, I wondered what would happen if I reminded Guru Dev of the events in Belgium in 2013. Bear in mind that at that moment, I was not aware yet of the stories of Marina and Olivia, nor was the outside world. In those days, to me, Guru Dev was still the right person to approach to request acknowledgment of the harm done by Hari and to ask for appropriate action to prevent similar abuse in the future. So, I decided to contact Guru Dev. Would he react differently eight years later? I emailed Fateh asking him to forward my message to the SNR master. It ended with these words:

In early 2014, the students who were abused by Hari approached you to start a conversation. You refused their invitation. Today, in 2020, there is a new opportunity to bring the impurities of the past into the light. They can be dissolved and healed, and everyone will benefit from that.

Looking forward to your answer.

My mail went out on September 30, and I did not expect a reply, accustomed as I was to silence as an answer on uncomfortable questions in both the Kundalini Yoga and Sat Nam Rasayan communities. They surprised me. One week later, Fateh informed me he had spoken to Guru Dev, who had formulated a response. Fateh shared his notes of Guru Dev's words as best he could.

I read your message, and I am sorry that I am the cause of any suffering. I take the position of this student. I observe the search for an act of purification, and the student has that right and the way that student reacted after the facts force us to ask ourselves several questions, such as What is the ideal way to overcome such an event? Do we confront the students and judge them? From what point of view?

Traditionally, in Europe, they would force someone to confess or help them confess their sins, and then you would get rid of them. There was this idea that the bad could be eliminated if we showed the criminal, and it would get publicly punished, and then we would all feel sure that we were the good guys and that we have one more minute of peace. This seemed like a form of justice, and it kept everyone aligned on the right path.

I am not one of the good guys. I also believe that the people that study a spiritual path are also not the good guys. Unlike the rest of the world, those people are doing something to overcome themselves; I can't judge them; what I can do is not reject them but instead help them grow if they wish to do so. I am not here to impose rules because your conscience can't be controlled by such rules.

Right now, we all want to speak. Women want to regain power, but you can't regain power by being a victim because it doesn't make sense. Once you're a victim, you're a victim, you're part of the game, and there's no way out. To be successful, women have to regain their power, and not their power against men per se, but the power of being a woman. That is a power on its own. When frustration is the motor that pulls you towards regaining power, you're starting from the wrong place.

The purity of the teachings won't happen thru those that are pure. The purity of the teachings is built, and it's built by the impure. We need to speak of compassion and observe that all of us are walking either towards or away from our demons. I don't judge them. I am not the Inquisition. I don't see the bad guys or the sinners. I teach and what I teach is empathy. Every moment is a moment for a decision, and the decision has to be what is best for everyone.

I don't believe women are weak. I also don't believe men are weak. They fall into a thought, one of thousands of ideas that are crossing their minds, and one of those thousands of ideas becomes an action, and if that action takes place, there are consequences, and then what do we do? You can't control the consequences of your actions. Nobody can control that. That's why there's theft and slavery and murder and sex. It all starts from a basic thought put into action. How do we control it? By causing fear of being burnt and reprimanded? How are we fair? Do we punish or vanish people? Or do we control it with our intuition that allows for empathy and compassion for others?

It's the story of the Buddhist monk and the thief. Once a monk saw a thief climbing up a tree to steal peaches from a tree, so he ran and got him a ladder. The thief asked him why he would do that if he knew he was stealing. He responded, "Because you could hurt yourself. I can live without my peaches but not with you getting hurt."

Always in your service.

I responded to each paragraph individually and ended my last communication with Guru Dev with these words:

The story of the Buddhist monk is beautiful. He prevents the thief from hurting himself. At the same time, he offers him an opportunity to grow. He lets him experience the calming effect of love and compassion. The monk is far from controlling and judging.

With their stories and reflections, the abused students show you and your SNR community where the ladder can be found. Sexual transgression should be unacceptable in your programs. In recognizing that, you would provide your teachers and students with a ladder. By remaining silent, you keep it from them. A code of ethics about relationships between students and teachers would be a good ladder, don't you think?

I understand from your response that we should not expect an answer to our question, "When will you take responsibility?"

It is fine, as that is your choice, and it is now clear.

Thank you for making this exchange possible. It was necessary and enlightening.

Wishing you all the best.[222]

On April 5, 2021, six months after this email exchange and twelve days after Olivia spoke openly about the sexual abuse that he had inflicted on her, Guru Dev Singh died.

ACKNOWLEDGMENTS

When the cover of this book tells you that I wrote it "with" Guru-Nischan, it means that we were working side by side, which felt natural and good. Her *Uncomfortable Conversations Podcast* lies at the heart of *Under the Yoga Mat*. We share the drive to keep scratching the wound until justice occurs. I am deeply grateful for the richness of our partnership.

I consider all the survivors who chose to be guests on GuruNischan's podcast—or of people like Mina Bahadori or Rachel Bernstein who conduct abuse-revealing interviews—heroes and role models for all of us. They take responsibility for bringing the truth about their sufferings to light, even when it is uncomfortable and painful, and they are scolded and humiliated by deniers. I honor their courage and strength as they consciously relive painful memories, testifying before the world about the senseless damage inflicted upon them by a narcissistic sociopath.

In connection with this book, I owe special thanks to Guru Bir, Gur Siri, Tej, Siri Nirongkar, Meeri, Mani, Gigi, Olivia, SatHanuman, and others who prefer not to be named, for giving their approval to use parts of their *Uncomfortable Conversations* with GuruNischan.

We could no longer ask Kirantana, George Craig McMillian, as he died on July 26, 2022. Still, I found validation in his writings on abuse-in-kundalini-yoga.com from April 2021: "I feel it is my responsibility to get these stories out there because they [SSSC, KRI, 3HO, SDI] have taken no responsibility to do so themselves, and there are still predator teachers involved and teaching for the organization. There are still young people in danger."

Under the Yoga Mat is dedicated to him and his beloved, Kirn Jot. I am so glad he shared his memories in which their love continues to live and breathe and is still tangibly present. Not even an army of Yogi Bhajans can destroy that, which is rejoicing and good to remember.

I feel a similar deep respect and appreciation for Sat Pavan, who married the love of her life despite all the power tricks YB played on her. Listening to Sat Pavan's utterly sad story is hard, and it infuriates me again and again. Still, it also moves me to see that the essence of us human beings, Love, is indestructible. I am so grateful Sat Pavan allowed me to share her story in such detail because it dissects the tactics of the power-hungry master to the core.

I am honored that renowned meditation teacher Tara Brach agreed to allow her 3HO abuse story to be part of *Under the Yoga Mat* as it shows how she turned her pain into new insights that form the basis of her current teachings.

Many thanks also to the second-generation adult who sent me letters and communications that the leadership used in the 1970s and 1980s to educate Bhajan's devotees about distance therapy and children's education. Similarly, I am indebted to Stephen Josephs for allowing me to use his interview with KartaPurkh and to an ex-3HO member who gave me access to his vast media database and other Bhajan-abuse-related information. Along the same lines, I am grateful to historians Philip Deslippe and the late Dr. Trilochan Singh for their relentless energy proving that Bhajan was a liar with little knowledge of Sikhism.

I am also grateful to Peter Blachly for granting permission to use vivid excerpts from his book, which paint a colorful picture of life as he experienced it in 3HO. I thank the host of Wacko World of Yogi Bhajan and Gursant for allowing me to use stories they published.

Had Marina from Italy not reached out to me, GuruDev's abuse would likely still be quietly hidden beneath sheepskins. I admire her courage to speak out, knowing that many in the Italian community will contradict and reject her. Likewise, I bow to the two Belgian ladies abused by Hari. They gave me permission and continue to support me to use their stories aiming to open the ears and eyes of the Sat Nam Rasayan community hoping that one day, the harm done may be acknowledged, and SNR leadership will recognize that abusing students under the guise of healing is disgusting and cannot be justified in any way.

I like to thank Suzanne, the moderator of the private Facebook group Beyond the Cage, for her unwavering commitment to allowing survivors a space that feels safe to share their stories. And in addition, I am grateful to her for our exchanges as members of the Compassionate Reconciliation process and appreciate her interest in this book throughout its making.

My respect equally goes to other moderators of social media groups set up before and after the mass disclosure of Bhajan's abuse who invested precious time and energy to provide a platform for like-minded people of different generations to share information and find support.

It is a blessing for a writer to have people review your work as it evolves. I was fortunate to have Pamela Dyson do that, reading parts of the manuscript and correcting me if, for example, I confused Ram Das Puri land with the Española ashram or the Ranch. But foremost, she encouraged and motivated me and allowed me to quote from her blog and include anecdotes she shared in our private communications. Indeed, her book *Premka* has helped many individuals step out of their isolation and discuss the injustices they experienced for the first time—some dating back years or even decades. We can't thank her enough for that.

Julia, my dear British friend, was by my side from the beginning. I had never written a book in English before, so I was delighted when she offered her support. She read, reviewed, and reread the pieces I sent her and patiently accepted the reality that I kept making the same spelling and grammar mistakes. Not only was she a buddy in language, but she also acted as my coach clearing away the doubts that eagerly surfaced at regular intervals.

My dear friends Pol, Koen, Marc, and Filip were instrumental in maintaining my morale. Each, in their own unique way, indulged my incessant ramblings about this book during long walks or over a lunch or dinner. They helped me alleviate the stress associated with writing a book that is essential, yet not necessarily enjoyable to write but needs to be written. In this case, the writer turned out to be me.

Izzard Ink publishing came to me through ALLI, the Alliance of Independent Authors. Izzard Ink's CEO, Tim McConnehey, promised to distill the best possible book from my writing to serve the intended purpose. He warned me that our relationship could be one of tough love. I experienced caring, dedication, professionalism, relevant feedback, and creative suggestions. Our communication was smooth, clear, to the point, and friendly. Therefore, a warm and heartfelt thank you to the Izzard Ink team, who was the best match I could have dreamed of.

I needed no creative brainstorming or AI intervention to come up with a title for this book. Instead, celebrated Dutch-language author Kristien Hemmerechts spontaneously blurted out *Under the Yoga Mat* as I explained what this book would be about. The title revealed itself, channeled by Kristien in a memorable moment that makes me smile when I recall it.

Something similar happened with Yogini, the figurine on the cover. In April 2021, on a beautiful spring morning, my bosom friend Henny stood at my frontdoor, holding Yogini in her palms as if it were a fragile baby. "I made this," she said, looking at the earth-colored figurine like a mother taking her child to daycare for the first time and already feeling the pain of parting. "Don't ask me why, but it's for you." Since that day, Yogini humbly and graciously welcomed my visitors from the low cabinet in the hallway. Then came the time when plans to gather ideas for a suitable book cover failed one after another. I whined to Henny about this.

"What about Yogini?" she said.

At that, I opened the door to the hallway and looked at the figurine.

Her gaze fixed on the ceiling, she muttered, "Yes, of course. My dear creator is right. That's why I'm here. I'm so glad you finally figured it out. Free me, please!"

NOTES

1. Gina Piccalo, "A Yogi's Requiem," *Los Angeles Times*, October 23, 2004.
2. There are multiple examples of cults and cases of known abuse or malpractice involving Eastern spiritual masters who arrived in the late 1960s and early 1970s in the West. Bhagwan Shree Rajneesh, later calling himself Osho, had to flee the US in 1985 and travel to India to escape a court case related to immigration fraud. Yoga masters who sexually abused their students include Pattabhi Jois from Ashtanga Yoga, Vishnudevananda from Sivananda Yoga, 2 (*continued*) Bikram Choudhury and Greg Gumucio from Bikram Yoga, and Manouso Manos from Iyengar Yoga. While many incidents date from decades ago, it is only since the #MeToo activist movement wave in 2017 that survivors in the yoga world have started sharing their stories.
3. Time, "Religion: Yogi Bhajan's Synthetic Sikhism," September 5, 1977.
4. An assistant district attorney (ADA) is a law enforcement officer representing the state government on behalf of the district attorney in investigating and prosecuting individuals alleged to have committed a crime.
5. Guru Bir Singh and Gur Siri Kaur, interview with GuruNischan, *Uncomfortable Conversations Podcast: The Untold Stories of the 3HO Kundalini Yoga Community*, Ep. 1, November 22, 2020.
6. Piccalo, "A Yogi's Requiem."
7. US Congress, "United States Statutes at Large 2005," Vol. 119, Part 3, Concurrent Resolutions, 3631. A link to the Google digitalized version can be found on https://www.abuse-in-kundalini-yoga.com/media.
8. Gurumustuk Singh, "Yogi Bhajan Memorial Highway," April 29, 2006, https://www.mrsikhnet.com/2006/04/29/yogi-bhajan-memorial-highway; Roswell Daily Record, "Memorial highway in northern New Mexico should be renamed," July 2, 2022, https://www.rdrnews.com/memorial-highway-in-northern-new-mexico-should-be-renamed/article_8517b28e-f962-11ec-baf8-27ba7e77202a.html.

9. A corporation sole is a legal entity consisting of a single incorporated office, occupied by one natural person.

10. Information from https://www.espanolaashram.com/pages/history-ashram/.

11. Since 2008, the RishiKnots website and blog have published testimonies and stories from children born and raised in the community: https://www.rishiknots.com/ and https://www.instagram.com/rishiknots/. Since 2001, The Wacko World of Yogi Bhajan's old site: https://forums.delphiforums.com/kamallarose/start/; new site: https://wackoworldofyogibhajan.com/. The Gurmukh Yoga Forum managed by Gursant Singh has been active since 2009: http://gurmukhyoga.com/forum/.

12. An Olive Branch Associates, LLC, "Report on an Investigation into Allegations of Sexual and Related Misconduct by Yogi Bhajan," August 10, 2020. Available at https://epsweb.org/an-olive-branch-report/.

13. Alexandra Stein, "Report on Themes and Impacts of 3HO Childhoods. Prepared for the Independent Healing & Reparations Program," October 2022, released January 2023. Available at https://www.alexandrastein.com/uploads/2/8/0/1/28010027/childhoods_in_3ho.pdf.

14. The website compassionatereconciliation.com informs readers about the project of healing, repair, and transformation for the 3HO, Kundalini Yoga, and Sikh Dharma community.

15. EPS, The SSSC Office of Ethics and Professional Standards, "Acknowledgment, Apology, and Reparations Program Announcement," https://www.epsweb.org/reparations/.

16. Harvard Divinity School, Program for the Evolution of Spirituality, Spring Conference "Uses and Abuses of Power in Alternative Spiritualities," April 26–29, 2023, Cambridge, Massachusetts, https://hds.harvard.edu/faculty-research/programs-and-centers/program-evolution-spirituality/uses-abuses-power-alternative-spiritualities-conference-spring-2023/.

17. Nirinjan Kaur Khalsa-Baker, "The Painful Process of Awakening: Harm and Healing in the Healthy Happy Holy Kundalini Yoga Community," *Sacred Matters Magazine* (n.d.), https://www.sacredmattersmagazine.com/the-painful-process-of-awakening-harm-and-healing-in-the-healthy-happy-holy-kundalini-yoga-community/.

18. Second Generation Advocates, petition, June 11, 2023, https://www.change.org/p/communities-supporting-the-healing-of-3ho-kundalini-yoga-sikh-dharma-abuse-survivors/.

19. Yogi Bhajan Kundalini Abuse Facebook page, June 17, 2023, https://www.facebook.com/yogi.bhajan.abuses/.

20. Gothe, Neha P. et al, "Yoga Effects on Brain Health: A Systematic Review of the Current Literature," December 26, 2019, https://content.iospress.com/articles/brain-plasticity/bpl190084/.

21. Carol Merchasin, "The Bad Buddhist Podcast," March 25, 2022, https://shambala.report/news/sexual-abuse-in-buddhism-an-interview-with-carol-merchasin/.

22. The analysis of the 3HO Kundalini Yoga cult according to the BITE model can be found on https://www.freedomofmind.com/blog/; and on https://www.abuse-in-kundalini-yoga.com/bite-model-analysis/.

23. Stein, "Report on Themes and Impacts on 3HO Childhoods," 23.
24. Steven Hassan, *Combating Cult Mind Control* (Newton, MA: Freedom of Mind Press, 2018), chap. 3, "The Threat. Mind Control Today," 82.
25. Alexandra Stein, *Terror, Love, and Brainwashing: Attachment in Cults and Totalitarian Systems* (Routledge, 2021), 2.
26. Jajna Lalich, *Bounded Choice: True Believers and Charismatic Cults* (University of California Press, 2004), 14–15.
27. Interviews hosted by:
    • Mina Bahadori, from July 2020 to November 2020, Instagram account series *"Discussing Abuses in the Kundalini Yoga Community"*, thirty-one interviews in total, https://www.instagram.com/minamorphosis/.
    • GuruNischan, from November 2020, *Uncomfortable Conversations Podcast* and YouTube channel, more than fifty episodes, https://www.gurunischan.com/.
    • Rachel Bernstein's IndoctriNation podcast, covering cult issues in different organizations, 3HO sessions on November 11, 2020, December 20, 2020, and May 11, 2022, https://www.facebook.com/indoctrinationpodcast/.
    • Generation Cult podcast interviews with people born and/or raised in cults, 3HO interview on September 16, 2019, https://generationcult.libsyn.com/ep-1-no-horses-in-india/.
28. Doris Jakobsh, "3HO/Sikh Dharma of the Western Hemisphere: The 'Forgotten' New Religious Movement?" *Religion Compass* 2 (2008): 10.1111/j. 1749-8171.2008.00068.x.
29. Guru Bir Singh and Gur Siri Kaur, interview with GuruNischan, *Uncomfortable Conversations Podcast*, Ep. 1, November 20, 2020.
30. Siri Nirongkar, interview with GuruNischan, *Uncomfortable Conversations Podcast*, Ep. 11, December 30, 2020.
31. *The Man Called the Siri Singh Sahib* (3HO: 1979), 44–46.
32. *The Man Called the Siri Singh Sahib*, 18.
33. *The Man Called Siri Singh Sahib*, 32.
34. 3HO, "3HO History & Timeline," https://www.3ho.org/3ho-history-and-timeline/.
35. The "ji" in "Yogiji" is a gender-neutral Punjabi suffix used at the end of a name or title as a sign of respect.
36. Peter Macdonald Blachly, *The Inner Circle: Book One; My Seventeen Years in the Cult of American Sikhs* (Sheep Island Press, 2021), 65, 68–89, https://www.amazon.com/gp/product/1737228009/.
37. MSS Guru Terath Singh Khalsa, "The Siri Singh Sahib's Directive for after His Death," Lecture by the chancellor of Sikh Dharma, October 13, 2004.
38. Bachittar Singh Giani, "Dr. Trilochan Singh: A Tribute to the Author," October 25, 2012, https://www.sikhiwiki.org/index.php/Dr_Trilochan_Singh/.
39. Philip Deslippe is a historian of American religion with a background in American studies and literature, https://www.religiousstudiesproject.com/persons/philip-deslippe/.
40. The S.G.P.C. is the Shiromani Gurdwara Parbandhak Committee, the Supreme Gurdwara Management Committee, an organization in India responsible for the management of Gurdwaras, Sikh places of worship in Punjab, Himachal

Pradesh, and the union territory of Chandigarh. SGPC also administers the Golden Temple in Amritsar (source: Wikipedia).

41. Sikh Dharma International, "About the Siri Singh Sahib," https://www.sikh-dharma.org/about-the-siri-singh-sahib/.

42. Trilochan Singh, *Sikhism and Tantric Yoga: A Critical Evaluation of Yogi Bhajan's Tantric Yoga in the Light of Sikh Mystical Experiences and Doctrines* (August 1977), 121–122, https://archive.org/details/SikhismAndTantricYoga/mode/1up/.

43. Philip Deslippe and Stacie Stukin, "How 'Siri Singh Sahib' Yogi Bhajan Created an Empire," BaazNews, *July 19, 2022,* https://www.baaznews.org/p/yogi-bha-jan-siri-singh-sahib-expose/. BaazNews is a medium for the Sikh and Punjabi diaspora.

44. T. Singh, *Sikhism and Tantric Yoga*, 5–8, 153–154.

45. B. Singh, "Dr. Trilochan Singh."

46. T. Singh, *Sikhism and Tantric Yoga*, 5–8.

47. T. Singh, *Sikhism and Tantric Yoga*, 8.

48. T. Singh, *Sikhism and Tantric Yoga*, 15, 20–23.

49. T. Singh, *Sikhism and Tantric Yoga*, 125.

50. T. Singh, *Sikhism and Tantric Yoga*, 4.

51. Time, "Religion: Yogi Bhajan's Synthetic Sikhism," September 5, 1977.

52. Shakti Parwha Kaur, "Ten Years of Highlights in 3HO History," *Beads of Truth*, April 30, 1979, https://studentsofyogibhajan.com/wp-content/uploads/2021/02/3HO-History-1969-1979.pdf, 58.

53. *The Man Called the Siri Singh Sahib*, 15.

54. Gursant Singh, *Confessions of an American Sikh: Locked up in India, Corrupt Cops & My Escape from a "New Age" Tantric Yoga Cult* (Kindle Edition, 2012), chap. 21.

55. Vice, "True Believers: The Dark Empire of Yogi Bhajan" (documentary), April 12, 2022; Roswell Daily Record, "Memorial Highway in Northern New Mexico Should Be Renamed," July 2, 2022.

56. Philip Deslippe, "From Maharaj to Mahan Tantric: The Construction of Yogi Bhajan's Kundalini Yoga," *Sikh Formations Religion Culture Theory* 8, no. 3 (December 2012), 369–387, DOI:10.1080/17448727.2012.745303.

57. Deslippe, "From Maharaj to Mahan Tantric," 382.

58. Deslippe, "From Maharaj to Mahan Tantric," 372.

59. Deslippe, "From Maharaj to Mahan Tantric," 377.

60. A few sources describing the 1970–1971 trip to India: Pamela Dyson's book *Premka*, Philip Deslippe's article "From Maharaj to Mahan Tantric," Trilochan Singh's book *Sikhism and Tantric Yoga*, the commemorative book *The Man Called the Siri Singh Sahib*, and Peter Blachly's book *The Inner Circle: Book One*.

61. Deslippe, "From Maharaj to Mahan Tantric," 377, 379.

62. Deslippe, "From Maharaj to Mahan Tantric," 380.

63. Yogi Bhajan, "Teachers: Talk to – I Am a Teacher," Los Angeles, March 23, 1990, video, The Yogi Bhajan Library of Teachings, 41:11–42:54, https://libraryof-teachings.com/.

64. Shanti Kaur Khalsa, "Sant Hazara Singh - Yogi Bhajan's First Teacher," KRI September 2017 Newsletter, https://www.sikhdharma.org/sant-hazara-singh-yogi-bhajans-first-teacher.

65. Shanti Kaur Khalsa, "Sant Hazara Singh, Yogi Bhajan's First Teacher. Where did he come from?" (n.d.), https://kundaliniresearchinstitute.org/en/sant-hazara-singh-yogi-bhajans-first-teacher-where-did-he-come-from.

66. Juan Francisco Lafontaine, *3HO in the Light of Experience, A Study of Experiences in the Healthy, Happy, Holy Organization (3HO)*, Faculty of Arts at the University of Helsinki, (Printed by Unigrafia Oy, Helsinki, 2016), 27-46, https://helda.helsinki.fi/handle/10138/161022.

67. Rob Zabel, Bhajan's Yoga: *The Roots and Context of Kundalini Yoga As Taught By Yogi Bhajan (2021)*, https://chicago.academia.edu/RobZabel.

68. Tom Butler-Bowdon, *50 Spiritual Classics: Timeless Wisdom from 50 Great Books of Inner Discovery, Enlightenment, and Purpose* (Nicholas Brealey Publishing, 2005).

69. Self-Realization Fellowship, "The Transmission of Divine Consciousness: A True Guru's Ability to Transfer His Ecstatic Experience to Receptive Students," https://yogananda.org/transmission-of-divine-consciousness/.

70. Paramahansa Yogananda, *"Autobiography of a Yogi,"* https://www.academia.edu/34088250/Autobiography_of_a_Yogi_by_Paramahansa_Yogananda/.

71. Julien's Auctions, "Lot #483 Elvis Presley Owned Autobiography of a Yogi," https://www.julienslive.com/lot-details/index/catalog/124/lot/54188/.

72. Philip Goldberg, *The Life of Yogananda: The Story of the Yogi Who Became the First Modern Guru* (Hay House, 2018).

73. Guru Bir Singh and Gur Siri Kaur, interview with GuruNischan, Ep. 1.

74. Blachly, *The Inner Circle*, 1–2.

75. Blachly, *The Inner Circle*, 11.

76. Blachly, *The Inner Circle*, 167–169.

77. Blachly, *The Inner Circle*, 167–177.

78. B. T. Fasmer, "White Sun Wins 2023 Best New Age, Ambient, or Chant Album Grammy," February 6, 2023, https://www.newagemusic.guide/grammy-awards/.

79. Tej Steiner, interview with GuruNischan, *Uncomfortable Conversations Podcast*, Ep. 2, November 24, 2020.

80. Pamela Saharah Dyson, *Premka: White Bird in a Golden Cage: My Life with Yogi Bhajan* (Eyes Wide Publishing, 2020), 9.

81. Dyson, *Premka*, 16.

82. Dyson, *Premka*, 22.

83. Dyson, *Premka*, 23.

84. Dyson, *Premka*, 24.

85. Dyson, *Premka*, 25–26.

86. Dyson, *Premka*, 27.

87. Dyson, *Premka*, 39.

88. Dyson, *Premka*, 41–43.

89. Dyson, *Premka*, 43–46.

90. Pamela Dyson, author of *Premka*, shared the information mentioned in the sections "Designed and Decorated" and "Master of Deception" in a conversation with the author in December 2022.

91. Dyson, interview with author, December 2022.

92. Information shared by one of Bhajan's former secretaries with the author.

93. Sat Pavan, interview with author, December 2022.

94. Marina Rondelli, interview with the author, April 2023.

95. "Sat Nam" is a greeting 3HO Sikhs and yogis from Bhajan's Kundalini Yoga use to greet each other, as yogis from other styles use the Hindu greeting "Namaste." "Sat" means truth, "Nam" means identity.

96. G. Singh, *Confessions of an American Sikh*, chap. 26.

97. Blachly, *The Inner Circle*, 207–208.

98. Blachly, *The Inner Circle*, 66–67.

99. Guru Bir Singh and Gur Siri Kaur, interview with GuruNischan, Ep. 1.

100. Sat Pavan, interview with the author, December 2022; Sat Pavan, interview with Rachel Bernstein, *IndoctriNation* (podcast), May 2022.

101. Dyson, *Premka*, 130–131.

102. Tej Steiner, interview with GuruNischan, Ep. 2.

103. Tej Steiner, letter to Yogi Bhajan, March 25, 1988. A copy can be found at https:// www.abuse-in-kundalini-yoga.com/abuse-and-misconduct-stories/lies-and -deceit/tej-questions-yb/.

104. Tej Steiner, letter to the Khalsa Council, July 21, 1988. A copy can be found at https://www.abuse-in-kundalini-yoga.com/abuse-and-misconduct-stories/ lies-and-deceit/tej-questions-yb/.

105. Tej Steiner, interview with GuruNischan, Ep. 2.

106. Marina Rondelli, part 2 of testimony published April 21, 2021, https://www. abuse-in-kundalini-yoga.com/abuse-and-misconduct-stories/sexual-abuse/ olivia-s-mother-marina-testifies/.

107. Sat Pavan, interview with Rachel Bernstein, *IndoctriNation* (podcast), May 2022.

108. Alexandra Stein, *Terror, Love and Brainwashing*, chap. 4, 76.

109. Sat Pavan, interview with the author, December 2022.

110. 3HO Magazine, "Education of the Future Generation," *Beads of Truth*, no. 24 (September 24, 1974). Shared with the author by a former 3HO member.

111. Sikh Dharma Brotherhood, "A World of Their Own" (1975), communication to 3HO members. Shared with the author by a former 3HO member and available at https://www.abuse-in-kundalini-yoga.com/abuse-and-misconduct-stories/ child-abuse/3ho-children-programs/.

112. Sikh Dharma Brotherhood, "Children of the New Khalsa" (1975), communication to 3HO members. Shared with the author by a former 3HO member and available at https://www.abuse-in-kundalini-yoga.com/abuse-and-miscon-duct-stories/child-abuse/3ho-children-programs/.

113. Sat Pavan, interview with the author, December 2022.

114. Yogi Bhajan, "Teachers: Speech to LA teachers," Los Angeles, August 31, 1975, text, The Yogi Bhajan Library of Teachings, https://www.libraryofteachings. com/.

115. Sikh Dharma Brotherhood, "Summer Solstice Lecture to Mothers by the Siri Singh Sahib Harbhajan Singh Yogi" (1975), communication to 3HO members. Shared with the author by a former 3HO member and available at https://www. abuse-in-kundalini-yoga.com/abuse-and-misconduct-stories/child -abuse/3ho-children-programs/.

116. Yogi Bhajan, "Lecture – Duality of Human Growth," July 20, 1977, audio, The Yogi Bhajan Library of Teachings, 17:13–19:37, https://www.libraryofteachings. com/.

117. Yogi Bhajan, "Los Angeles Lecture," March 14, 1983, video, The Yogi Bhajan Library of Teachings, 08:08–22:10, https://www.libraryofteachings.com/.
118. Yogi Bhajan, "Gurdwara – Technology and the Guru," November 20, 1983, voice, The Yogi Bhajan Library of Teachings, 40:35–41:29, https://www.libraryofteachings.com/.
119. Sikh Dharma, "RE: Announcement of Education Program in India Beginning March 1985," letter sent out July 1984, shared with the author by a former 3HO member, https://www.abuse-in-kundalini-yoga.com/abuse-and-misconduct-stories/child-abuse/schools-in-india.
120. Yogi Bhajan, "KWTC Lecture" Española, NM, July 25, 1984, video, The Yogi Bhajan Library of Teachings, 36:36–43:50, https://www.libraryofteachings.com/.
121. Siri Nirongkar, interview with GuruNischan, Ep. 11.
122. Meeri Bylund, interview with GuruNischan, *Uncomfortable Conversations Podcast*, Ep. 4, December 11, 2020.
123. Anonymous testimony shared with the author by a former 3HO member.
124. Anonymous second-generation adult, interview with Mina Bahadori (October 2020), https://www.instagram.com/minamorphosis/, series "Discussing Abuses in The Kundalini Yoga Community."
125. RishiKnots Instagram account, "Children's Camp circa Early 1980s," June 11, 2021, https://www.instagram.com/rishiknots/.
126. An announcement by the program head of the Khalsa Youth Camp in the Yearbook of 1982, 14, shared with the author by a former 3HO member, https://www.abuse-in-kundalini-yoga.com/abuse-and-misconduct-stories/child-abuse/schools-in-india.
127. RishiKnots Instagram account, "Ram Das Puri, Española NM," August 23, 2021, https://www.instagram.com/rishiknots/.
128. GuruNischan, *Uncomfortable Conversations Podcast*, Ep. 36, July 26, 2021.
129. Sat Pavan, interview with Rachel Bernstein, *IndoctriNation* (podcast), May 2022.
130. Mina Bahadori, Instagram interview, October 2020.
131. Siri Nirongkar, interview with GuruNischan, Ep. 11.
132. Story told by a second-generation adult, its source is known to the author, Jasbir is a pseudonym.
133. Dr. Alan's letter to the parents on February 7, 1982, handed over to the author by a former 3HO member, https://www.abuse-in-kundalini-yoga.com/abuse-and-misconduct-stories/child-abuse/schools-in-india.
134. Siri Nirongkar, interview with GuruNischan, Ep. 11.
135. Report by the program director of Sikh Dharma Foreign Education, related to a visit in November 1986 to the school in India, December 29, 1986, shared with the author by a former 3HO member, https://www.abuse-in-kundalini-yoga.com/abuse-and-misconduct-stories/child-abuse/schools-in-india.
136. Yogi Bhajan, "Yogi Bhajan Talks to Young and Adults," Fort Lauderdale, Florida, December 30, 1988, video, The Yogi Bhajan Library of Teachings, 02:06–05:46, 1:19:50–1:24:56, https://www.libraryofteachings.com/.
137. Sikh Dharma Foreign Education Newsletter, (November 1989), shared with the author by a former 3HO member, https://www.abuse-in-kundalini-yoga.com/abuse-and-misconduct-stories/child-abuse/schools-in-india.

138. Yogi Bhajan, "Khalsa Council," Los Angeles, April 9, 1991, text only, The Yogi Bhajan Library of Teachings, https://www.libraryofteachings.com/.

139. Siri Nirongkar, interview with GuruNischan, Ep. 11.

140. GuruNischan, *Uncomfortable Conversations Podcast*, Ep. 7, December 17, 2020.

141. Siri Nirongkar, interview with GuruNischan, Ep. 11.

142. This message was posted on https://www.ssscorp.org/. By the time of the publication of this book, it was removed.

143. Vice, *True Believers: Empire of Yoga* (documentary) (April 12, 2022), 21:30–...–26:00, https://www.vicetv.com/en_us/video/empire-of-yoga/62339b3f36e9-dd07e52b53ac/.

144. Vice, *True Believers*, 22:31–...–26:29.

145. Vice, *True Believers*, 23:13–23:52.

146. Vice, *True Believers*, 18:40–...–23:52.

147. Testimony shared by a survivor with Pamela Dyson, author of *Premka*, on March 4, 2020. She was requested to bring the story into the open, hoping that this story might inspire other survivors to speak out.

148. Vice, *True Believers*, 26:55–...–32:09.

149. Sat Pavan, interview with Rachel Bernstein, *IndoctriNation* (podcast), May 2022.

150. Katherine Felt v. Harbhajan Singh Khalsa Yogiji, Civ No. 86-839 HB (US district court for the district of New Mexico, 1986), https://www.culteducation.com/group/795-3ho.html, under the heading "Litigation Against 3HO and/or Leaders." In this book, we use the survivor's spiritual name: KartaPurkh.

151. KartaPurkh, interview with Stephen Josephs (1985). The interview transcript was shared with the author by a former 3HO member.

152. S. Premka Kaur Khalsa v. Harbhajan Singh Khalsa Yogiji et al. (US district court for the district of New Mexico Civ No. 98-0838 M., 1986), https://www.culteducation.com/group/795-3ho.html, under the heading "Litigation Against 3HO and/or Leaders."

153. Pamela Saharah Dyson, "The Lawsuit" (blog post), April 28, 2020, https://www.pamelasaharahdyson.com/blog/.

154. Yogi Bhajan, "KWTC Lecture," Española, NM, July 4, 1986, video, The Yogi Bhajan Library of Teachings, 5:20–6:25, 10:53–13:25, 41:11–42:54, 56:42–58:35, https://www.libraryofteachings.com/.

155. Bhajan, "KWTC Lecture" (July 4, 1986), last part of the transcript of this lecture.

156. Mani Niall, interview with GuruNischan, *Uncomfortable Conversations Podcast*, Ep. 18, February 5, 2021.

157. Dyson, "The Lawsuit."

158. Albuquerque Journal, "Legal Battle Causes Split among U.S. Sikhs," July 19, 1987.

159. G. Singh, *Confessions of an American Sikh*, chap. 59.

160. Brice Watson, "Gursant Singh: Whistleblower & Survivor of Yogi Bhajan's Kundalini Yoga Cult," YouTube, 2023, https://www.youtube.com/watch?v=efiA995nM1A/.

161. GuruNischan, *Uncomfortable Conversations Podcast*, Ep. 29, April 29, 2021.

162. Dr. Steven Hassan mentioned this in his interview with Pamela Dyson on April 18, 2020. https://freedomofmind.com/former-3ho-official-pamela-dyson-discusses-yogi-bhajans-use-of-sex-money-and-power-to-deceive-and-control/. NLP is also mentioned in Gursant Singh's *Confessions of an American Sikh*, chap. 17.

163. Yogi Bhajan, "KWTC Lecture," Española women's camp, April 26, 1978, video, The Yogi Bhajan Library of Teachings, 1:00:00–1:05:34, https://www.libraryofteachings.com/.

164. Yogi Bhajan, "KWTC Lecture," Española women's camp, July 11, 1989, video, The Yogi Bhajan Library of Teachings, 18:45–19:45, https://www.libraryofteachings.com/.

165. Yogi Bhajan, "KWTC Lecture—Celestial Communication," Española women's camp, July 22, 1988, video, The Yogi Bhajan Library of Teachings, 9:37–10:21, https://www.libraryofteachings.com/.

166. An Olive Branch, "Report of An Olive Branch into Allegations of Misconduct," August 2020, https://www.epsweb.org/an-olive-branch-report/.

167. An Olive Branch, "Report," 56–58.

168. George Craig McMillian (Kirantana Singh), interview with GuruNischan, *Uncomfortable Conversations Podcast*, Ep. 12, December 31, 2020.

169. Meeri Bylund, interview with GuruNischan, Ep. 4.

170. Mani Niall, interview with GuruNischan, Ep. 18.

171. Yogi Bhajan, "Winter Solstice—Orlando, FLA Tape 7 of 8," December 26, 1974, voice, The Yogi Bhajan Library of Teachings, 1:15:15–1:17:00, https://www.libraryofteachings.com/.

172. Yogi Bhajan, "KWTC Lecture," Española women's camp, July 22, 1980. KRI. https://www.libraryofteachings.com/.

173. Yogi Bhajan, "KWTC Lecture Celestial Communication," Española women's camp, July 22, 1988, video, The Yogi Bhajan Library of Teachings, 28:09–29:18, https://www. libraryofteachings.com/.

174. Peter Macdonald Blachly, *The Inner Circle: BOOK ONE*, 73.

175. An Olive Branch, "Report," 58.

176. Yogi Bhajan, "Kundalini Yoga, KWTC," Española women's camp, July 22, 1983, audio, The Yogi Bhajan Library of Teachings, 00:00–10:34, https://www.libraryofteachings.com/.

177. Anonymous testimony shared with the author in 2020.

178. Tara Brach, "Tara Brach: Trusting Who We Are [retreat talk]," November 6, 2019, https://www.youtube.com/watch?v=iisZEbIq3U8&t=2273s/.

179. Siri Nirongkar, interview with GuruNischan, Ep. 11.

180. Guru Ram Das, the fourth guru of the Sikhs, was considered by Yogi Bhajan as his personal guru. He is considered the guru of the heart, of compassion.

181. SatHanuman Singh Khalsa, interview with GuruNischan, *Uncomfortable Conversations Podcast*, Ep. 19, February 10, 2021.

182. Vice, *True Believers*, 14:50–15:15.

183. Kushwant Singh, "Keeping America Secure," The Global Sikh Trail: Stories of Eminent Sikhs, September 2005, https://theglobalsikhtrail.com/stories_posts/gurutej-singh-khalsa/.

184. Philip Tanzer, "Questions on Akal Security. Should a Non-profit, Tax-exempt Church Oversee a For-profit Security Contractor Tasked with Enforcing ICE

policies?" Medium, August 27, 2018, https://www.medium.com/@philliptan-zer/questions-about-akal-security-8bcf932bb42d/.

185. Fatehbir Kaur, "Child Separation and Kundalini Yoga," YouTube, https://www.youtube.com/watch?v=hsjnzjFjA0Y&t=1s/.

186. Tell Akal to Sever Ties with ICE (website), https://www.akalandice.weebly.com/.

187. Akalandice, "Official Response to SSSCorp Statement Regarding Akal Security," Aug 26, 2019, Tell Akal to Sever Ties with ICE, https://www.akalandice.weebly.com/response-to-ssscorp.html.

188. Voluntary Work Program Agreement of the Service Processing Center, El Centro, California, based on the ICE standard that mentions a compensation of at least $1 per day, https://www.ice.gov/doclib/detention-standards/2011/5-8.pdf.

189. Cult Education Institute, "3HO aka Healthy, Happy, Holy Organization," https://www.culteducation.com/group/795-3ho.html. See topic "Litigation Against 3HO and/or Leaders."

190. Vice, *True Believers*, 16:40–17:15.

191. Mary Frei, "Former Sikhs Tell Why They Left New Mexico Religious Community," *Santa Fe Journal*, 1985, https://www.abuse-in-kundalini-yoga.com/abuse-and-misconduct-stories/fraud-and-more/1985-leavers.

192. This is how GuruNischan remembers the myth being told in 3HO.

193. Bill Garland, "Woman Gives Sikhs $1.3 Million; Mother Asks Sanity Healing," *The New Mexican Journal*, October 7, 1977.

194. Bill Garland, "Sought Sikh Woman 'in India,'" *The New Mexican Journal*, October 9, 1977.

195. Gigi Kaur, interview with GuruNischan, "The Ram Das Puri Land Purchase Story," Uncomfortable Conversations Podcast, Ep. 46, June 22, 2022.

196. Yogi Bhajan Kundalini Abuse Facebook post on April 27, 2021, https://www.facebook.com/profile/100066720483964/.

197. Rodney King was an African American who was the victim of police brutality in March 1991. The incident was filmed and shown on local news. King was unarmed, on the ground, and beaten. It caused a public furor. (Source: Wikipedia.)

198. Guru Bir Singh and Gur Siri Kaur, interview with GuruNischan, Ep. 1.

199. The house of Guru Ram Das is what 3HO members called their community, as YB considered Guru Ram Das, the fourth guru of the Sikhs, his personal guru.

200. George Craig McMillian (Kirantana Singh), interview with GuruNischan, Ep. 12.

201. A *hukam* is a ritual in the Sikh tradition whereby you receive a message from the Holy Book of the Sikhs.

202. Anonymous, "Yogi Bhajan Sent Me to Work for 3HO 'Toner Bandits' when I Was 24 Years Old!" December 4, 2011, https:// www.gurmukhyoga.com/forum/index.php?id=394/.

203. G. Singh, *Confessions of an American Sikh*, chap. 17.

204. Hector Gutierrez, "Toner Bandit Gets Prison Term," *Rocky Mountain News* (Denver, CO), August 17, 2000.

205. BT Fasmer, "White Sun Wins 2023 Best New Age, Ambient or Chant Album Grammy," February 6, 2023, https://www.newagemusic.guide/grammy-awards/.

206. Gursant Singh, "Yogi Bhajan's Chief of Protocol: MSS Hari Jiwan Singh Khalsa," The Gurumukh Yoga Forum, June 24, 2011, https://www.gurmukhyoga.com /forum/index.php?id=324/.

207. G. Singh, "Yogi Bhajan's Chief of Protocol."

208. G. Singh, *Confessions of an American Sikh*, chaps. 17 and 31.

209. Federal Trade Commission, "Gemstone Marketers Agree to Pay Monetary Judgment to Settle FTC Charges," August 18, 1998, https://www.ftc.gov/news-events/news/press-releases/1998/08/gemstone-telemarketers-agree-pay-monetary-judgment-settle-ftc-charges/.

210. "Khalsa Financial Services, Inc., Gurujot Khalsa and Darshan Khalsa Sanctioned," SEC News Digest 93, no. 190, October 1, 1993, https://www.sec.gov /news/digest/1993/dig100193.pdf.

211. Mani Niall, interview with GuruNischan, Ep. 18.

212. United States of America v. Albert Ellis and Gurujot Singh Khalsa, aka Robert Alvin Taylor, Case No. 3 88 0144 FW (US District Court for Northern California, February 19, 1988). This lawsuit was filed by a special agent of the Drug Enforcement Administration from the US Department of Justice in San Francisco. https://www.yogibhajan.tripod.com/id19.html; https://www.culteducation.com/group/795-3ho/32-gurujot-singh-marijuana-and-machine-guns-.html.

213. United States of America v. Albert Ellis and Gurujot Singh Khalsa, aka Robert Alvin Taylor.

214. Cult Education Institute, Lawsuits against Yogi Bhajan, https://www.culteducation.com/group/795-3ho/35-katherine-felt.html.

215. Guru Bir Singh and Gur Siri Kaur, interview with GuruNischan, Ep. 1.

216. Eugene Newspaper, "Victim Found in Car Trunk," September 1986, found on the site "The Wacko World of Yogi Bhajan," http://www.forums.delphiforums.com/kamallarose/messages?msg=325.1/.

217. Sat Nam Rasayan International School, "Guru Dev Singh," https://www.satnamrasayan.it/gurudevsingh/.

218. The story of the abuse by Hari Singh in the Belgian Sat Nam Rasayan training is described at https://www.abuse-in-kundalini-yoga.com/abuse-and-misconduct-stories/sexual-abuse/sat-nam-rasayan-teacher-sexually-abuses-2-students.

219. Marina Rondelli, extracts from Part 1 of her story, March 9, 2021, https:// www.abuse-in-kundalini-yoga.com/abuse-and-misconduct-stories/sexual-abuse/olivia-s-mother-marina-testifies.

220. Olivia Taglioli, interview with GuruNischan, *Uncomfortable Conversations Podcast*, Ep. 25, March 24, 2021.

221. Marina Rondelli, extracts from Part 1 of her story, March 9, 2021, https://www.abuse-in-kundalini-yoga.com/abuse-and-misconduct-stories/sexual-abuse/olivia-s-mother-marina-testifies.

222. Author's reply to Guru Dev of October 6, 2020, can be found on https://www.abuse-in-kundalini-yoga.com/abuse-and-misconduct-stories/sexual-abuse/sat-nam-rasayan-teacher-sexually-abuses-2-students.

CPSIA information can be obtained
at www.ICGtesting.com
Printed in the USA
LVHW042048210723
753026LV00001B/132